GOLD AT RAINBOW'S END

GOLD AT RAINBOW'S END

TONY JENKINS

Best wishes Jean

Tony Jenkins

Aug 18th 09.

ILLUSTRATIONS BY
ROWENA CASS

A. G. JENKINS
STAINTONDALE, SCARBOROUGH

iii

Books previously written by the same author:
Revised and adapted for inclusion in this one

The Story Unfolds (1991)

At a Price That's Very Nice (1992)

Planning to Crack a Nut (1995)

Horse Magic (2000)

© Tony Jenkins 2004

ISBN 0-9539420-1-5
Published by A.G. Jenkins, Shire Horse Farm, Staintondale,
Scarborough YO13 0EY

Printed by HPE print Pickering. Tel: 01751 473578

ACKNOWLEDGEMENTS

This book is dedicated to our family, our friends and the many visitors we welcome each year.

I have to thank many people but chiefly two builder friends of mine, Bill Jackson and Des Berridge, for without their tuition and skill the building and restoration of this small farm enterprise would not have been possible.

Also the many friends far too numerous to mention but who's help and support got me through some difficult times. And not least, the wonderful staff I have employed over the years. Truly dedicated and not a weak link amongst them!

Finally my wife Ann, who has been the 'Miss Smith' in my life since day one of our marriage. A secretary, an organiser and a friend, all in one.

Dony Jenkins

INTRODUCTION

When our eldest granddaughter was small and it doesn't seem so long ago, she had asked her Mum – our daughter 'Was it really like that in the olden days?' I think this sums up the timescale relative to our life at different stages.

In childhood a year is a decade, and the space between us and our parents seems to be a century. I used to listen to my father, 'When I was your age…,' it usually started, and then he would tell me of his escapades, which to me, had happened in the dim and distant past.

Life, as you get older, is nothing like that at all and those long summers and seemingly, endless school holidays, when the sun shone every day, not much more than a myth. The past is never more than a recent memory away and with this in mind I intend to recapture some of the carefree, happy days of youth, set out my dreams and ambitions as the story unfolds.

The theme running through this book is essentially horses because they have played such an important part in my life and continue to do so. Everybody has a dream to fulfill. It can be sheer ambition to become powerful and wealthy or it can be in a more peaceful and secure way of life. On the other hand, it could be a yearning for a way of life you had read about, enjoyed as a child or just simply, as they say, 'something in your blood'.

There is a lot of truth in the latter because your genes do play a big part in influencing your ambitions and your future. Only one other ingredient is necessary – luck.

I have said many times that I have been one of the lucky ones, but I can tell you also that luck does need to be reinforced by determination and hard work.

The book starts when I was a small boy, when in my case, 'our heroes really were cowboys'. The Second World War had just broken out. My life revolved around the surrounding countryside, and my simple ambition seemed to be just owning a horse.

Little did I know just how many of my dreams and ambitions were to become reality. This book is going to span a large slice of a lifetime. It is a written adaptation of previous books which proved to be remarkably successful. They have been revised and compiled to tell the whole story. In response to the many request for such a book - here it is - enjoy it.

Tony Jenkins

CONTENTS

T. J.

I call him T.J. that's Tony Jenkins to you
Like his hero Roy Rodgers he did what a man has to do
A vision, a dream, call it what you like
With his love for the horse so great
He worked hard till he got it just right

In the days of the old wild west gone by
With a homestead horse and some land
Good old T.J. would have fitted in just grand
Sitting high in the saddle guitar in hand he sings to his four legged friend
This Staintondale cowboy lives his dream it's all just as he planned

From sunrise to sunset the man, the horse and the land do blend
No time to waste on fools or folly there's work to be done and a fence to mend
Not just a pretty face and a winning smile
Oh no! there's more to this friend of mine
On dark winter nights as the snow does fall he writes a book or two
Then come the summer he will sign it and sell it to you.

How can you resist this friend of mine with that twinkle in his eyes
With heart as big as a bucket you've got to give him first prize
His knowledge of the past the Knights and Kings of old
Tales of smugglers and their bounty he'll eagerly unfold
Come sunshine or come showers the show will still go on
In the yard full of beautiful flowers he pleases the gathering throng

Now come the new Millenium, what will it hold in store?
Could this man come up with even more?
Yes, he's written a song so you can sing along
Now he'll be more famous than before
But he won't sell his horse to drive round in a Porsche
No, that would fill his heart with remorse

So you call him Mr. Tony Jenkins and that will do just fine
I always call him T.J. and I'm proud to say he's a friend of mine

Margery Parkinson

X

CHAPTER ONE
Early Recollections

Childhood memories are someone else's history and should be faithfully recorded. I want to start mine for the purpose of this book, in the late 1930s. We were living with my grandparents at 157 Cresswell Road, Clowne, in Derbyshire and horses were very much in evidence. Nelmes Bakery was just at the bottom of the hill and even at my tender age I was aware of the magical sound of their address – Spring Vale. In my mind it conjured up a fantasy world – a world I wanted to live in. It would be thirty years at least before I was to realize my dream, but luck was to play its part and my dream eventually came true. It wasn't to be Spring Vale, it was to be Stainton Dale.

I had a close relationship with Nelmes Bakery but they were not to know it. They delivered bread and cakes around the village with horse-drawn vans. These vehicles and the horses were kept on land just behind a lane at the back of my grandparent's garden.

It was this area that was the focus of my attention and I used to spend hours talking to the horses and revelling in the smell and atmosphere. Roy Rogers came into my life about this time and it came about through a comic called Radio Fun. Each week Roy Rogers had a fan club page and wrote about his life with his clever Palomino, Trigger. I was fascinated – in fact I determined that was what I wanted to be – a cowboy.

Each week, a list of numbers was published, with the opportunity to win a Sheriff's badge if your number came up. Well that's life, I took that comic for four years only to be disappointed. Sixty years later would you believe, some friends from Woodbridge in Suffolk bought me one!

I made a friend at school called John Williams and in the evenings or at weekends I used to take him to my 'ranch' behind Nelmes bakery and show him 'my' horses. I sat on the fence and fantasized with an imaginary lariat and a ten gallon hat on my head. He never caught on.

'I made the mistake of my life.'

We went to school in what was known as the Rectory Barn. I suspect it was an old tithe barn because Clowne was mentioned in the Domesday book and has some historic connections.

At the start of the Second World War there was a shortage of teachers at the school so we only attended for half days – either morning or afternoon. To us children it was wonderful and we could spend the rest of the day either flying kites, playing whip and top or marbles.

The whip and top bit was the best I thought, and with a top called a window breaker (windabrekker) you could be a serious threat to Warren's shop window as we whipped them up in the air on their shopfront – until we were chased off, that is.

My grandad was a keen gardener and in addition to going to work and tending the garden round the house, he also had an allotment some one and a half miles up a lane called Gapstick. In the garden round the house he grew roses and carnations. He very rarely went out in his 'best suit' without a carnation for a buttonhole. Horse manure was always in demand and I can truthfully say always to hand because horses delivering bread, milk, fruit and vegetables, transporting furniture and a host of other commodities were frequently passing his front garden. It did not go unnoticed.

I used to escort him to his allotment on a regular basis especially at weekends. The walk up the lane was particularly interesting for me because again, horse power on the land was the order of the day. The jingling and tinkling of chains and harrows was always evident and I could hear the ploughmen and waggoners talking away to the horses or whistling a happy tune. At harvest time on a summers day I thought it sheer paradise.

These were never to return days and I look back with wonder at such a demanding, yet seemingly gentle way of life. Life in the 1930s was hard for most people and wages were as poor as the people who worked for them. It did not seem to make people any less happy and it is a credit to them that they made what they could of life. They did not seem to envy anybody anything.

My first encounter with horses had come about a little earlier when we had lived in a mining village called Langold, near Worksop in north Nottinghamshire when I was five years old. Horses were commonplace and my obsession already overwhelming. I had watched the milkman each day delivering house to house with his bucket and measures - anybody remember a gill?

This was before the Co-op dairies and the rattling of crates and bottles! The horse used to stop at intervals and the dairyman farmer would make the morning calls. I had waited and planned my move. As the milkman disappeared down the path to a row of houses, I pounced. Jumping on the float I clicked my tongue. The sensation has stayed with me from that day to this. The horse walked on! It was a very short lived affair because I was spotted from the window of our house, and worse still, the horse only walked on to the next call. I was in trouble! My father shouted something almost incoherent, but the meaning was clear. At the same time, the milkman emerged from the pathway to the rear of the house. I was out of the float and off like a shot! I hadn't gone far, when I made the fatal mistake of my life - I looked round to see how far the opposition were behind me, and simultaneously I ran face sideways into a gas lamp post! My nose bleeding, I was in great distress, but that was nothing compared to the good hiding that followed.

I remember the next few years very clearly, my appetite and obsession grew and my dreams were constantly of horses and having one of my own. At the time of my encounter with the milkman's horse the prospects of ever owning one were remote.

My father worked on the pit top, he was a surface worker, making and repairing the steel tubs used underground to bring out the coal. For those who cannot imagine what these tubs looked like, they were oblong in shape and on wheels that ran on narrow gauge railway lines. From memory they would be about five feet long and two to three feet wide, with sides about three feet high. I should think they held about a ton of coal. I mention these in particular, because they were pulled underground by the pit ponies. Sturdy little creatures that lived and worked down the mine for a whole year at a time. They were intelligent and incredibly canny. It was commonplace for them to stop and refuse to go forward, either sensing a roof fall or that one was about to happen, using their noses or sixth sense. Whatever their station in life or their size, horses are still horses, and seem to have remarkable perception. Many a man's life has been saved by these devoted creatures in industry and in war.

To return briefly to the tubs. They were hooked together by a coupling to form a train or chain, and then diverted and controlled by a points system to get them in and out of the coal faces and on to the cage. The cage of course, being a large lift working up and down the mineshaft to bring out the coal. The ponies got used to the routine and learned to haul these tubs wherever they were needed.

The highlight of their lives was their holiday each year for a pit week. This was the week when the mine closed down for the annual week's holiday and the ponies were 'brought up'. At this time word went round the village, spread by the excited youngsters like wildfire - 'Pit ponies are comin' up!' The whole child population was there to witness this spectacle. You can imagine this situation, the shaded glare and shadows of the oil lamps suddenly became bright sunlight and green pastures. These ponies went wild. Contrary to popular belief, they were not all small and uniform in size. In fact their size and colour varied tremendously, and what a sight to see. I stood and closed my eyes, daydreaming that if I could only own one of them...

My thoughts and dreams were stimulated by the fact that my father used to tell me that for one reason or another, these ponies were occasionally sold or even given to a good home. Where do you keep a pony in a backyard measuring only 20 feet by 10 feet at the most, and this usually accommodating a mangle stood outside and a tin bath hanging on the wall.

CHAPTER TWO
Wartime Childhood

As we moved into the 1940s my awareness of the war became more clear. We had moved from my grandparents home to our own house in Worksop, Nottinghamshire. It was a town terracehouse built on the back-to-back style in rows. No garden, just a small back yard.
It seemed far removed from the fields and farms I had grown accustomed to and I saw the prospects of ever owning a horse fading fast.

Oh yes, the street deliveries were still mainly made by horses but what did you do with horse manure here?

I still had my old wind up portable gramophone and my few records and I can remember the Regal and Parlaphone labels. My favourite was 'Old Faithful' and I rode my bike with two bits of string tied to the handlebars pretending it was a horse. I sang and played that song so much I wore the record out.

The war had its compensations, not least the Autumn holidays for potato picking. Tractors had started to appear on the land as the farmers were encouraged to grow more food. In spite of a small influx of them, horses were still the main power on farms and I revelled in that.

The potatoes were spun out of the ground with a spinner made up of spring tines which was driven by the tractor. I say driven but I suspect that these spinners were of the old horse drawn variety and actually driven by a ground wheel. Hydraulics had not yet arrived on the farm.

Anyway the length of the field was marked out in stints and each of us kids assigned one. We were given a skip to collect the potatoes and get the stint cleaned before the tractor made its return trip.

The best part was the collection of these skips – this was a job for the horse and cart. As the cart travelled up and down the rows, the skips were tipped in. When the cart was full the driver took it over to the edge of the field where it would be tipped into what was called a 'pie'. It was basically a large soil excavation which would be eventually covered by straw. This protected the potatoes from frost until they were required. Potatoes were an important part of the war effort and people were encouraged to eat more. We used to sit under the hedge to eat our dinner and the fresh air made us ravenous. The horses were given nosebags and I used to rush my sandwiches so that I could go and talk to them.

The other love in my life at that time was the canal, which ran right through the town centre and under a bridge across the main street. Warehouses lined the tow path and locks regulated the water levels. Horses provided the pulling power. We spent our time playing 'Commandos' along the banks of the river Ryton – and at times, wreaking havoc. I remember once when we had decided to build rafts we realized that the water in the river wasn't deep enough. To raise the level we took down a stone retaining wall running along the side and re-built it across the Ryton. To completely stop the flow we plugged the gaps with grass sods. It was an amazing success. Within an hour the river level had risen two feet and what panic it created.

Further up the river it was running back into drainage holes and flooding people's back yards and threatening their houses. It was seeping over the banks in places and running on to pavements. It didn't take long for somebody to alert the police and fire service and we were on the run – and how. 'Just William' had nothing on us wartime kids and with a lot of mums working in munitions and dads on active service, it was a wonderful world, at times...

One such event was the formation of a smokers' club – I was eleven at the time. We had been in the habit of sharing a packet of Woodbines – I think they were five for five pence halfpenny (about 2p). Anyway since we all lived within a stone's throw of the Town Football ground, we decided to locate our club in a room above where the pitch markers were kept. I should add that supervision of any kind during the war was thin on the ground and we seemed to have the run of most things. It was at this point that we realized that we had an inexhaustable supply of tobacco all around us – cigarette ends! With all the camps and American bases around, they were plentiful. Cautious of the fact that hygiene (or the lack of it) might be a problem, we came up with a plan. The burnt end had to be cleanly cut off, the paper and tipped ends removed and the remaining content sterilized. You might well be

'Old faithful'

excused for wondering how this was done? Well it might not have been the ideal solution but at least we felt better. Our mixture of Camel, Lucky Strike, Three Castles, Woodbines, Players, Capstan, Black Cat and Park Drive at least got blended. This is how we did it. Everybody it seemed had access to seven pound tins of jam which found their way from the surrounding Army camps to various households – we only needed an empty jam tin. Into the tin we carefully shook out the 'shelled' tobacco and dry mixed it. We then put it in somebody's oven – a munitions mum not mine! We cooked it until the water had evaporated and the moisture had dried out. After that it was simple – a Rizzler cigarette roller and some papers and hey presto!

I must add for the benefit of young readers that I gave up smoking at twelve and no longer smoke. At about this time and soon after I got friendly with a boy who had a pony. The pony was like a magnet to me and it certainly helped to keep us friends. More than that, his grandfather had a farm right on the edge of the town and he had even more horses up there. At the time I had no idea why he had all these horses but years later I realized the awful truth. These horses were all destined for slaughter. The end of the horse era was drawing to a close and mechanisation had already begun. It wasn't too evident just yet, but soon the flood gates were to open and millions of horses would go this way. Anyway I loved the opportunity to go and see these horses and ride the pony.

We camped out in a field using saddles for pillows and cooked over a fire – this was heaven on earth. Some days we took some of the farm's working horses to the Farrier. His name was Lomas and the forge was situated on the canal bank. It was an education just to visit and usually we had to join a queue. The barge horses seemed to be given priority because barges had to keep moving to meet strict timetables. If one lost a shoe the job stopped. Mr Lomas soon had it moving. His colourful language intrigued me as well – he didn't seem to be too polite towards some of the horses being shod.

Our days were filled with activity. There wasn't time to get bored. We once had a brilliant Circus come to town and as usual all the local kids were there to help erect the giant big top. Sometimes we got free admission tickets but usually just promises – but we got our own back on such occasions.

I remember once when such a situation arose and we hadn't been adequately rewarded, we saw a chance of getting even.

This particular Circus had a wonderful collection of horses and did some remarkable acrobatics on horseback. They called some of them liberty horses and they were immaculately turned out. Further away from the main area they also had a very attractive spotted pony stallion – and he seemed anxious for his liberty.

It was a bit naughty, but fair's fair and we were giving the pony his freedom. You can imagine the effect his freedom had upon the various horses assembled at the big top. Again we had to run – for our lives.

CHAPTER THREE
Country Boy

During a recent TV interview on the Yorkshire Television network programme 'Tonight' I was asked by Ian Clayton 'How does a lad like you whose father worked in the coalfields of North Nottinghamshire know about nature?

I think the answer to that should have been that in spite of living in the centre of town for my early childhood I was never far from woodlands, ponds and leafy lanes. We all had bikes of one sort or another but nothing like the variety on the roads today. Most had no gears, some had three and the majority were either too big or too small. I am sure that you have got the picture. We rode miles, and Worksop was in easy reach of places of local interest now developed as tourist venues.

One of our favourites was Edwinstowe and Sherwood Forest. We were fascinated by this gnarled, aged oak tree with its spreading branches and hollow trunk. It stood in a small clearing called a glade and the ground was carpeted by grass and ferns. There was never anybody there, and we shouldered each other up to climb its lofty branches.

Like all children, we questioned its legend, and as we all crushed ourselves inside the tree, comments like, 'well he never got all his merry men in here' and even more critical 'Friar Tuck must have got left outside!'

They were happy, carefree days and the smell of the bark, the leaves and the dankish atmosphere gave you a feeling of splendid isolation from the rest of the world. It was our world anyway and tourism hadn't even been invented for working class people. I was to find out much more about it as the pages of this book will reveal.

It goes without saying that we all had bows and arrows and selecting saplings for the bow was a task taken seriously. We knew exactly what

11

we were looking for, even to the trees that produced the best arrows. I think the most expensive component for this particular day's activities would be the string for the bow. If we couldn't salvage some, we probably had to chip in a penny to buy a ball.

I had a friend called Jimmy Rayner and his father was chauffeur to Captain John Farr, who owned the Worksop Manor estate. Jim lived with his parents in the gate lodge alongside the impressive entrance to the Manor itself.

Compared to our house in a back street in the town this was another completely different world. At the time during the early 1940s, our hero was Johny Weismuller in the Tarzan films and the environment in Manor Woods, as they were called, lent itself to our fantasies. The woods seemed huge and wild with young saplings growing among mature trees and an inpenetrable carpet of dead branches and undergrowth.

This was indeed our jungle.

Most Saturdays I walked up Mansfield Road for something over a mile and went to spend the day with Jim. Their 'house' was at the top of a stretch of road called Hawksnest Hill. I used to borrow the small axe that my father used for chopping the sticks to light our coal fire, which was the only heating for the whole house. I mentioned the cooking range earlier at my grandparents – this was exactly the same. It also boasted a side boiler and many is the time during the winter, when it was necessary to take a ladle of hot water up the yard to the outside toilet to thaw the water cistern. Even this was not an easy task because it was high on the wall and I had to stand on the old fashioned wooden toilet seat to perform this task, to flush the 'loo'.

Anyway I digress – back to the woods. Armed with an axe and a knife, we used to explore the 'jungle'. It was certainly big enough to get lost in, which we very often did, and it also gave up its secrets.

The secrets were ponds now and again, and various wild fruit trees bearing anything from crabapples to nuts and berries. It was just like in the film and of course we practised our yodelling to call up the wild elephants – I don't remember many appearing though, although we never gave up hope. We lit fires, made dens with fern leaves for the roof and cooked our tin of baked beans in a billy can. It was sheer delight and we had made our own plans that if the Germans did invade we would escape into these woods and live in hiding. At that time it was more than a possibility that Hitler had in fact talked about living at Welbeck Abbey when he won the war. Welbeck Abbey was only about 3 miles away. I think the most exciting thing we did in the woods was to try and emulate Tarzan when he was seen swinging through the jungle from tree to tree.

We used to climb the very tall willowy saplings that were growing up between more mature trees. They were being drawn up towards the light and grew fast and lean. Our party piece was to shin up these trees right to the top. We then hung on tightly as we projected ourselves sideways causing the tree to bend. It was brilliant, the trees used to bend like a bow and you came down to the ground as if by parachute. Well mostly – if it snapped and you came down a bit quicker, the yodelling ended abruptly!

This was how I came to know about nature, and of course these experiences motivated my ambitions and dreams. I wanted to live in a natural environment although that phrase alone would be a foreign language to me at that time. To have a pond of my own, perhaps a small woodland and hedgerows, and a field or two – even own a horse. I pulled up my socks, stuffed a few crabapples into the pocket of my short trousers and picked up my Dad's axe.

Another Saturday, another dream but little did I know how much of the dream would become reality. We shall have to wait and see.

I mentioned Welbeck Abbey earlier and Adolph Hitler. It's amazing really that he should refer to it because Welbeck had been requisitioned by the Army. It was used because of its labyrinth of passages. These were used as dumps for ammunition of all kinds. I can't describe them accurately because to us kids they were all bombs, shells and grenades. But there was tons of it. If Hitler had blown that lot up there wouldn't have been much left of Welbeck Abbey for him to live in!

Looking back I am amazed that we were let into these passages unchallenged. I am sure that today's young people wouldn't have been allowed within a mile – knowledgeable as so many of them are.

Anyway this wasn't the case with us, as a gang of girls and boys alike rode in on our bikes. All we got was a cheery wave from the Sentry who recognised us as local kids. It was another haven in the grounds of the Abbey. The former grandeur of the gardens and orchid houses was evident everywhere. The lovely paths, grottos and lakes were in a world of their own. The world of the Dukedoms of the Dukeries.

At this time they were ours. There was nobody about as we explored every nook and cranny. I think I proposed to my first childhood sweetheart in one of the grottos. They called her Betty Bowler. At thirteen I thought I was definitely destined to be a Duke and I would need a Duchess. That wasn't all, there was a boathouse by a beautiful lake. It housed boats and crafts of all kinds from rowing boats to canoes. All the boats had their rowlocks removed but that was no deterrent.

We sailed around the lake in many a craft using the oars as paddles – it impressed the girls and I am sure that spurred us on! We also took out a superb canoe which was a wonderful experience. Nobody ever challenged us or chased us. This really was our secret garden and what a secret.

I look back now with wonder and incredulity and I can't imagine situations like that could ever happen again – especially to town kids. We did live in a wonderful world even during the war. We also put everything carefully back where we found it and would never have dreamt of damaging anything.

CHAPTER FOUR
Bucking Broncos

It's hard to believe but during the war there was a riding stables right in the town centre of Worksop. It was behind an Inn called 'The Marquis of Granby'. They were using the stables and coach yard which had formerly belonged to the Inn in its coaching days. Worksop was once a busy coaching route for traders and travellers.

I loved the whole atmosphere of the cobbled yard, the smell of the stables and of course, the horses. The clip-clopping of their metal shoes ringing out was music to my ears. To ride these horses cost three shillings an hour, on today's currency that would be 15p. At that time it was far beyond our reach.

I had several after school jobs which averaged around five shillings a week, from delivering wine and spirits for Gunns who were merchants, to working at a shoe shop called Barlows on Bridge Place. Imagine in todays world taking shoes to a shoe shop to be repaired and having them delivered by a boy on a carrier bike (shades of 'open all hours'). Even new shoe purchases were delivered to your door in those days.

At Gunns they had a special carrier bike with a huge front basket carrier and a small front wheel. I reckon it could carry a hundred weight of booze! At Christmas time when deliveries were on the elevated side of town – in more ways than one, I had to push this bike for up to two miles because with the sheer weight and no gears it was impossible to ride it. The war wasn't quite as hard on some people as others and I used to gaze inside those elegant entrance halls decked with glittering decorations, holly, mistletoe and wrapped parcels. These were scenes we usually only saw at the cinema.

I started this chapter at the Marquis of Granby in Bridge Place, Worksop and so let us return there. As I explained, as kids we couldn't afford horse riding by the hour but for me anyway, I couldn't resist the call of the stables.

A man called Sturdy ran them and through hanging about – my usual ploy – I got into conversation with him. The horses were turned out in a field beyond the town football ground (of cigarette end fame) and the cricket ground. It was quite a long way really and they had to be brought in on a daily basis. I plucked up courage, 'Do you need any help to get the horses in Mr Sturdy?' I asked. He had scrutinized me well before answering 'Can you handle horses?' 'Oh yes,' said I boldly, 'My granddad's a farrier.' He looked me up and down again. 'These are quite big horses and although you're fairly tall, you are a bit skinny.' 'Oh I'll manage them all right!' By now I was a confident fourteen year old and cocky with it.

'Right,' Mr Sturdy said, 'you can help Saturdays and Sundays,' he paused, 'I will send one of the stable girls over with you and she will show you what to do.'

Friday night I couldn't sleep wondering whether or not I would get a chance to ride, but in the event it would have been wiser not to have ridden – well not the way I eventually did. On the Saturday morning I got up early and went round to the stables. Mr Sturdy was expecting me. 'I am letting Sarah go with you this morning. She's a very capable young lady and so just do as you are told.'

It was fantastic. We had walked across the main street, down the side of Woolworths and down a lane towards the football ground. Sarah was quite a character. 'What we do,' she said, 'but don't tell Mr Sturdy, is to catch up the horses – there are five, and then we mount one and ride it bareback and lead the others. You have two, I will take three.' My eyes must have been as big as saucers. 'But be careful and remember we have to dismount when we get past the football pitch,' she told me.

All was fine, and after some initial nervousness I soon got fairly confident. After a few weekends working with the horses I got very confident. Well, it was going to happen sooner or later. Can I just have a gallop round the field Sarah before we take them over? 'Oh go on then,' she had said, 'but make sure you stick on.' That morning I had already broken off a piece of willow to use as a stick – riding school horses can be a bit lazy sometimes. I took off – 'C'mon lad,' I yelled doing my fantasy cowboy bit, 'get on!'

As the stick came down on the horse's hip, up he went – back end first and then a gigantic buck with all four feet off the ground. With no saddle and only a single halter rope for control, I didn't have a lot to hang on to. I grabbed some mane. Up I went – up into the air like a rag doll. But this horse hadn't finished with me yet. On the downward descent he lashed out with a hind leg and caught me on the arm. Sarah was there in a flash, 'I wouldn't have missed that for the world,' she said – and that was the extent of the sympathy I got.

'Come on – let's get them over and then you had better go and get that arm seen to.'

A very deflated Tony Jenkins went home that morning, and knowing I should be in trouble for not telling my parents what I had been doing at the stables, I went into the kitchen and ran the cold water on my very swollen arm. It came up like a football – and it hurt.

The next thing I was round at the Victoria Hospital (which has now been demolished) and was awaiting the X-ray results. My hopes of a simple sprain were a forlorn hope.

I walked back home, my arm firmly ensconced in plaster and a sling to boot. Suddenly I began to feel a bit proud of it – a bronco buster in the making. Better not make too much of it though, I thought to myself, some of the lads at school wouldn't see it quite the way I did. Ah well, at least it was my left arm.

About this time, I had persuaded my mam to buy me a pair of knee breeches – partly funded by my delivery job. I thought they were the bee's knees. A real pair of breeches.

They laced up just below the knee and then you pulled your turnover top socks over them. When you consider that in our day most boys of my age wore short trousers, I did manage to stand out in the crowd! I didn't care – these were the nearest thing that I was going to get to riding breeches, and I just had to put up with the jibes and jokes. It's amazing to think back and try to see myself as the other boys saw me. In a back street of Worksop it would be hard for them to imagine me riding into the sunset. In fact, I did it every day! I called my horse 'Old Faithful'. Remember Johny Cash and 'A Boy Named Sue'? – Well I had to live with my breeches and deal with the consequences.

CHAPTER FIVE
A Horse called Dusty

We are now going to fast forward this story for the next twenty years or so. After a remarkable career from motor mechanic, to shop keeper, business man and builder, my life had been fairly successful. At last I was in a position to buy a horse. The whole thing had been triggered off by our younger daughter Anita, caring for a pony. I don't think there could ever have been a more deserving case, and her love and care for her pony, Smokey, plus her relentless quest for knowledge on the subject of horses, was insatiable. She became quite an authority by the time she reached her teens and a very capable rider as well.

I think my childhood enthusiasm had been dampened by the pressures and demands of business, and even time for leisure was grudgingly allotted. In fact, without realising it, I had become an ambitious workaholic. Things had changed a little bit recently, influenced by new acquaintances, I had realised there was more to life than proving yourself successful.

Anita's interest in her pony had aroused new passions. The smell of horses, the stables and the quite distinctive smell of leather had taken me back to my youth.

Our elder daughter Shirley, had also taken an interest in riding. I am not really sure if that didn't influence the next move, because the next suggestion I think came from me. 'Why don't we buy a family horse and then we can all ride?'

It met with unanimous and spontaneous approval. Shirley was almost two years older than Anita and quite tall. This meant that we could look for a cobby type of horse at around 15 h/h. The year was 1967 and we were living at Carlton in Lindrick. Not too far away from Worksop and still in Nottinghamshire.

We decided to look in the columns of a local newspaper called the 'Sheffield Star' and were not to be disappointed. On the very first Friday night, there it was. 'Quiet grey mare, four years old, good to box, shoe and catch. Make family ride.' What were we waiting for? I picked up the telephone and rang the number – we all held our breath – had it been already sold?

'Dusty was everything we could have wished for'

Our prayers were answered – yes the horse was still there and we could go over and ride her, although they didn't have a saddle. Her name was Dusty and she sounded really nice. The horse was at Killamarsh, not too far away and we soon found ourselves in love with her. She was apparently an Irish Draught crossed with a T.B. and stood at 15 h/h 2". A little bit wide for Shirley but she obviously didn't mind that and she was soon astride her.

Dusty was everything we could have wished for. I got on her back and the old enthusiasm was re-kindled. In the U.S. Cavalry they have a saying 'There is nothing so good for the inside of a man, as the outside of a horse.' A sentiment I would endorse. Now there would be a stable to build, and some grazing to find. You will gather from this that we bought ourselves a horse.

At that time I had a friend called Phil Sparke and he rented a small piece of ground at Manton – quite near the town. In addition to having a tractor and trailer and other items of agricultural equipment, Phil also had a horse. It is remarkable how incidents in your life in some way help to influence it and I am sure one such incident certainly influenced mine.

Once we had Dusty and of course Anita's pony, Smokey, we really did need some grazing for them. The obvious solution seemed to be selling our almost newly built home and buying a house with some land. In a rural area there were quite a few options available so our search for something suitable began.

At one of these properties that we viewed the lady vendor just happened to mention that she had a field of standing hay to sell. This was in fact the adjoining paddock to the property. Although the house wasn't really suitable for our purpose, my ears pricked up when she mentioned selling the standing grass in the paddock for hay.

Phil Sparke, I immediately thought he would know what to do with it. It was a wonderful experience for me and the smell of new mown hay making is the true scent of summer. It is intoxicating.

The sun really shone for us, and the end product was several hundred bales of leafy green hay. It really did smell good enough to eat. Phil had cut the hay, turned it a few times and then borrowed a baler to bale it. There could not have been a better hay making time.

Luck was still on our side after we had removed what we needed for winter feed. A car had pulled up whilst we were loading bales and the driver, a local man from Blyth, asked if we had any to sell. He actually bought all of the remainder which left us a handsome profit. Phil and I patted each other on the back and laughed at the sheer pleasure of what we had done.

Now all of these things were fuelling my own thoughts and dreams. Just to own a meadow for the horses to graze and a house even, with outbuildings and stables. I have said in a previous book 'If you have a dream, dream it every day.' Well we shall have to wait and see, but things were going to change fast, in a very short time.

In the mean time we were going to enjoy having Dusty. I had built a stable next to the house and the pleasure of hearing horses quietly munching hay, is a sound of contentment and it does have a very therapeutic effect on people.

We all rode her – that is Shirley, Anita and myself, at local shows. Shirley, at thirteen, was a bit like a pea on a drum on her back, but what she couldn't manage to do, Dusty did for her. It was years after when we discovered the truth about the long gallops over stubble fields, Dusty, it seemed, had what they called 'taken off' with Shirley on endless occasions and they thought that was wonderful. Flat out gallops with little or no control with the wind in her face, Shirley, it seemed, was in her element.

It was at this time that I began to realize that horses really did respond to care and comfort. Our daughters loved them and this was evident by the way they were cared for and looked after. In return, Dusty in particular, had recognized her stable at our house as her comfort zone. One day a really bad thunderstorm had errupted with heavy rain, flashing lightning and frightening crashes of thunder. It really was dreadful and we were worried about the horses. They were turned out about half a mile away in a field down what was called 'Water Lane.' It said everything.

Suddenly through the mistiness of the heavy falling rain, came Dusty accompanied by the sound of galloping hooves, she came careering through the drive gates, rocketed up the winding drive, took a short cut across the corner of the lawn, straight round the back of the house like a tornado, and shot into her stable. I think we almost heard her breathe a sigh of relief – she was home. Dusty had clearly jumped a fence to get out of the field, which we learned later had partially flooded, and headed for safety.

Lesson one in this book – 'Horses know which side of their bread is buttered.'

I experienced the power of Dusty's galloping one day when I had gone out for a ride with another friend, Peter Rossington. We had gone for a hack out at a place called Hundred Acre. Later this area, I believe, was to become the location for a film about farm life in the 1920s called 'Brother to the Ox.' A very moving story about a young lad who went to 'live in' at a farm at twelve years of age, and the poverty and work load he had to endure. It really was dreadful and nothing like my childhood. My dad had a saying to describe that as well, 'You don't know you're born.' I didn't even understand what he meant, but I do now.

Anyway, back to the ride.

We were quietly walking the horses along a narrow lane in a partially wooded area. It was a lovely day and the birds were singing as we soaked up the smell of pine needles and the fragrance of other trees. I could tell Dusty was starting to get excited. She had either picked up some special scent or was anticipating what might be in store – possibly even my thoughts, of where we were going to have a good gallop. Horses can do this, their inexplicable sixth sense seems to give them powers far beyond human comprehension.

Lesson two – Never underestimate your horse's ability to read your mind. He is a prey animal and his survival depends on his ability to outwit his predators – and humans sometimes!

Pete had said at that moment, 'Let's have a canter.' I squeezed Dusty on and away we went. Just ahead the path opened out into a wider area with ploughed fields on either side. Dusty was in take- off mode and needed some restraining. I tried to check her but to no avail 'bombing off' as the girls called it, was more than imminent. At that moment Dusty's legs came under her body and the impulsion and power of a heavyweight four year old reached maximum thrust. Talk about a jet engine!

I saw my opportunity. To the left of us a deeply ploughed field stretching away up a steep incline – just what I needed. Taking my inside leg off her side and reigning sharply to the left, I turned Dusty up the field. Snorting and squealing with delight, she took the incline like a rocket. There were soil, stones and clods flying as we catapulted to the top, and quite a considerable distance it was. Pete looked on in amazement. I turned back down. 'That was spectacular,' said Pete, 'never seen anything like it.'

'Well,' I said, 'that should take the wind out of her sails.' Dusty thought otherwise. With an amazing twist of her body which caught me completely unawares, she took off up the ploughed field again, accompanied by more squeals.

My thoughts this time were of regaining control. I put a bit more pressure on the bit and tried the see saw action. The upshot was a disaster. Dusty's bit was a vulcanised pelham with a curb. It was an ordinary white metal affair which had nothing like the strength of stainless steel. The bit ring on the left hand side snapped and that was my rein control gone. How I brought Dusty to a halt I shall never know but fortunately a lot of the steam had gone out of her. I rode her down towards Pete with more than a sigh of relief.

The words of wisdom from our farrier sprang to my mind when I had bought Dusty. 'You would have been better with a gelding. Mares are like women, you never know when you've got them.' A sexist remark if ever I heard one. Was it the time of year I wondered? It had been a bit out of character even for Dusty. And it did not end there either.

We had stopped to try and make something of the broken bit, and foolishly I had removed the bridle. Dusty had been standing quietly at the side of us and then suddenly a repeat performance happened. With a squeal and a snort, she suddenly spun round and galloped away. We were flabbergasted. When I say galloped away I meant it. She quickly disappeared out of sight, and after that, we just caught glimpses of her winding her way towards the summit of a hill top. She must have been a mile away by the time she got to the top and then we could see her seemingly looking down towards us. Chasing after her didn't seem to be a good idea. Then a flash of inspiration suddenly entered my mind. 'I read in a book somewhere,' I said to Pete, 'that horses are herding animals and don't like to be left on their own. I think we should try walking away from her and see what happens – we have nothing to lose.' LOSE! It was magic. We had walked for about 5 minutes when suddenly, we could hear the sound of galloping hooves, and Dusty re-appeared as fast as she had gone – more than that, she just came up and walked quietly behind us.

Lesson three – 'It is worth learning something about horses' behavioural patterns.'

CHAPTER SIX
At a price that's very nice

We had been lucky in every sense of the word. A nice house, four lovely children and a successful business. The business had developed over a ten year period and with both Ann and myself involved, a lot of hard work, and some very good staff we were expanding.

It was our home, our anchor and our investment for the future. In fact it was the investment bit that was indirectly to change our lives!

In 1968 the 'Never had it so good' years seemed to be running out. Credit was being tightened and the banks were closely watching developments. I, in turn was watching the bank - my bank.

It had suddenly occurred to me that they owned my heart, life and soul and called it collateral. The foundations of the new house hosted my blood and my sweat, and the few silver coins thrown in for luck as we topped out the gables, did not seem to be sufficient insurance against the poor economic climate. Suddenly my business interests were not keeping pace with my ambitions and the profitability was out of step with the enthusiasm and effort I was putting in.

The economic situation in the country was getting worse (was it ever any different?) and I saw my particular world under threat. I seemed to be gambling with our security and I didn't like it.

We, like many people had suffered a sad bereavement in the family and it hit my wife Ann particularly hard. A quiet holiday seemed the answer so I booked a self catering cottage for a week in a lovely Dale in North Yorkshire. I had my own problems. Selective Employment Tax had been introduced and Purchase Tax was to go on some previously exempted goods that we sold.

The beautiful Moors and Dales and the tranquil environment was a tonic to us all. We breathed it like oxygen. I had taken our two girls pony trekking - an experience in itself. These ponies could even

These ponies could even climb walls

climb stone walls. We thought it was out of this world. The freedom, the freshness, the adventure!

My mind was working overtime. Here I was, never having enough hours in the day, seeing very little of my children and with grave doubts about the system (they call it stress these days). And this newly discovered world had a twenty four hour day and the opportunity to lift your head up and look around. It probably didn't hold entrepreneurial opportunities for building empires but for quality of life it must be unrivalled.

The ponies we were riding were a motley selection of misbehaved equine rejects. In fairness to them I should think some of them had been victims of bad behaviour and ill treatment. The tack was undescribably poor and bits of old carpets served as saddle blankets to cover up saddle sores and scars. Old binder band seemed to hold the tack and the ponies together. Fortunately today as I write this book those days are gone for good. I spoke out loud. 'What about looking for a small farm with a few acres and setting up some stables for Pony Trekking - I am sure we could do a better job than this!' We already owned a family size horse and pony.

The whoops of joy sang in my ears. My two daughters were ecstatic. 'Do you mean it Daddy, really really mean it?'

I meant it all right. Here was the opportunity I had dreamed about all my life. To actually own a green field and run a business working with horses and ponies.

'What would Mum say.'We walked home full of it. With the girls' enthusiasm overriding all logical thought and my determination to change my lifestyle, we put together a strong case. Well in our minds anyway.

Back at the cottage I let Shirley and Anita spill out their excitement. They didn't hold it back either, Ann was reeling under the onslaught. We could do this Mum, do that Mum and isn't it marvellous Mum? At last I got a word in. "Well it's certainly got a lot going for it and recessions don't last for ever". Although the area seemed very quiet ' I was convinced it was a holiday growth area. I didn't even know it was a National Park:

We persuaded Ann to agree to the idea in principal but subject to finding a suitable property within our price range. No big borrowings!

Suddenly it became an exciting adventure. With four young children what isn't. The prospect of looking over old farm property and a

Four pairs of eyes scanned the columns

possible purchase stimulated our, enthusiasm still further. We suddenly couldn't wait. That week we bought, every local newspaper we could lay our hands on. In fact any newspaper, covering the entire area. There had got to be something!

The papers' property pages were spread all over the floor as four pair of eyes scanned the columns. We were like sleuths looking for clues. By now we were hooked. The funny thing is at the time it didn't occur to us to go to an estate agent. There weren't many in those days and most kept a fairly low profile. Property booms were unheard of. We eagerly awaited the weeklys on Friday and Saturday but still nothing.

By now desperation was creeping in, it was becoming a treasure hunt. The week ended as a failure. Nothing. Well nothing in the small acreage, reasonable price and in need of restoration bracket

Well my mind was made up. We needed more time and I knew once at home over a hundred miles away the idea would die the death of all holiday good ideas. We discovered a caravan to let at Ugthorpe in Whitby and I persuaded Ann to agree to an extension of another week. 'But that's it, we go home and forget the idea.'

Now the second week was almost over and despair was in our hearts. Was there nothing in need of restoration with green acres and a suitable price tag!

That Friday we bought the Whitby Gazette and down on the floor it went. All eyes down we willed a property to leap out of the pages.

There was a property for sale that sounded nice. "Too nice," Ann lamented, 'I bet they want a fancy price.' 'Interesting beamed roof area' the advert stated 'In secluded position'.

Shirley was in paradise.

'Ring in the morning Mum, Ring in the morning Mum!'

To the children it was like Christmas Eve. Ann agreed but said she still wasn't hopeful about the price.

The next morning I had gone round to the village pub to return a few empty bottles and was having a chat with the landlord. Ann had gone to find a telephone. Suddenly in shot a small whirlwind with flushed face and eyes as big as saucers. Shirley was kicking my ankle and reciting a popular at the time television jingle. "At a price that's very nice. At a price that's very nice". she sang out. I got the message. Back at the caravan Ann had packed our luggage. It looked a formidable mountain.

The Triumph Herald had a roof rack. With four young children we

A flurry of disturbed geese

could have done with a trailer. I loaded up slowly and carefully and roped it all down. The children watched with growing impatience. 'Hurry up, Dad.

Ann was in no hurry, A two bedroomed cottage with a granary above didn't really appeal. Not with four young children.

"It has no mains water, no mains sewerage and goodness knows how secluded it is, the Estate Agent wished me luck finding it."

"And what about school?". My wife's opposition was gathering momentum.

"Well it's on the way home," I almost faltered.

"Yes and good job too." (Anybody remember Al Read?)

We found it all right but not before ending up at two other farms first. It's amazing and it still hasn't changed much, nobody bothers about having a farm sign, even though you can wander miles along a track only to find yourself at the wrong place - we did.

One section of the road, and if you are a visitor you know exactly where I mean, is something of a challenge. To my heavily overloaded and grossly underpowered 1200cc Triumph Herald it wasn't a challenge it was an offensive against the impossible. We ground slowly up, bottom gear and fingers crossed. At last we were on the farm track crossing a field no less. A flurry of disturbed geese had projected themselves at the car as we slowly drove alongside a pond and then nothing. We climbed a rise in the landscape and then we could see the farm.

It really looked a picture and I immediately fell in love with it.

We drove though the gate into seventeen acres of open pasture. A few sheep and a few bullocks grazed in the sunshine.

This has got to be God's little garden I thought.

CHAPTER SEVEN
Northward Bound

The morning of my departure from Carlton-in-Lindrick was as heavy and overcast as it was miserable. At 7 am it was barely light and the cloud and drizzle almost clung to the ground.

With the negotiations and transactions just about completed it was to be a complete change to a totally new and different way of life, but it would be ours - all ours. It hadn't been particularly easy, even to sell our lovely house - a typical casualty of economic decline. The sale had eventually gone through but only after we had some very -uneasy moments and not always concern for ourselves. The people who were selling Ease Side Farm were emigrating to Australia. Because my wife Ann (her real name is Anita but I have always called her Ann) had agreed that we buy the farm only on condition that our first offer be accepted, I was not to get a second chance at what she saw as sheer madness, by negotiating further!

Our offer had by now of course been accepted, but it was subject to completion and that depended on being able to sell our house. At the time it did sometimes look a little doubtful. The Hitchenors however, the vendors, accepted the offer and on the strength of it, started to make arrangements for their journey to Australia - they even sent most of the furniture! You can imagine our horror at hearing this news and the grave concern we had for them, should our house not sell. It did not bear thinking about.

During our conveyancing arrangements the usual answers to questions were sought and searches made. One of the most significant, and especially after our much publicised planning dispute, was one question our Solicitor asked of the Vendors. 'Was the property in a National Park or similar situation and what conditions if any, were imposed on the property in view of this?'

Answer. Yes, National Park and No, no conditions. Ah well the

It was primitive and cold

halcyon and oblivious day of 1969!

Back to this dim and dismal morning, the 15th December 1969. John Hardasty, a bricklayer and builder friend was accompanying me to Staintondale to make a start on the fabric of the house. We called it gutting and getting -rid of some of the muck and rubble. We were to live in the house for just over a couple of weeks and make a start on the restoration prior to the family moving in. I have described the move in my first booklet.

Our tools and equipment were loaded into an old single horse trailer hitched to the car. My zest and enthusiasm for not forgetting anything proved to be bordering on the ridiculous - the car struggled to get the thing moving. It was as heavy as my heart and we had over a hundred miles to go - mostly in third gear. A saga of a journey made worse by deteriorating weather.

As we approached Scarborough travelling over the Wolds, the drizzle gave way to sleet and rain and the whole situation was one of creeping misery - at least that is what it felt like.

We passed Scarborough by and were now on the final leg of the journey, the A171 Whitby road, at a village called Burniston. On the right hand side I spotted a Pub, 'The Three Jolly Sailors.' Without consulting John I pulled across the road and into the car park. A pub lunch was what we needed and a pint of good old fashioned bitter, a sheer necessity. Inside it was everything we could have dreamt of. A cosy room, a roaring fire licking up the chimney and a feeling of warmth and serenity with every flicker of the shadows on the beams. Sanity had been restored.

Lunch and beverages over we left the sanctuary of this most welcome hostelry and continued Northwards towards Staintondale. We left the A171 at Cloughton and took the minor road which hugs the coastline. It was sleeting quite hard by this time and the scene to the right of us looking out to sea was distinctly inhospitable. A grey and cold mass of water, and a coastline looking rugged and desolate.

What had I done? I thought back to the friends and comfort left behind. As we turned the final turn along the road leading down the dale, I had the most serious misgiving of my life. The road narrowed, turned left and plunged down a steep hill through the trees. It made it dark and forbidding. My heart sank into my boots.

At the farm things only got worse. We went to the barn door which was to take us through to the back of the house and a vicious bark greeted us, as a dog threw itself against the door on the inside. Its barking and snarling continued to the extent that we decided to forget the back door and make for the front. I shall return to the dog later.

Once in the house my fears and doubts about this move became infinitely worse. It was very dark on such a day due to the weather and the small windows, but worse, the smell of damp and I suppose the smell associated with cold and old property was overwhelming. I looked down at the floor - a mixture of flagstones and concrete patches lying on virgin earth. Damp was an understatement.

I thought of my wife Ann and her nice new house that I had helped to build. I thought of central heating and fitted carpets. I thought what the devil am I going to tell her?

A rusting old cast iron AGA Cooker that had looked so homely on our many visits had long since gone out. The damp had already got to work on the iron and started the rusting process. The electricity had been disconnected and I peered into the gloomy corners trying to adjust my eyes. There was no respite to my inner thoughts they were gloomier than the situation.

John spoke. "Your description fell far short of my mental picture - you must be mad. I can't believe anybody could swap your much envied life and lifestyle for a place like this." I joked back, or was it a choke? "Just give it time, by the summer you won't recognise the place. "Again my thoughts drifted - it really is idyllic in the summer, I consoled myself.

We got to work straight away on re-building a lean-to kitchen made out of railway sleepers and tarred boarding. After propping up the roof we demolished what was left. This gave me a big kick, swinging a fourteen pound (6.5 kilo) hammer alternately with a pick axe I burned up my inhibitions and frustrations. I would make it work.

After the demolition we had to start digging new footings, but by now it was snowing heavily. Just what we needed on our first day. "We shall have to rigg up some protection," said John. "These trenches will be full of water." Fortunately we had a big roll of polythene D.P.C. sheeting and we were able to hang some of this from the roof and form a tent. It is hard to believe now, but that day with the aid of a paraffin tilley pressure lantern we worked on until 9pm. Time was at a premium

I cooked some hamburgers and made some instant mashed potato. We ate it with lots of bread and butter and a mug of tea. It was primitive and cold but (excuse the expression) we could have eaten a horse!

At IOpm with the food eaten and the temperature dropping towards freezing our Aladdin Blue~ flame oil heater seemed totally inadequate. The thought of kipping down in a sleeping bag was even more unacceptable at the time. We decided, to head for the local - The Shepherds Arms. I suppose it was an average sort of night, mainly locals who seemed to hardly notice our entry. A table echoed with the sound of dominoes being shuffled and the steady throb throb of darts hitting the board were the only sounds rising above the muted sound of country conversation. I suspect we were no more than a couple of bricklayers or labourers passing through.

"Two pints of bitter please," I said. Dick Lockey, the Landlord looked enquiringly into our faces. If he was curious about our presence or our purpose it didn't show. He purposefully pulled two pints of beer with expert precision and put them on the bar. I handed him the money and with a well practised 'Thank you' he gave me the change.

The huge fire, packed to capacity with both coal and logs drew us like a magnet. We moved closer soaking up the heat and revelling in the comfort of old fashioned (by today's standards) Public House hospitality. An institution fast disappearing.

Soon we were withdrawing back from the flames, the intense heat starting to penetrate our clothing. A move we were to repeat many times over the years to come.

In 1969 an abundance of fancy obtrusive outside lighting was a rarity. Indeed driving from Cloughton to Ravenscar was like a drive over-uninhabited Moorland. Barely a light flickered in the Dale below, the only lights glinting were those of fishing boat lanterns dancing on the dark waters.

To approach the Shepherds Arms out of total blackness on a dark and cloudy winter's night was like a page from Jamaica Inn. A single light illuminated a sign on the gable end and another over the entrance guided you in.

Shepherd Arms, the name of the pub, is a clue to the sort of terrain this area is made up of. For centuries it would be sheep grazing, originally owned by Monks and later by the Knights hospitallers of St. John.

The Manor of Stainton in Blackmoor was given to the Order by King Stephen in the Twelfth century and would no doubt boast a huge flock of sheep both within and without the boundaries of the Royalty. The Shepherd Arms is a known meeting place of Ancient Shepherds well

A page from Jamaica Inn

into the Nineteenth Century and less ancient shepherd to the present day!

The fire mellowed our thoughts and to me the situation less hostile. We sat back and enjoyed the atmosphere, the ale no doubt, giving it a rosy glow.

A large clock face just above the bar on the right gave away its secrets. The fingers now stood at twenty past eleven and the remaining company looked in no hurry to disperse. A resident or two perhaps!

John stood up, looked towards the landlord and enquired "What time do you close?" Dick Lockey'looked up and without a flicker of an eyelid replied "Half past ten!"

In a flash John retorted "Just time for one more then?" "If you're quick," said Dick as he reached for the empty glasses.

The fingers stood at twenty past eleven

CHAPTER EIGHT
The likely lads

East Side Farm is a small traditional Dales Farm built of local stone. The house itself consisted originally of two downstairs rooms and a small dairy with two bedrooms above - one on either side of the staircase. Above that in the loft area of the roof was the granary. Access to the Granary was on the south eastern gable up a flight of stone steps.

The house nestles snuggly into a bank and is sheltered from the north and east.

A range of farm buildings built round a courtyard forms complete protection for wintering stock and a through barn stored the grain and fodder.

Through doors (Thurff Duers) was the name given to these purpose built buildings. In the days of hand threshing corn and wheat a flail would be used. The husks were separated from the kernel by riddling with the wind blowing through the open doors. This cleared the dust and the separated husks. It was a cleaning process. Sometimes the gathered up grain from the stone floor would be bagged and pulled upside down-towards the apex of the roof. The band or thong tying up the neck of the sack would be released. As the dusty grain gushed downwards the wind again helped to separate the wheat from the chaff. Deeds show that the house was rebuilt in 1814 - A new farmhouse is referred to in the deeds. These date back to 1770 and all in original vellum and manuscripted by hand.

The farm deeds are a complete encyclopedia of its own history. Within the deeds and documents the wills of several former owners are to found. All telling their own story. Pictures of a way of life long since past but steeped in tradition and full of intrigue. Even the manorial and wreckers rights are referred to.

Local legend has it, that if a shipwreck occurred on a Sunday, word would be sent to the local church and the news quietly passed along the rows of pews. Anyone attending the service who had claims to the wreck, equally quietly filed out - until they reached the door!

A good mental picture of the original layout of the interior of the house should be recorded. The front door itself was in the centre front of the building. There was no porch. Inside the house, the door opened into a small hall area and a passageway which went through to the back of the house. Out of the hall a door on the left took you into a small sitting room and another door immediately in front led up the stairs. At the far end of the passageway a door on the right led into the main living room - a quite narrow room. On the left and under the stairs landing, was the dairy or pantry. Although the floor has been re-surfaced with mastic asphalt, it is worth mentioning that underneath lie the lovely old stone flags scrubbed almost white and with the centre tread area worn away to give a gentle concave hollow to the stone. Nearly 200 years of straining and skimming milk, separating cream and making butter had left its legacy behind. The meat hooks still look down from the beams above, but on a totally different scene. If only walls could talk.

Let us return to the Shepherds Arms. Variously referred to locally as 'Dicks', 'The Sheps', or the 'Shepherds' in something of that order. It is situated on the roadside looking out to sea and probably commanding one of the finest coast views in North Yorkshire. The Pub had formerly belonged to Mary Lockey's father and Mary had come there as a little girl so being the Landlord's wife held no surprises. She knew the business and the customers and she knew them equally well. Dick kept a good house and many's the time, after pulling a half pint glass, he would hold it up to the light. "Too good for the general public" he would observe! He placed the newly filled glasses on the bar. North Yorkshire born and bred, a man of few words was Dick Lockfey.

John by now relaxed and talkative, pursued the conversation. Looking straight at me he said to the Landlord, "You want to look after this chap if this is to be his local, he's a rugby player and" (at this point looking round the pub in a challenging sort of fashion) he carried on, "He could drink more beer in one night than this lot could drink in a month!" I looked down at the floor - there were only two of us!

My fears of this remark upsetting somebody were groundless. The remaining customers responded with spontaneous enthusiasm. Why, how, where and for what reason was on everybody's lips.

John bolder by now and in the chair, "Tony's bought East Side Farm and he's bringing his family up soon to live here. We are just doing some alterations and re-building the kitchen and they will be moving in come January!"

At that point my fears, anxiety and all previous misgivings were dispelled in a flash,. Everybody was talking at once "Oh Roger Hitchenor's place - he played rugby - grand little spot - one of the best spots in the village. Anything you need, any help - just ask you'll love it, nice to meet you - It just went on and on. You could call it a rural exchange of friendliness but it did the trick. I knew we could make it our home. A few more drinks and we were all the best of friends - after all it was approaching Christmas.

Somebody nicknamed us the likely lads, so our password for a pint became a couple of swift halves - it stuck and 22 years later it still stands.

We left the pub eventually and headed for the farm. A sharp frost had descended and the ground and the verges glistened. As we headed down the dale I was aware of a slippery incline ahead - "hold on," I said to John, "You'll enjoy this." I shot the car downwards and over the bridge, at the same time accelerating gently, we flew up the bank and way on without a problem. John said "And my wife thinks you're a nice steady bloke." We both laughed!

The next day after a pretty miserable night in sleeping bags we woke to discover that the water was frozen up. In typical building site fashion we lit a cement bag fire round an outside stand pipe and then filled our kettle.

We decided life was going to be a bit rough for a while but consoled ourselves that at least we had the Pub now, and our newly acquired friends.

We had the footings dug out, awaiting the concrete but inspite of our plastic sheeting the melted snow and rain had percolated into the trenches. "Only one thing to do," I said to John, "bale out what we can, dry mix some strong concrete and wop it in. God'11 provide the water."

I have got to say that we were already down to solid blue clay - the only foundation the entire house is built on. So anything that could improve that is a bonus. Our method worked and worked well.

The rest of that day we carried round all the blocks and facing for the new kitchen. They were stored in the hay barn to keep dry and had to be brought up the front of the house and right through it to the back. All was ready for a flying start the following morning, so after getting ourselves cleaned up it was a bowl of hot soup, bread and cheese and Shepherds here we come!

That night at the Pub everybody seemed in festive spirit, I suppose the old legend about strangers in your midst had something to do with it.Mary had a small music centre and a couple of small speakers stood onthe mantel piece and some of the sixties favourites rang out. We had a real party and decided there and then it was to be a rave up every night until   Christmas. "Just wait until your wife gets here I am surprised she lets you out of her sight."

But it was all good harmless fun and anyway had they any idea what my wife was like? I told them that a friend had told me that if I found myself a young strong Irish lass, I could sell the horse!

This had proved useful advice and my wife, although a big strong sort of a lass was really quite nice, and I was sure they would like her. What sort of a mental picture this had conjured up I dare not think but Mary the landlady told Ann later that they were in dread of meeting her, they really did fear the worst!

Fears totally unfounded of course and my description so far from the truth that Mary later confirmed to Ann and said what a smashing person she was and what was she doing with a husband like me?

If

If you can keep your head when all about you
    Are losing theirs and blaming it on you,
If you can trust yourself when all men doubt you,
    But make allowance for their doubting too;
If you can wait and not be tired of waiting,
    Or being lied about, don't deal in lies,
Or being hated don't give way to hating,
    And yet don't look too good, nor talk too wise:

If you can dream — and not make dreams your master;
    If you can think — and not make thoughts your aim:
If you can meet with Triumph and Disaster
    And treat those two impostors just the same:
If you can bear to hear the truth you've spoken
    Twisted by knaves to make a trap for fools,
Or watch the things you gave your life to, broken,
    And stoop and build 'em up with worn-out tools:

If you can make one heap of all your winnings
    And risk it on one turn of pitch-and-toss,
And lose, and start again at your beginnings
    And never breathe a word about your loss;
If you can force your heart and nerve and sinew
    To serve your turn long after they are gone,
And so hold on when there is nothing in you
    Except the Will which says to them: 'Hold on!'

If you can talk with crowds and keep your virtue,
    Or walk with Kings — nor lose the common touch,
If neither foes nor loving friends can hurt you,
    If all men count with you, but none too much;
If you can fill the unforgiving minute
    With sixty seconds' worth of distance run,
Yours is the Earth and everything that's in it,
    And — which is more — you'll be a Man, my son!

Rudyard Kipling

CHAPTER NINE
Rising Damp

The dismal day of our arrival was still fresh in my mind and the scene which met us as I opened the front door vivid. The interior of the house, now stripped of its furnishings and floor covering was a depressing sight. The patched and broken flags of the living room which I have described earlier still stared up at me. I had opened the door leading on to the staircase and another visual broadside hit me. The old original staircase was a mess, something I hadn't even allowed for in our work programme. Evidence of woodworm was very apparent but worse than that, the treads were in a terrible state. It looked like the wear of years of going upstairs to bed still wearing hobnailed boots. The rounded nosings of the treads were chanelled away. To make it usable, and I have no doubt that it wasn't deliberately done to hide anything, rubber protectors had been nailed over the front edge of each tread. These together with pads on the stairs themselves had allowed a stair carpet to be fitted. This had now gone of course, and as I saw things now, the entire flight of stairs would have to go!

I had telephoned Ann at what we still call home, and gently broke the news. There was no hesitation in her response, "Well something's got to be done about it before we move in. There is no way we can lay carpets or anything else in that situation. "She was still not convinced that we were making a good move and who could blame her. From a lovely new house we had lived in for only seven years to this. I eyed the scene before my eyes. The old Aga even rustier by now and with our crude cooking arrangements and sleeping bags lying around, I think poverty stricken summed it up. Well a primus stove stood on an old oil drum wasn't exactly the scene of a Corden Bleu cook. It was a challenge anyway and I consoled myself with this thought. The amazing thing about it was that it didn't worry me too much. I knew exactly what I was going to do and I had a lovely mental picture of what the end product would look like.

The thing to do first was to get a price for laying mastic asphalt over the entire ground floor area. I reached for Yellow Pages.

Nearly all the firms were around the Leeds area and they were all very efficient and co-operative - Yes give me the floor area and we will get an estimate in the post. That was until I got through to one particular firm - a veritable entrepreneur, a man going places - I liked his style. "Give me the area, I willgive you a price now and we'll get over there sharpish and get it done."

The price was right and I accepted.

"I am assuming that this is an old farm property with no damp proof course, so to take full advantage of our flooring process I am suggesting that you remove all skirting boards and any door casings and architrave running down to ground floor level. Then, and this is the reason for it, if you rake out all the joints in the stonework near the ground we can run the mastic well in." He added "Mastic asphalt is not just a good flexible and resilient floor it is also a good damp proofer so you are getting the best of both worlds."

Demolition wasn't the word! If you can try to imagine the scene, it was organised vandalism at its best. The living room was half boarded with matchboard nailed on to battens secured to the wall. We decided to rip the lot off! God, the awful smell of rising damp and rotting timber hidden for donkeys years behind a fresh coat of paint. Out came the wooden wall partitioning which separated the room from the staircase. Off came the interior doors and skirting boards and finally we ripped out the stairs lock, stock and barrel. What a mess - we couldn't see for muck and dust. The front door was wide open to let some air in, but it was also providing the exit for all the woodwork - most of the house seemed to be going outside. John joked, "We shall only be left with a pile of stone, shall we pull it down and start again?" By now we had a massive pile of debris on the front lawn massive by any standard.

At that point Roger Hitchenor arrived to leave a bag of dog biscuits (Oh, yes the dog was still in the barn!) He looked at us in amazement but even more so when he took stock of the situation and saw the great pile of the former contents.

"Do you think you will manage to get it all back?": Grinning, I said, "Roger, it isn't going back, it looks like its got to be a complete refit."

45

Most of the house seemed to be going outside

He was a really nice bloke and he and his wife and three young sons had enjoyed living at Eastside. "Well it was ready for it," he said "We have already done a lot, there was no bathroom when we came and the whole of the outside had to be repointed. Our resources couldn't manage much more and I certainly didn't have the know-how to tackle something like this. It has always been a happy house though and I am sure you will make it a showpiece. He wished me luck and I returned the compliment. They were off to seek their fortune in Australia.

It was nearly dark now and so I lit the old pressure lantern. What a complete disaster area we had created. The lamp threw a mixture of light and shadows into the gloom and settling dust. It looked like a dungeon! We eyed up ihe newly exposed plaster clinging to the wall and the damp areas where the house is actually built into the bank. It was like exposing history. An unusual shade of blue, reminiscent of a Reckitts blue bag (for those who remember them) had been used at sometime to try and decorate the walls. It looked like a hundred years ago but it seemed to bring the past and probably the poverty into our lives at that moment.

"It looks like cow dung and lime put on with a shovel," laughed John. We both laughed. What was so funny I don't know but there was never a dull moment. Well there couldn't be, could there? "It will all have to come off," said John picking up a flat bladed pick.

The following day with the walls stripped and the place swept out we waited for the Asphalt men arriving. It was snowing hard.

At 11.15 am through the swirling snowflakes we heard the sound of a vehicle. Sure enough our contractors had arrived. A battered old lorry towing a trailer which was actually the tar boiler to melt the blocks of mastic asphalt.

They tried to drive up the bank to get the vehicle and equipment up to the front door. It was hopeless, the wheels just skidded in the snow. We went to help. Fortunately we had a pile of sharp sand lying just inside the barn, purchased for even more concreting at a later date. Grabbing some shovels we quickly got some grit under the wheels and with a bit of brute force and shunting the vehicle was manoeuvered into position.

Our plan was to leave these men to it and return after the weekend when our nice new shiny floor would be laid. We went into the house and they followed us. "God, who would want to live in a God forsaken place like this," was the first comment. I grinned inwardly - "It takes

47

all sorts." We were just a pair of bricklayers to them. Picking up our transistor radio I made for the door. "Don't take that way please - leave us some contact with the outside world!" said one.

The snow had thickened and the sky was heavy with more. It was bleak mid winter all right.

As we drove down the track we looked back, even their vehicle was obliterated now in that short distance. "What's the betting they're still here when we get back," I said to John.

"We've got to get home yet - come on lets get the hell out of it!"

CHAPTER TEN
A dog's life

The inventories of the small amount of remaining 'live and dead' farm stock was something like a condensed version of Noah's Ark. There were two sheep, both mature ewes now but both reared as pets by Ann Hichenor. One was a pure Suffolk by the name of Jane and the other a Dorset Down cross, Susan. Both were very friendly and tame.

There was two cats. One called Apache and one called Cheyanne. They had immediately taken to John and myself and had lived with us in the house prior to the family moving in. Well we fed them their daily bread and whatever else was going, from our crude but adequate menu.

There was also a pair of bantams - they perched high up in the roof of the barn adjoining the house at night and scratted around the yard and haybarn during the day. Bantam eggs are very tasty but this was December and the hen wouldn't be laying much before February.

In addition to these few animals we also took over two galvanised iron pig troughs, one sheep trough, a yard brush and a muck fork!

Oh yes, there was an old rulley (flat bed waggon on rubbers). It's amazing the difference in names given to farm vehicles in different parts of the country. In Nottinghamshire, Derbyshire and South Yorkshire it would be called a dray but in other parts a trolley. Men delivering beer with horses were usually called draymen - in fact still are.

The small, quite comical looking vehicle I had acquired was my first real piece of horse drawn equipment. We had no previous experience of livestock or farming or indeed anything connected with agriculture. My only claim to any connection with the land was that my great grand parents, on my father's side lived near Crich in Derbyshire, were farmers and corn chandlers later to become carters and haulage contractors. They were called Flint (Joseph and Mary) and we suspect

49

they were of Irish origin.

My obsession with horses which I described in my first booklet was also associated with a love of green fields, woods and natural surroundings. I had to make it all happen. If you have a dream, dream it every day.Roger Hitchenor had a dog called Sally, a chocolate and white border collie. We had seen it and played with it on our many visits to Eastside before we actually bought the property. It seemed very friendly like all border collies, but it did have a streak of aggression towards strangers, especially on our earlier visits. Ann was wary of it.

It was a contentious issue for the period leading up to the arrival of John and myself at the farm. Roger, obviously not wanting to have the dog put down was both persistent and persuasive that we should take it on. Ann was quietly determined that we should not. "I just wouldn't trust it with the children, you have seen how aggressive it can be - anyway its got peculiar pink eyes. Don't you be talked into it!"

I have already described the arrival of John and myself at the farm and the fiery reception we got from the dog. Things hadn't changed much. Each day a boy from the farm at the back came down and fed the dog. Sometimes he would hold it while we got equipment or building materials out of the barn. It never seemed to give up on its total distrust of us and neither did we give it a chance to show it! God, how that dog could snarl.

The days had gone by. Roger promising to take the dog away but for one reason or another, he didn't. What goes on in a dog's mind is difficult to imagine but I suspect Sally was missing her owners and especially the three boys who no doubt she loved.

Inside she would probably feel abandoned and deserted. Pining for familiar voices. Who were we, and what was our purpose. She neither knew us or trusted us.

One night in our by now, favourite local hostelry, spirits were running high and no doubt the beer was running somewhere! Christmas was getting closer and the farmhouse was taking on a new dimension. Our restoration was well on course and I was feeling happy. The subject got round to the dog, Sally. "Is Roger's dog still down there?" enquired Dick. "It's still there all right," said John, "but it's not getting any friendlier." "Tell you what," Dick leaned over the bar, "It won't do. It's a queer dog that, not many people round here trust it. It's got a reputation has that dog!"

So forlorn, so miserable, so dejected

The beer and the conviviality of the surroundings, the glowing coals of the fire and me in good spirits, pushed me into the conversation. Against my better judgement I just had to get myself involved. "Oh, I don't think it's that bad. It was quite friendly when we used to come and look round. I think it's just because its been abandoned - or at least thinks it has!"

"Well," said John, "Tomorrow is your big chance to prove it. We have all that timber to get out of the barn and that young lad won't be around."

The morning dawned its usual grim and foreboding presence. It never seemed to get light at all these days. Cold and grey was normal and a few snowflakes occasionally helped to lighten the gloom. It was miserable first thing every morning. We lit the tilley lamp and then the oil stove - Roll on civilisation. I poured the methylated spirits into the reservoir of the primus stove, hands shaking with the cold. "Don't forget you've got a job to do today." John had just returned from the outside standpipe with the kettle filled with water. "Don't remind me," I shivered inwardly. "I was hoping nobody took much notice of what I said." John laughed, "You were on good form last night, you even sang them a few song s, they lapped it up. There is no way you can go back up there without sorting that dog out."

I carried on cooking breakfast. It was the usual bacon on fried bread and several mugs of tea to get our circulation going. It was dark this morning though. I decided to wait for more light before going anywhere near that dark barn.

We made a start. By now after only a week the new kitchen was built and plastered out and we had even got a new flight of stairs in place. John was a damn good worker.

At 10.30 1 decided to make my move. After thinking my strategy out carefully, I opened both ends of a large tin of dog meat. With one end still in position I pushed the meat right though the tin and sat it on my hand. The theory was, that if the dog did want to bite something, it could have a go at this large cylindrical section of dog meat. Balancing the meat on my left hand I made for the barn door. I deliberately kicked against the door calling the dog's name. A bit more deliberate bravado really, but I wasn't feeling very brave.

There was no response! I just couldn't believe it. I kicked again, "Sally, Sally?" I enquired. No sound. My hands closed on the door handle. I squeezed the sneck. Still no sound. Pushing the door slightly open, I peered into the darkness. It was very dark inside this old building. The walls were of grey stone and the floor (at that time) of earth. No sign of the dog and no sound. I was worried. My immediate thought was has the dog pined away and died! I felt sick inside.

John was stood behind me and seemed to sense my anxiety, "I'll get the lamp."

I shone the lamp round the clutter of building materials and tools. "Sally, Sally," I called out. And then I saw her, the light picking up those distinctly pink eyes. She was crawling towards me on her belly. No hint of aggression, no sound. She looked so forlorn, so miserable and so dejected that my previous fears vanished. I put out my hand and stroked her head. She responded with a gentle whimper and licked my other hand. I had made a devoted and loyal friend.

It goes without saying that we kept Sally. And whenever my wife Ann was in the house alone she was always on guard outside the back door.

Equally, Ann who was originally so opposed to having the dog became as attached to Sally as she has to Eastside Farm. I mentioned this in my previous book, 'The staunchest supporter of our new way of life.'

CHAPTER ELEVEN
Stone Town

Stone has always held a strange fascination for me and never so much as the day Roger Hitchenor was escorting me on a walk over the farm.

"These walls," said Roger pointing to some with particularly large pieces of stone built into the bottom, "Are said to be very old, ancient in fact. I don't know exactly how old but certainly hundreds of years."

We both marvelled at the size of some of them and speculated where they had come from and how they were manoeuvred into position. Some must have weighed a ton!

"I suppose they just littered the surface of the landscape until someone decided to clear them up and put them to good use", was an idea put forward. "Yes," said Roger, "And it's amazing how much shelter they provide, especially for sheep."

Shelter was all important, particularly where we were standing just north of the farm. Roger pointed to a Quickthorn bush. "Look at that, it's spectacular."

It was indeed. Standing on the lea side of a stone wall it looked like a one sided umbrella. The foliage was almost horizontal with a flat top, all the foliage to the south. The wind had created a natural sculpture.

"That's seen some wild and windy winter's nights - and days." Our thoughts were mutual.

Walking inland we came across a chimney, the house itself completely hidden from view until we were literally on top of it. "That's Rigg Hall - Ethel and Bob Taylor," Roger went on, "Salt of the earth with a heart of gold, that's Ethel, and Bob's a smashing chap as well. If you get stuck with anything or need some help, they are the people to ask. Bob'll always pop down."

We soon got introduced and became good neighbours. Ethel Taylor was and still is a character - you could hear her raucous laugh all over the dale. Mind you she said that about mine!

"A lot of history too," said Roger. "Staintondale was once the home of the Knights Hospitalers of St. John and legend has it that King Stephen was sheltered here by those same Knights. In return he granted them a Charter!"

Little was I to know at that time just how interesting this information was going to prove and useful too, and how much more of the background and the story I was going to unearth. History, both legendary and factual is another weakness. What better place on earth to pursue my curiosity.

Ye Manor of Steynton in Blackamore -'A Stone Town on a bleak moor!' This is the description given in copies of the old Charter which I now have in my possession. The boundary of the Manor is also graphically described using named landmarks and the position of bounder stones. Becks are also referred to and a clear indication of the entire township can be visualised.

It is fascinating stuff and the amazing thing is some of the gifts and considerations granted by King Stephen way back in the Twelfth Century still hold good today. For example all our carts and wagons bear the inscription 'Toll and Tax Free' and I was told on the good authority of the last of a line of Village Joiners and Wheelwrights, the late Mr. Arnold Leonard that Staintondale wagons had borne that inscription for centuries. The rights to claim exemption from toll charges was exercised as recently as 1958 when Staintondale wagons were allowed to freely lead sand off Scarborough beaches.

The craft of making traditional agricultural equipment including ploughs, carts and wagons had been previously carried on by Arnold Leonard's father and grandfather.

The old Smithy is close by the premises previously occupied by the Leonards but that too no longer rings with sounds of hammer and anvil. Nor do we hear the whinney of impatient horses.

One item of interest at the farm and one that is on display is a North Cave plough. It's interesting because the plough sock or point came off the last of this type of plough to be actually made in Staintondale in 1958. Not so many years ago really when you compare it with the centuries since King Stephen was put on the throne in 1135.

Arnold Leonard, giving me the sock for the plough I had acquired elsewhere had said, "Oh yes its a North Cave sock. It came off the last plough my father made in Staintondale and nobody wanted it. I only sawed it up a year or two ago - got sick of falling over t'handles!" This would be about 1978. A lovely bit of local history I am proud to record.

Arnold Leonard also did a lot of work for me on the Dales Waggon prior to its final restoration. I spent so much time up at the joiners shop Mrs. Leonard used to give me lunch. I think I rated as- an improver but it taught me a lot about horse drawn vehicle construction.

This Chapter is called 'Stone Town' so let us not get too far from the subject of stone. In the inclosure awards of 1829 there were 3 stone quarries in the village, all faithfully recorded and awarded to the Lords and Ladies of the aforesaid Manor.

The Lords and Ladies of course being the freeholders who had in fact by this time purchased the Manor, and were Co-owners. As Staintondale freeholders these manorial nights are conveyed to us in our Deeds which I referred to earlier. I am hoping to get some of these interesting documents photocopied and put on display very soon.

Stone is a beautiful commodity. Its colours are both striking and subtle. You need to photograph a stone wall at sunset and study the picture, to really appreciate what you probably see every day of your life. A lot of stone used locally is sandstone but occasionally you pick up a piece of marble limestone - a natural gemstone really. Something worthy of admiration and used as a decorative architectural feature for centuries.

Progress on the farm was now becoming both rapid and rewarding. We had returned to the house after our departure in the snow, to discover that the asphatlers' lorry wasn't buried in a drift,but had gone. What was left was a first class job and the creation of a shiny black pitch mastic floor. It looked so good we felt like walking on it in stocking feet! What a transformation. By now, and we were only into our second week, things were really shaping up. Another flight of stairs running parallel to the first had replaced the old worm-eaten loft ladder to the granary and a small stone block fireplace built in what we now called the small sitting room.

"Tell you what," I said to John, "Do you fancy building a big stone chimney breast to house a blacksmith made dog grate?" The manorial rights and title had already gone to my head. I could see the crossed swords and coat of arms already, in my mind.

"I'd like to build one," said John - "Leave my mark on the place, well there's loads of stone - it will just need humping in. It will take a few ton you know."

That night I roughed out a basic design and we decided to make a start.

If you can imagine something ten feet square with a great slab of a hearth nearly four feet long and nearly a foot thick, it will give you some idea of what we were taking on.

We got this great fire place built up to lintol level - that's the great slab needed to carry the stonework over the huge dog grate opening

This monument of stone was built basically by choosing the pieces as we went along from the piles of stone which seemed to be everywhere. Most I had trundled or rolled down the front garden path or if smaller, barrowed. But all through the front door. Pitch mastic flooring is tough too!.

We needed a lintol about five feet long. A nice clean piece of stone squared and faced. It was decided that we go on a search mission. This piece was not going to be easy.

Round the farm, down the track. Up and down the walls in the fields. In and out of buildings. Nothing. Nothing even near to what we wanted. "It's an old gatepost we want," said John, "But even then its got to be a good one. They usually taper at the top."

We returned to the track and farm gateways - the thought of digging up one of these posts seemed a bit desperate.

And then we saw it. As if put there by a guiding hand. This post stuck in the ground. We must have walked past it twenty times. It wasn't a gatepost - what was it?

We decided it was a marker stone put in by some ancient freeholder or hospitaller to guide travellers possibly to the old Hospital or Chapel? It was after all at the side of the track leading northwards.

We started digging, it just had to be the right length now. The post was over two feet in the ground and as it turned out, exactly the right length. How lucky can you get?

It would be difficult to say how heavy that stone was, but we reckoned three or four hundred weights at least.

We fetched a barrow and after endless attempts to lift it on we finally managed it. Measuring sixteen inches by six by five feet, it must have been twice the weight of a comparable piece of sandstone.

I got hold of the handles of the barrow - with difficulty I could just lift them. The pneumatic tyre looked decidedly flat and fit to burst but worse that that I couldn't even push the barrow. "It's a rope we need,"

The barrow over the stone, me over the handles

John suggested, "I will slip up and get one."

He was soon back and with the rope tied on to the front he started to pull and me push.

"Keep her rolling," he yelled, "Don't stop!"

We got up speed and our enthusiasm took over. Then it happened. The stone slid off the front, dropped in front of the wheel. The barrow stopped dead and shot right over the stone. The barrow over the stone, me flying over the handles and the whole situation became farcical. I picked myself up off the ground, we just stood and laughed. Our breath spent, what else could we do?

I said breath spent, and I meant it. We tried in vain to pick up that monster piece of stone again. It was hopeless. Every ounce of energy in our bodies was spent.

We left the stone lying in the middle of the track and just hoped nobody came. A cup of tea seemed a good idea to re-charge our batteries. After that, we returned to the scene and this time we succeeded, the stone was eventually manhandled through the front door!

Getting it into place must have been similar to the building of the pyramids. We built a ramp of stone and timber and slowly, inch by inch we walked it into position!

At that precise moment a neighbour walked in. I was to experience at first hand a piece of real North Yorkshire local dialect. "Wheears thi fetched staines fra?"

It is difficult to put in writing the way this enquiry was expressed. it could have been a foreign language. I looked blank

Our neighbour looked puzzled 'Staines' he said pointing at the baronial edifice, "Wherefrae" It dawned and I laughed out loud. "You had me there, I'm going to need somebody to interpret for a while."

Some of the words still used in this part of the World were brought over from the Scandinavian countries and are very much part of the local vocabulary. It is not surprising they are difficult to understand - Anyway 'Staines, of course, Stone Town'. I should have known.

We got this great fireplace built

CHAPTER TWELEVE
Historic speculation

What I have found truly amazing is the profound interest people show in my daily talks with regard to the historic connections. Not just one particular section of the audience but a broad spectrum of wide ranging age groups.

History at school to most people is a dry subject. You could say dead almost to the majority. Only one date sticks in most people's minds - well at least of my generation, 1066.

Little did I realise that this date was to recur so predominantely in my life years later.

I do not profess to be an historian, nor do I claim to be an authority on the subject. Any serious minded scholars reading this please note ` This is my story based on historic speculation and possibly not without a touch of added colour.

Colouring a subject and I think I do this by a good application of sheer enthusiasm and of course the use of the horses, brings the history to life.

Almost a ton of might and muscle. Oh yes they definitely carried the Knights in Armour. They were bred, and at considerable expense and even in those days, trained for it.

I expand further. At the end of the era they literally outweighed their usefulness, became hopelessly ineffective and eventually the mighty war horse was no more.

Cavalry, dressage and maneouvrability became the order of the day. Strategic warfare had arrived. It is the year 1135, King Stephen was on the Throne and newly crowned. It has led to bitter rivalry and constant warring between the Scots and the English. Stephen's accession was in dispute, the Scots claiming Matilda should be monarch.

What really intrigues me as a layman, is the timescale and the distances travelled in those days in the absence of a road network. 1135, only sixty nine years after Norman invasion and the Battle of Hastings. Wars are ranging over the length and breadth of Britain and all by foot soldiers and mounted cavalry. Ships were also used to great advantage to transport armies to various vantage points, but from these it was mostly footslog.

Another remarkable piece of history is the fact that Harold marched his men all the way from York to Hastings to confront William the Conqueror. A distance of 400 miles. A veritable marathon even today, considering most were on foot.

The Battle of Hastings was certainly an historic landmark and a different outcome would have changed history.

Harold, who had been so successful in previous battles allowed William to outmanoeuvre him, using tactics that had contributed so much to his previous victories. Ironic really but as we say in most situations, "On the day, William's troops deserved to win."

You are probably wondering what all this has go to do with Staintondale and Shire Horses? Relatively I would say a great deal.

At the time of the battles raging openly between England and the Scots, King Stephen was sailing up the East coast in what I think historians have previously described as the 'White Ship.' Please don't quote me on that.

Just off the rocky and rugged coast of what later was to become North Yorkshire, a great storm blew up. We can safely say that this was nothing unusual, as a massive graveyard of sunken wrecks exists all along the stretch between Scarborough and Whitby.

Let us allow our imagination to take over for the time being. The ship's progress was being closely monitored by the coastguards of the day. Possibly brethren of the Knights Hospitallers. Although in peaceful times their role was to help the sick, poor and needy they would be very aware of any threat of invasion from the sea. This was not the case at the moment, but the weather was turbulent and ominous. Constant look out was being kept.

At sea, Stephen's crew were struggling to steer a course for some shelter. No doubt the haven of the sheltered inlet of Hayburn Wyke was uppermost in their minds. The vessel, now battered by the strong wind, its timbers strained and creaking was being blown northwards. It was getting precariously close to the rocks, the shelter of the Wyke fading fast.

A great wave rose and plunged, the ship with its splintered rigging and torn sails was about to flounder. With blinding spray and heavy sea lashing over its decks and bow it was only a matter of time.

Suddenly a great violent impact was felt as the wooden hull struck rock, timbers splintering she lurched and listed, savaged by the gale force wind. The cry to abandon ship was both unnecessary and futile, men and cargo were being swept overboard like so many pieces of flotsam.

The sea was like a cauldron.

King Stephen was well attended, his life must be secured. His master at arms and several lieutenants pulled him into a boat.

On the clifftops at Ye Manor of Stainton the brethren prepared to descent the cliff. Strong ropes and slings at the ready, they were soon on the rocks below.

The great rescue had begun. It was to be an historical success. This was the King of all England.

Legend has it, and I have personal word of mouth knowldge that this history was actually taught at Staintondale School many years ago, that Stephen was rescued and sheltered by the Knights Hospitallers of St. John and in a rock outcrop not too far from Eastside Farm. Its closer identity shall remain a secret.

The King, grateful for his rescue and the saving of his life rewarded the Order by the granting of a charter.

It is a rare document conveying the freehold of Ye Manor of Stainton in Blackamore to the Order, their brethren, their families and successors forever.

He made one condition that the Chaplain should give divine service daily and that at twilight a bell should toll and a horn be sounded to carry the weary and poor travellers and strangers, to the shelter of the hospital.

We leave my little story there because the rest of this chapter is very much in the present.

It is my privilege to be able to research and write about our unique historical connections. The horses lend themselves to the situation remarkably well. After all it was the first heavy horses to be brought over to England, the Destrier, that helped William the Conqueror defeat Harold. His small native ponies were certainly no match for these great.continental Stallions.

They became the first front line defence for the Normans and were to remain so for another two hundred years. It is worth recording that as chain mail gave way to plate amour, these horses were bred heavier and stronger. Ultimately up to a capacity of carrying 400lbs on their backs - nearly 200 kilos.

Revenge for Harold's defeat came later at Agincourt when the French with their grotesquely over burdened and excessively armoured horseman were routed. Their sheer weight, lack of maneouvrability and clumsy weapons proved totally ineffective.

These pieces of history really illustrate my subject as it is easy to relate a horse of King's stature to the picture of heavily armoured cavalrymen, I refer to our King of the present day, King, our Shire gelding.

We have also another link with cavalrymen - the Cromwellian horseshoe I dug up from deep down in the ground.

Cromwell was an acknowledged master cavalryman of some repute. He was an authority on the subject of maneouvrability and thinking warfare. His troops at one time stormed Scarborough Castle so it was no real stretch of the imagination to identity the shoe I found to one of his followers. A horseman possibly touring the farming areas to buy food. The old shoe can be seen in our dairy museum in a glass case, it is about 350 years old.

Because of the influence and importance of the Medieval Order of the Knights of St. John in Staintondale both at the time of the existence of the hospital, and also to the present day, I have got to include a few paragraphs about my own personal fascination with the subject.

A subject so intriguing that it persuaded me to research some of it in Malta, the scene of the great siege of 1565 and a monumental example of gallantry and fortitude. Originally the Order was divided into three elements, the most powerful of the three, the Templars had been suppressed in the early fourteenth Century. The second, the Teutanic saw their demise after Tannenberg in 1410 when they were defeated. It was only the Order of St. John of Jerusalem that had survived into the sixteenth century.

The Knights of St. John were unique in their concern for the sick and needy and their prime concern was the building and maintenance of Hospitals such as the one in Staintondale. They had a commitment after joining, to their Christian Vows of Chastity and Obedience and became novices for their first year. They then joined a Convent as it

It is easy to relate to a horse of Kings stature

CHAPTER THIRTEEN
My wife's arrival and two donkeys

My wife Ann's arrival at East Side Farm was to say the least spectacular. It was January 6th 1970, one of the worst winter days for years with wind born particles of ice dusting fiercely across our open fields. You could hardly open your eyes.

A friend of mine who had spent a couple of weeks helping me start on what was to become almost a lifetime's building and restoration programme was getting anxious as we both stared across this antarctic landscape. The removal van together with my wife and family of four children - two boys and two girls in a small car were making the 100 miles or so journey in apalling road conditions and, as we kept hearing on the radio, road after road was getting blocked by snow. They should have arrived hours ago.

At just before 3 pm when my own anxiety level had just about gone through the roof, the telephone rang - it was one of those caught off guard, urgent tones of the call we had been waiting for. I grabbed at the receiver. Our new neighbour's voice was unmistakable 'I think your furniture vans arrived - he's stuckin t'beckbottom.' John and I gathered up our coats and opened the door - a great gust of wind blasted it towards us, at the same time discharging the coating of snow into the room. Hell, I thought, what a day to move in. I hoped it wasn't to be an omen for our future!

The next few hours restored my faith in human nature - we arrived at the snowbound bridge in the beck bottom and what a sight greeted us. A large pantechnicon van with its very limited traction was being manhandled and manipulated by a small army of neighbours and local farmers who had miraculously arrived as if by bush telegraph. They had shovels, ropes, tractors and a willingness that country people muster in times of trouble. I was overwhelmed, my previous misgivings were well and and truly laid to rest.

Not only did they beat, batter and overcome the odds, they persuaded the vehicle across the 3 fields to the farm and stayed to help unload it three hours later. Some of the downstairs furniture ended up in the bedrooms and vice versa but we didn't care, we were home. A big fire was blazing in the grate and the weather was firmly shut outside.

The next few years were a challenge. First of all there was the granary or loft area of the house to convert to two bedrooms. As Ann had pointed out when being wholeheartedly opposed to the idea of buying East Side Farm.'Tony it's ridiculous - only two bedrooms, we do have four children!' Opposition that later turned to unequivocal support and affection for our newly adopted way of life. After restoration of the house came the buildings;some to repair, some to build. I loved every minute. During the early seventies the country's economical problems worsened and this affected the farming community around us. It was soon to get a lot worse - the gulf crisis and its subsequent effect on oil prices brought about a new threat to the country's industrial and agricultural economy. Energy conservation and the search for alternatives was to start. We had four young children and self sufficiency was uppermost in my mind.

Between our neighbours we joked about some of the problems and always came up with the observation 'well we can grow a few taties and a bit of corn - we shan't starve'.

In 1973 1 was looking at something nearer to my heart - call it a bit of self indulgence. 'What about getting a couple of Shire Horses? We could really be self sufficient?' I was asking myself the question. With typical runaway enthusiasm my ideas blossomed 'I could start to breed a few and start a small Shire stud?' Well, alternative source of energy? This could well be the answer for us! It was no longer an idea, I decided to do it.

Today was the day. After searching the columns of the leading horsey magazines I had located two Shire filly foals for sale in Oxfordshire. As show quality they were not impressive but then I had a lot to learn, and in any case was it all that important?

I had been down to Oxfordshire and made the purchase. Not only that, I had taken the self sufficiencies bit really to heart and bought from the same vendor a trio of Oxford Sandy and Black pigs. They were all to arrive together.

It was October 1973 and we once again surveyed the landscape, this time for any sign of the cattle truck that was to deliver our hopes for the future.

With great excitement we heard the rumble of a vehicle on our farm track, everybody rushed out to the front of the house. They were here. The tail gate was lowered to the ground and there at the top stood our own two Shire foals. One grey with four white socks later to be called Grace and one black with very little white, later to be called Carmen. (Ann my wife's choice -'Because she's got Spanish eyes.') We led them, looking very frightened and nervous down the ramp. Carmen was only 4 months old and Grace a week or two older. They looked a bit sorry for themselves, they had travelled a long way.

Ann looking on couldn't hide her caution -after all they were part of her future too -'Are you sure they are Shire foals? They look more like donkeys to me!' We all laughed but I had to admit they didn't look much like the Beswick variety.

Now for the pigs - they had been penned right at the back of the container and a dividing gate had to be removed. Pigs are characters and none so more than these. They were a kind of sandy gold colour with big black splodges and hairy - well hairy was an understatement, they were hairy in every sense of the word. The boar had a long tapered snout which looked almost telescopic with small deep set eyes almost hidden by rolls of skin - and tusks! He looked wild and ferocious. The three of them which included a sow and gilt, just stood and refused to negotiate the ramp. In fact any attempt to remove them brought squeals of protest and some not too friendly looks from the boar. They were supposed to be very friendly and docile but like a dog you don't tempt providence.

The driver who had helped load them was a livestock haulier and used to handling stock,just find me a length of corrugated sheeting or an old door - I'll soon get them down - pigs won't run into a wall!' He used the sheet to cut off their vision and sure enough after spreading some of their own straw on the ramp - down they came.

They were indeed friendly pigs and we had them for several years. The boar we named King Ogg. Oggy for short. There is a photograph in our Tea Room of some piglets and a sow taken in 1990 - the sow is a great great grandaughter of the pigs I brought to Staintondale in 1973.

By 1976 the scene had changed again. My original plan to open a riding stables and treking centre had to be abandoned. My two daughters so enthusiastic about the idea were now young adults. It

70

Frightened and nervous down the ramp.

71

Pigs are characters.

wouldn't be long before they were making their own ambitions become reality.

CHAPTER FOURTEEN
Opportunities abound

Right out of the blue a telephone call quite late at night changed all that. A friendly Irish brogue said, 'Is that Tony, it's Terry Keegan here'. We exchanged our usual light hearted greetings and discussed some items of mutual interest.

'Tell you why I rang'said Terry 'l wondered if you would consider becoming a member of the World Ploughing Match Horse Committee?

The year was 1984 and a lot of interesting things had happened in between. Mascot, our black stallion was born in 1980 and was now part of the family. David our eldest son and Anita our youngest daughter were married in 1981 and Glenn our youngest son in 1983. This led to another interesting incident involving Nobby and the wedding cart appearing at the Great Yorkshire Show - I shall refer to this again later.

Back to the telephone call. Terry Keegan is a man dedicated to the history of working horses, and in particular their harness and decorations. It was not surprising that he was involved with the World Ploughing Contest.

He came to the point! 'The thing is, the horse ploughing section has to raise its own sponsorship monies, this could be quite considerable. We thought' went on Terry,'that you might be a likely candidate to help raise it!' I laughed - thought there must be a catch somewhere!

'Anyway have a think about it and come back to me - any ideas would be welcome' - he rang off.

My flashes of inspiration were becoming a habit - like pennies from heaven I could seize on this golden opportunity. Here was a chance to have a trial run to test public interest in my idea and at the same time help the horse ploughmen to compete in the World Ploughing Contest 1984.

I rang Terry back. I would set up an open day to be called Horse and

74

Cart Sunday, the date would be Sunday May 6th. If Terry and local Ploughing Societies and any other interested organisations would help publicise the event, I would give the proceeds to the Ploughmen by way of sponsorship.

At this point I can do no better than include a report of the day's event which I wrote for 'The Heavy Horse' magazine Summer 1984.

"It was 3.00 a.m. I heard the grandfather clock ring out; not the deep throated gong of a modern version but a clear and precise sound of a bell being struck. Today was the day' After years of talking, several months of planning, and the last few weeks of hard slog by every member of our family, the big day had arrived our Horse and Cart Sunday and our 'Trial Run'. David and Celia, our friends from Everton, Nr. Bawtry, had arrived the night before and earlier that same evening, Toll (other friends), David and myself had put down 20 tonne of stone to repair the farm road, make the customers happy is our password!

Back to today. Carmen, our foundation mare, was already twelve days overdue to foal. I wasn't really expecting it this morning but the prospect of a few hours' old foal, a very possessive mare for a mother, and a lot of curious and devoted horse enthusiasts trying to get a peep, was really something we could do without at least for a couple more days. I willed myself into consciousness and slid out of bed. It was a lovely calm morning with all the prospects of a good day ahead - we were going to be lucky. I really do believe you make your own luck in this world, but I do give way to old Mother Nature and her weather.

. I got dressed quietly and made my way downstairs. No point in waking the whole household. Picking up a lamp I made my way outside and walked through the barn. Yes its was a soft sort of morning. The cold wind the previous day had eased and I walked across the field looking for Carmen. It was a pleasant feeling, and I soon established that we had a few more days to go and made for the house. I decided a couple more hours of sleep wouldn't do any harm, so back to bed I went. It was hopeless. I lay there planning the day ahead, making a mental list of priority jobs for 6 a.m. when David (Hirst) and myself made a serious attack on them. The very first job was a couple of glass pantiles on the dairy roof so that spectators had more light. At six minutes past 6 a.m. we were on the roof - the day had begun.

The horses had to be fetched in from the fields. The in-foal mare moved to another pasture to make room for a temporary car park-this

75

One to a leg

really upset our stallion Mascot, who lives out in an adjoining field because he couldn't see her, so he started to gallop himself into a real sweat - soon to be covered with a thick layer of dust, which in turn reduced his beautiful glossy presence to something of a nondescript. We quickly fetched him in but the damage had been done. Anyway no time for an inquest, still a lot to be done. Hoped to get back to him later and closed the stable door.

Legwashing next for our working pair, which went smoothly. Phil (our son-in law) made a start and was soon joined by the others, and Toll, our waggoner for the day, took charge of the stables, assisted by Bill Bailey and later Frank Stainthorpe who plaited their manes, while Celia (David Hirst's wife) did up their tails. All hands on deck now. Our family of ten plus friends and helpers were now desperately setting up direction signs for the car park and entrance, and manning the pumps! At 10 a.m. precisely the first customers were coming through the gate.

The sun was shining - so good was our organisation we had it shining straight on to the Heavy Horse Magazine stand situated in front of our Hay Barn. I joked with Sylvia that sun blinds would be provided if required. I don't know if it's the same sun that shines in the South of the country, but it just seems bigger in Yorkshire!

Sunny Staintondale is the way we see things here. Set in the dale bottom in something of a panoramic landscape, we are sheltered from the sea and the moors, and yet enjoy this superb view all around us. A real suntrap in Summer.

It was the sort of day to start us off in the right direction, and soon Mr. & Mrs. Beeforth from Westerdale were setting up their corn dolly displays and demonstrations, and alongside the workmanship and skill of Gordon Flintoff, with his hand carved and superbly finished sticks and crooks. Our refreshment mobile provided by Pippins Restaurant (Scarborough) was adjacent, and all surrounded by a picnic area complete with a sandpit for the kiddies (Bairns in Yorkshire). By now people were streaming in and making their way towards every individual display and exhibition.

Just beyond this point we had our big implement shed where our old lady of the farm stood in silent contrast to all the comings and.goings. She is an 1890 Ruston Proctor 5 h.p. Eccentric Cam Finishing Machine or Thresher to the men who toiled in dust and sweat when she was in her heyday. Today was a day to remember them, and many of the men looking around her remembered all too clearly, with a fond memory or a touch of sad nostalgia for happy days of youth.

Alongside, a display of horse ploughs; the main attraction being our Ransomes R.N.F. 7 plough,which all being well will be ploughing at Wispington (Lincoln) with our team in the hands of Toll Harrington. (Godfrey really but nicknamed many years ago).

Further along this route is the waggon shed, which housed our completely rebuilt 1900 McCormick Self Tie Binder (made in Chicago, U.S.A.); a North Cave Wood Beam Plough; a large Chop or Chaff Cutter, driven by an old Lister engine; a wheelwrights early band saw (used for cutting shafts and felloes), a Bedfordshire Tumbril or Tip Cart, which we restored to show condition; and a fine example of a 1918 Dales Waggon which has received the same treatment; various poles, swingle trees, lined the beams above.

The stables were alongside, and at one end of the stalls we keep the harness. Here we had our Saddler and Harness Maker, Mr. Brian Reeves from the Longdale Rural Craft Centre, Mansfield, Notts, who demonstrated filling and lining horse collars, amongst other things, and created a lot of interest.

In the stable yard our Dairy housed a complete range of old fashioned equipment, from a milk cooler to butter churns and milking stools. A modern innovation was provided by Mr. Bob Marley, a local dairyman, who sold ice cold milk and real farm butter. (Sold out in fact).

Next to him our real showpiece - a complete cottage layout, with cooking stove and pegged rugs, and a whole range of domestic byegones, all brought to life by the inclusion of two static models dressed in period costume. Affectionately called Smithy Cottage, the Blacksmith's Shop is right next door.

Unfortunately our farrier couldn't make it on the day so the hearth was glowing away in vain. Some highlights of the shop are the old hand bellows made by Lindley of Sheffield, over 100 years old and still connected and working. Also two really old anvils, one about the same age, and the other very much older. The shop itself was adorned with a large assortment of implements and items in for repair at that time.

Our old Cow House was set out for a spinning wheel display of handcraft given by Mrs. Janice Carter, and, alongside a cake stall provided by Mrs. Irene Harrington, who actually baked them all! She also sold out in record style.

Thresher to the men who toiled in dust and sweat

The old cart shed, with its pantiled roof and stout oak lintel, was the setting for our collection of farm hand tools and implements. Items of interest included an instrument for docking horses tails- a really cruel process! Our own Veterinary Surgeon said he was glad the practice was made illegal - he couldn't stand the sound of the bone crunching. I personally maintain that it was cruel in more senses than one. If people thought as much about a horse's welfare as they do about their appearance, tails would be left long!

Another interesting relic was an old pit saw, which was used to plank a whole tree trunk set over a pit sometimes in the forest itself. The sawyer stood on the trunk while his assistant was below in the pit doing most of the work pulling this great seven-foot long saw through in a cross cut motion.

There were peat cutting spades, drainage tools, and a host of other things, all aptly being described by our neighbour, Mr. Geoff Edmondson.

Finally to the yard with its old fashioned hand water pumps, and on display more horsedrawn equipment, including our 1894 Charabanc which seats twenty people on the one single deck.

All around was an air of yesteryear, and the lovely crowd of around 700 people made it just perfect, which was our reward and complete satisfacton, not to mention a large donation to the World Ploughing Contest horse section, which will be printed in the catalogue.

Another very good friend of mine Bob Lomas was editor at the time and I think, when going on a visit to North America. He once described me as 'Our Northern Correspondent'. The magazine has since ceased publication unfortunately, and I have lost contact with Bob although I am sure we are still good friends. There will have to be a second booklet to fully explore some of these interesting American visits: 1984 was a year of total satisfaction. It began with the visit to America in the early spring - even this was brought about through the columns of 'Heavy Horse'. I had started to correspond with the then Secretary of O.R.S.C.A. (Ohio Regional Shire and Clydesdale Association) a lady called Smokey Lynn Bare in response toa letter printed in that magazine. This led to several visits to America and many friendships. It also established our prefix 'Staintondale Shires' in the States and a win at the Ohio State Fair for two horses we bred here. Just prior to the visit our Stallion Mascot who was sire to these two horses, was awarded a premium at the National Shire Horse Show at Peterborough in March. Pride was an understatement that day, I don't know who stood the tallest Mascot or me!

During our stay in the States and only a couple of weeks later our Mother and Son team Princess and Nobby in the capable hands of another friend Toll Herrington, won a small local ploughing match at Ravenscar.

We returned home to set up the Horse and Cart Sunday which I have already described in detail and then of course later that year the 31stWorld Ploughing Contest at Homcastle in Lincolnshire. Probably the wettest ploughing contest of all time!

The ploughing match over, it was now getting uncomfortable close to 1985 - A year of destiny. These were pioneering days and that spirit prevailed throughout. I had broken my ankle during hay making in July 1984 and only just got reasonably mobile by the time of the Ploughing Match. This had restricted progress a little bit, but again, with the help of a young man I shall call Udi, we cracked on regardless and my pot leg became increasingly less of a problem. There was fences to erect, a barn roof to finish. Trees to plant, hedges to cut back and ditches to clean. Once when Udi had got the tractor almost submerged in the mud of an overgrown ditch, he came up and said'I have problem' I was laughing, 'But this is big problem' he insisted. He was right! The top of the exhaust was almost glugging through the mud. Right through that winter we continued to make progress, toilet facilities, car parking space. The tea room to set up, leaflets to be printed. An amazing variety of things that you hadn't even thought about. And then there was advertising - we needed to spread the word. Being off the beaten track has its advantages but passing trade potential isn't one of them - there isn't any!

It was 1985 now and spring was blossoming forth, with all the splendour and determination that only nature can provide. The big flowering cherry bursting with buds, the ambitious honeysuckle clambering and flowering all over our front porch roof.

The day grew nearer - Spring Bank Holiday Sunday dawning, the year of achievement and personal fulfillment. I think of it as my year, these were pioneering days all right and we relished every minute. More than that the public loved it. Success was to be ours.

CHAPTER FIFTEEN
Vicar to the rescue

At this point I think a few amusing incidents very worthy of a mention should be recorded. Horses are not mechanical creatures and they can be quite unpredictable - never underestimate their reactions.

One particular friend I shall call Bernard, taught me quite a lot about handling and harnessing a horse, although at the time I don't suppose he realised. His quietly spoken manner and his very obvious love and devotion could work miracles. This is how we gentle our horses, it isn't called breaking here. Trust is the keyword and trust is mutual, break it and the horse won't let you forget.

The Dales waggon we have, as I said, once belonged to my old friend Robert Pearson of Egton. It is measured and recorded in a book by Joan Ingleby and Marie Hartley called 'Life in the moorlands of North Yorkshire'. Over the years it has gone a full restoration and today it was to be the wedding carriage for our eldest son David's Wedding. This led to it being featured on the front cover of 'Horse and Driving'magazine in 1981. I am going to relate what is now a very amusing story. At the time it was near disaster.

On the morning of the wedding we were up very early. Nobby our gelding, still the character we have come to love, was the subject of our attention. He had to be brought in and prepared for the big day. We began by washing his legs down with stock shampoo and carefully removing any traces of mud from his heels. We then washed out his mane and tail using the same solution and then the whole mass of nearly one ton of horse was rinsed down with warm water and squeeged. After getting rid of most of the water the drying process continued with the use of white wood flour worked into the feather. (hair on legs). This helps to separate and fluff out the hairs and present that larger than life hairy legged look that Shire horses are famous for. You can understand why an early start is necessary.

Once Nobby was immaculately toiletried - mane and tail combed and brushed to perfection, the harness was brought out and unwrapped from pieces of old blanket which protected it, all brass shining like gold, the leather gleaming like an advert for Cherry Blossom boot polish. It goes through your mind how do we put this lot on without making finger marks?'-well we don't, they are polished off afterwards.

Now the problem area. It is not possible to drive out of the dale with the horse yoked to the cart. The road is too steep and the metalled surface too smooth for a horse to grip with his toes.

So the horse is driven out by long reining him and the waggon taken to the end of Downdale Road by trailer. All very time consuming and by now encroaching on time we didn't have. I'll bet many of you appreciate what I mean, as on most wedding days, especially if you have had a modest family pre-wedding celebration the night before!

So far, so good. We are outside Bridge Farm, the vehicle has been unloaded and Nobby is stood quietly waiting to be 'put to' or sometimes called 'shutting in' into the shafts. He looked magnificent with his plaited mane and tail complementing the gleaming brasses.

Nobby was on his best behaviour as I quietly backed him into the shafts - this was a relief, today wasn't the day for humouring him out of one of his obstinate moments. I slipped the shoulder chains into the hooks and then coupled the britchen. Nobby seemed to sense the importance of his role today, his head was held high and ears well forward. Good lad I said - just stand still, you're doing well. I carefully buckled on the belly band and then took the reins from the nearside.

'OK Bernard' I said 'up you go.' Bernard had been busy hooking on the wooden bucket at the back of the waggon and making last minute adjustments to the floral decorations - he gave the shining waggon a final polish. He climbed up via the shaft platform and I handed him the reins. I was getting concerned about the time, I still had to get back to the farm and get washed and changed. I couldn't help feeling an uneasy sense of urgency.

With a click of the tongue and 'Get Up Nobby', Bernard started him forward. We were at the junction with the Cloughton/Ravenscar road and a right turn was taking the turnout towards its destination.

I watched the turn taking place and climbed into the car.

'Get on Nobby, Get on!'Bernard's sharp command was unmistakenly ominous. I looked round. Nobby was slipping badly on the smooth surface of the gradient and looked like going down. The only way to avoid catastrophe with a horse is to urge him on, Nobby was not responding.'Get on Nobby will you? Get on'.

But Nobby had decided otherwise - He made a U turn to the right and started to almost jack knife the vehicle. I couldn't believe it. It is called shock horror these days and that summed up my state of mind, but worse was to come. Sprinting the few yards to Nobby's head I grabbed the rein on his nearside close to the bit and pulled him over. I should explain that these waggons do not have a full lock, that means to say that the front wheels cannot pass under the waggon body. The result is that if you take a really sharp turn, the front wheel going into the turn jambs up against the waggon and over you go. By widening the turning circle this can be avoided but it is not easy from the driving position, especially with a young newly mouthed horse, and especially if he's called Nobby. I had him now and a sense of new relief began to asert itself.

To make sure the U turn was not going to be a problem I made a widecircle and turned Nobby into it - too wide!!

We were now on the left hand grass verge and it was all going well, or so I thought! My intention was to lead Nobby so far and help him up the incline.

The next thing I knew Iwas up to my waist in a ditch closely followed by Nobby closely followed by the nearside front wheel of the cart! Cursing my stupidity, I realised my error but the grass had concealed the ditch I knew to be there. I cannot put down in writing either the words or expressions that sprang to my lips or erupted from them! In my mind, all I could see was Ann my wife waiting to be driven to Church, and still down at the farm. Worse my future daughter in law and her father stuck at their home at Ravenscar wondering if there had been a change of plan - wrong day perhaps?

Any minute now I expected Nobby to want to rid himself of the whole charade, get out of the ditch, break leather and gallop away into the horizon. Never underestimate your Equine friends. 'Nobby, I said quietly'Don't panic'

I think it was more in hope and desperation than serious thought of expectation.

Nobby was implanted in a ditch up to the extent of his legs and me to my waist. I took a gigantic breath 'Keep cool' I said to myself. Bernard was beside me now. Our task was to loose Nobby as quickly and quietly as possible. We said a few prayers as the belly band and chains

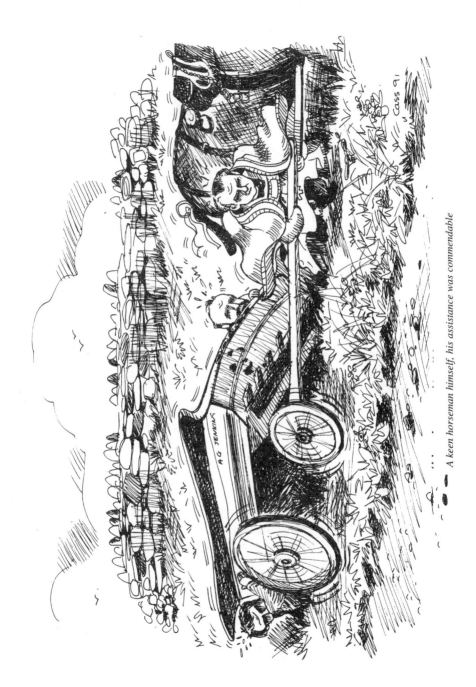

A keen horseman himself, his assistance was commendable

were released.

So far so good, Nobby was as calm as a cucumber - I have often said its the handler that panics the horse! At this point a lone car drove up towards us and came to a halt.

The Rev. Christopher Tubbs emerged from the vehicle and rushed over - I think I looked upwards, but I certainly felt the sinking feeling subside. Our local Clergyman was on his way to officiate the wedding and grasped our predicament in one. He quickly and capably came to our rescue. A keen horseman himself, his assistance was commendable.

Just about at the same time a local resident and his wife Mr. & Mrs. Richardson who lived almost opposite the scene of the accident also came over to help. With Nobby released without mishap we soon had the cart back on the road without so much as a broken buckle.

My respect for Nobby and his breed blossomed. This story has a happy ending, and as fairy tales unfold, so did this one.

The next half hour was like a fast forward function. I found myself one minute going in the back door of our house and seconds later coming out of the front. By now I was suitably clad and laundered for a wedding and of course accompanied by my wife Ann who was looking very radiant and of course unscathed by the morning's events. We headed for Ravenscar.

As we approached the Church what a sight greeted us. It seemed the entire population of both villages had turned out, not,to mention friends and relatives from all over the country. I breathed a big sigh of relief - at least we had made it, and I suspected a lot of people were here to see a horse and cart wedding. What a catastrophic let down it would have been if things had gone really badly wrong.

Dropping Ann at the church I turned back towards my daughter in law to be parents' home. A normal situation of wedding morning nerves and great expectancy prevailed. Liz and her father were waiting.

I hastily buckled on my driving apron, took hold of the whip and climbed aboard. The situation had all the aura of Cinderella going to the ball - I felt just like the coachman that my great grandfather in fact was.

With my charges in place everything was suddenly one of calm serenity. A snow white sheet draped the waggon's interior and Liz sat in magical splendour - the scene was set.

Our arrival at Church was equally spectacular. It seemed a thousand faces were turned in our direction as everyone strained to get a glimpse of the bride. It was a picture of sunshine and happiness.

The Rev. Chris Tubbs beamed down from the pulpit. Looking straight towards me and with a hint of a wink he said 'And I just happen to know that certain members of this family have had a fairly traumatic morning!'

At this point and since Nobby and Princess too, have participated in two more of our family's weddings, other less dramatic incidents should be recorded.

Only weeks after David's wedding (our eldest son) our youngest daughter Anita was to be married at Staintondale Village Church. She had chosen for her wedding the Victorian Charabanc - a large passenger carrying vehicle which we no longer have. It was designed to be pulled by a pair of horses, no less than Nobby and Princess on the day. Memories are of everything on these occasions but pictures in your mind are a little different, certainly more specific. My picture memory of that day was the bride and her maids in outfits that belonged to a fairy tale wedding. On board the 'carriage' the fairy tale became a reality. That was later

With the scene from weeks earlier still fresh in my mind I was helping to'yoke up' Princess and Nobby at a friend's farm (Church Farm, Staintondale), Geoff Bird my friend looked on. He watched with interest the buckling on and adjustment of the split driving reins - something of course not used with cart gears (harness)'Did you fetch them with you from t'West Riding he quipped!' I laughed -'I'm a Derbyshire man'. This fact usually gets me off this North and East Riding rivalry banter bit and the fact the Northerners think the West have strange ways!

Only one brief hiccup which was just about to happen made my pulse race that morning. We had just driven out of Geoff's gateway and turned uphill towards the Church. I was sat with my daughter Anita trying to appear relaxed.

I must emphasize here that this was a very heavy vehicle and it was designed to carry twenty passengers. As we started up the incline at a walking pace the vehicle began to weigh heavily behind the horses. Again through not being accustomed to road work and their shoes highly polished on the underside by the grass pasture, they both started to slip as they tried to dig their toes in for extra leaverage.

It was a flashback of a situation only too recently impregnated in my mind.

I leapt to my feet and stood behind the driver - another friend of mine Bob Pearson. Bob would no doubt have handled the situation, but I was taking no chances, 'Get up Nobby, Get up Princess' I yelled 'Get on, Get on!' They responded, Nobby's back legs bent to it like pillars of oak. Like a weight lifter his muscles strained and all was well. Good old Nobby. I think Princess was hardly in the collar. Princess by name..

At the reception I told the Rev. Tubbs a joke.

It seemed, years ago that the Parishes of North and South Cave then in the East Riding, only had one parson between them.

It was customary for this gentleman to conduct Sunday morning services at one church and then walk to the other for a repeat performance. On this particular Sunday as usual, the parson was walking along and hoping for a lift. He wasn't to be disappointed. A pony and trap pulled up and a cheery voice called out 'Want a lift Vicar?. 'Oh thank you, thank you' beamed the parson 'How very kind, how very kind.'

He climbed into the trap and off they went. They hadn't gone far when the young pony, obviously still pretty green started to play up. Just a few attempts to rear and then when unchecked a sudden surge forward and a few kicks.

The driver worked hard but to no avail, the pony got worse and a runaway was iminent.

'Oh dear, oh dear'said the parson in dismay.

'I would gladly give a pound note to be out of this vehicle'.

With characteristic wit and sarcasm the driver retorted. 'I can't let you waste yer money Vicar, we are both going to be out in a minute - and for nowt!'

Chris Tubbs laughed. It was not too disimilar a picture to one he had recently witnessed.

Moving on now to a third Horse and cart wedding. This time our youngest son Glenn and our daughter in law Sue.

Sue had deliberately elected to marry in the village for the sheer pleasure of a traditional village wedding and of course most of all - a horse and cart carriage. The preparations had started long before, when I had asked Glenn if he had any particular favourite for the wedding vehicle. He looked straight at the well weathered and worn two

I can't let you waste yer money Vicar

wheeled farm cart stood on the yard - I fancy that could we do that one up? It was a challenge I leapt at 'If you give me a hand to strip it down, we'll do it'.

When I said challenge I meant it - this vehicle needed new shafts making. I had purchased a great plank of Ash years earlier and was waiting for some inspiration.

CHAPTER SIXTEEN
Restoration of the past

As I am writing it is becoming increasingly obvious that one small booklet will be totally inadequate. At the moment, as I search the depths of my mind to stimulate my memory I discover that there is an untapped source of material just wanting to be included. For the time being I shall have to carry on with the thread I have chosen.

The cart we are discussing was purchased in Bedfordshire at a small village called Caldecote. It belonged at the time to a family called Price. If anyone at some future date should be reading this book and have knowledge of this family then the following story should be passed on.

When departing with the cart suitably loaded and roped on our trailer Mrs. Price remarked 'And when you have restored it - let us have a picture'. The year would be about 1976 and my Father who is now aged 90 was with me.

It was now 1982, and this well used and well worn cart had suffered the weather protected only by a couple of tin sheets. Great sculptures of wood had been taken out of the shafts with the constant rattle of loose chain ends during its working life and the paintwork was practically none existent. Having said all that, the cart had great character and a pride of workmanship now almost a thing of the past. What do they say 'gone with the horse and cart!'

Restoration gives me great pleasure - just to rub down the contours of the lovely old hardwoods give you a tremendous contact with the person who made it. All the love and care given by devoted craftsmen is once more in living hands. You can feel the pride and the workmanship. Glenn helped me strip down the entire vehicle. All ironwork was put in a couple of old buckets to be fettled. We did this by a grinding process with a small portable hand grinder. Any ironwork not re-usuable - some of it completely eaten away by rust we remade using our own forge.

After stripping, all parts were examined and one great thing in our favour was that the wheels were sound. 'Only just re-tyred'Mrs. Price had said 'Not long before it was laid up!'

The shafts of course were totally unusable - hence the nice piece of ash. The ash was purchased from a local timber mill, Harry Pennocks of Kirklees Farm, Harwood Dale. Harry has now retired and the mill has gone. I remember asking for this particular piece of timber and for a particular job. Harry knew exactly what I wanted 'Come on, let's go and have a look'. We walked along rows of timber neatly stacked and each sturdy plank separated by segments of timber to let it breathe and season. Something like a year for an inch of thickness. Harry stopped 'Here we are, that's a piece of nicely seasoned ash, you should get a good pair of shafts out of that.

You can see the cart now on display, but you can also see pieces of the offcuts of this ash on top of the old wheelwrights bandsaw sitting right next to it. Lovely old English ash, and grown locally. I was very lucky.

Another old friend of mine and one of the few retired craftsmen still willing and able to pursue his calling is George Watson of Sneaton. A wheelwright who actually featured in 'Life in the Moorlands of North Yorkshire' albeit as a younger man!

So far as my capacity and ability to do this work was concerned I have to regard George as my mentor. He carefully swung an adze, guided by his knee -'that's how you do it', he said simply. I had tried and tried to persuade George to make the shafts but now unfortunately he didn't have a big bandsaw to actually cut out the shafts. 'If you can find someone with a bandsaw' he remarked 'You could make those shafts yourself'. I grinned. 'You can do it he repeated. Well now was the opportunity. Was this the challenge I had been waiting for?

With Glenn's enthusiasm to help restore the cart and use it for his wedding, I was only too keen to get on with it.

As the weeks went by the picture changed. From a pair of wheels leaning against the wall, from a body stripped of its floor and shelvings, in fact from a variety of odd shaped pieces the cart began to take shape.

The work progressed into the pink primer stage to undercoat and then to the beautiful gloss of good quality coach paint. It was and still is a picture. I painted in the yellow strings - the grooves designed to give a

I knew exactly who I wanted for the drivers of this very special cart

planked effect down the sides.

It was sheer magic. 'Glenn', I said 'Your wedding is just before the Great Yorkshire Show, I think we'll enter it.'

The wedding day was approaching with that sudden speed that always seems to take you by surprise. One minute, several weeks - next minute, several days.

I knew exactly who I wanted for the driver of this very special cart. It was another friend now sadly passed away, John Whitehead. Complete with his Billycock hat and Dickensian presence he was the perfect choice.

John, his wife Pat and their family Christopher and Sarah were friends of a special kind and when it comes to real horsemanship and dedication theirs was a unique combination.

I rang John and explained what I had in mind. 'Great' he said 'we will come the night before and help get Nobby ready.' I was over the moon. I knew Pat was good at decorations with flowers and general presentation. They would be a tremendous help. The next morning the wedding ritual began again. Nobby having his bath, only this time one person to a leg! That was the scene on our yard as soapsuds splattered and splodged everywhere.

It was a very misty morning as summer days often start, but the sun would get out - wouldn't it?

I was hoping against hope that it would be a lovely day because I knew that a lot of my daughter-in-law to be's family were coming a long way. They had been impressed by stories of spectacular sea views from the churchyard.

The church is perched on the roadside and looks over this beautiful dale with its North Sea backdrop and lofty cliffs. It is now in fact designated 'Heritage Coastline', a name well befitting its splendour and serenity.

This apparition - like picture surrounded in mist

CHAPTER SEVENTEEN
Sea fret for a wedding

With Nobby immaculately turned out our morning progressed. The decorations were impressive. Nobby had small silk rosebuds plaited into his mane and more rosebuds and flowers bedecked his gleaming harness. What a magnificent sight.

Toll who had previously done the ploughing, mentioned earlier in the book, set off to lead Nobby to Church Farm for a re-run of past rituals. The rest of us got ready for the wedding. The sea fret now hugged the ground, it was worse if anything. These frets are really sea mist created by cooler air blowing off the sea into a warm front. They are a summer phenonemon on the North East coast and can sometimes last for days!!! And it did.

We stood on the grass verge outside the Churchyard peering into it. Somebody said'Is the sea really out there?'It was hard to believe anything was out there -we could barely see the wall across the road. Then suddenly out of the mist came the clip clopping sound of horses feet - we all stared in this direction. Although sunshine was what we wanted, the magic moment of seeing this apparition-like picture surrounded in mist, make its enchanting presence felt, was spectacular! It really looked like a ghost from the past.

The Bride looked radiant and the colour and majesty of the occasion shrugged off the dull of the day like a discarded cloak. The big red wheels, the green and gold of the cart and Nobby, he rose to it all. I think he quite enjoyed weddings.

Of course this chapter doesn't end there because Nobby and this resplendent cart had another venue - The Great Yorkshire Show.

We drove along Seamer Road towards the suburbs of Scarborough, the fret stayed with us - suddenly and without warning a great glaring light shafted a great hole in the gloom. Sunshine! It was almost nbelievable. More than that, it was hot, the temperature suddenly soared. After living for over two days in grey, misty and quite a cold world it was a shock to the system. We had forgotten it was mid July and summer, even though they kept talking about heatwaves on the radio. Well here it was.

The drive to Harrogate was uneventful. Nobby was being transported in the horse trailer behind the Landrover and I was towing the cart now securely mounted on our small low loader trailer. Our destination 'The Great Yorkshire Show.'

The main story is about Staintondale so I do not intend to deviate too far or for too long but an incident at this particular show is worthy of a mention. Particularly as it involved the wedding cart.

Our time had arrived to make our debut in the showring - the main and impressive area reserved for all main events. It is provided with a suitable large grandstand and observation tower.

The big moment came and we entered the access area. This is a collection ring where the stewards direct operations and soon we were parading round the outside perimeter of the main ring itself being scrutinised by literally thousands of spectators. I felt overawed, but very proud to be there. Nobby was really behaving himself and performed like a veteran. It was very very hot, we were in fact wearing shirt sleeve order and enjoying the brilliant sunshine. The crowd were loving every minute of it and soon to show their appreciation!

We turned into the apron area of the massive grandstand. A ripple of applause started to trickle across the rows of faces. Nobby, who up to now had been taking everything in his stride suddenly became aware of this new diversion. The clapping increased as we turned across this sea of spectators and became something of a crescendo. Nobby didn't like it. He had never heard anything like it before and he was off! Ears pinned back he took off across that ring like a rocket - Oh yes, cart horses can gallop.

Ben Hur had nothing on me that day. A large two wheeled farm cart precariously balanced on a single axle and no springs. It was a hair raising experience I shall not forget. Nobby's hooves thundered forward.

It seemed the wheels were only hitting the ground every several yards and now with my knees dug into the back of the front boards of the cart, I felt every bump. My elbows were well tucked in and I was keeping a good contact with Nobby's mouth and at the same time trying to keep my balance. He was responding by just leaning his almost one ton of bone and muscle against the bit.

Worse, I could feel the reins stretching and I found myself looking along every joint in the leather. Would they hold? One thing I did promise myself if I came out of this without being upshot, was a new pair of strong driving reins!

I continued talking to Nobby- appealing to his better judgement.'Steady boy', I said and released some pressure on the bit. 'Steady old lad, nothing's going to harm you.'Nobby started to ease back - partially running out of steam. It's a big ring at the Yorshire and providing nothing breaks there is always the tiredness technique! 'Whey old lad, whoa now steady as you go.' I could see Nobby's ears going forward and relief surged though my veins.

I decided there and then, if you are really committed to demonstrate total catastrophe, the Great Yorkshire Show, in front of thousands of people is not the place to do it.

By now we had completed the full circuit and we were approaching the dreaded grandstand once again. More clapping. This time with no reaction from Nobby, it was a relief, I raised my hat to the crowd, acknowledging that we had friends amongst them. Nobby, looking very composed and superior walked quietly on.

It was a few years after, when talking to some of my audience after a demonstration on the yard at home, a visitor said to me'Our friends were at the show that day and recorded your performance on Video'. I laughed. 'Yes and when you got the clap on your second lap, it was because they thought that you had done it on purpose in the first place.'

We were to visit the Yorkshire Show just once more in 1985 the year we opened our enterprise to the public. This time it was with both Nobby and his Mother Princess and the Victorian Charbanc.

The attendance there was not appreciated by our visitors to the farm so from that time onwards all our showing during our visitor season is done on our own yard.

Ben Hur had nothing on me that day

CHAPTER EIGHTEEN
Transitions of a Foal

Ann and I started married life in what you would describe now as a bed-sitting room. With a full time job, I had also started up a business in what was called 'spare time.' It was a joke really because there was no such thing as 'spare time' and most of my life seems to have been more about making time than spending it. Anyway we will not dwell on that too long. Suffice to say with good friends and hard work we, like many other people had made a success of our early married years. We had a family of four, two boys and two girls.

Success had provided us with the new house which I had built with the help of a staunch friend Bill Jackson, and, as I have said previously - a lot of sweat and blood.

It was this asset that was going inadvertently to change our lives. We were going to sell the house and move to a completely different way of life. This was the chance to realize all those childhood dreams and ambitions. It was a chance we had decided to take.

Most of this transition I have described in previous books, but now is the time to tell more of the story, which still continues. Horses continue to dominate and they still remain the centre-piece.

I have previously mentioned our horse called Dusty, so I shall pursue the story. We had bought this small farm to start a riding stables and although we did diversify later to breed Shire Horses, finding a house with grazing for a horse, outbuildings and stables was all part of my dream. It was to become larger than life reality. I converted what was once the stables for the farm's workinghorse into two separate boxes for Smokey and Dusty. It was ideal for them and ideal for our daughters Shirley and Anita, - they only had to saddle up and ride.

As usual I had taken on an amazing workload because all the buildings were in need of full restoration. Pantiles were missing from the roofs and walls were leaning at precarious angles. The crazy thing about all this, is that I was back to square one – still making time, and it didn't leave me any spare either. Never mind, once I get this job done…

I did ride though and had many a happy hour on Dusty. Anita pursuaded me to turn out with the local hunt, in fact, I did this on several occasions. This became difficult for me later because I really didn't have the time to care for a hunter in a stable. They need clipping out, keeping fit and plenty of exercise. In addition to renovating the house and buildings I also had a small business to run. Keeping a horse stabled for such a single purpose was out of the question and as I joked with Anita – 'I need a groom, dammit all!' Shirley, by this time, had gone off to Agricultural College – even though later and almost straight after, she trained to be a nurse.

At this point we decided to join the Hunter Improvement Society and put Dusty in foal. After much debating we took her to Max Abraham's stables near York. Go for the best I thought – he keeps the Queen's Cleveland Bays there.

It was not a success and we did not get a foal from this visit. We did see the Queen's horses though – albeit at a price. Our neighbour had a small thoroughbred which Anita liked. He probably could produce a nice foal just the same.

The acting stud groom at this neighbour's farm was Vic Dent who has had a mention in a previous book. His commentary during the service of a mare was hilarious – he was and still is a character.

To quote some printable comments – 'come on you lazy b…… you're not here for the view.' He wasn't talking to me. The period and events leading up to this foal is a story indeed.

Dusty, like most part draught horses was inclined to get fat during the summer months, and although after trying her several times with the stallion after the initial service, we were not totally convinced that she was in foal. It was a case of well she might be but on the other hand…

The gestation period for a horse is 350 days give or take a week or so. As Dusty approached this period of time, I asked our local Vet to take a look at her. He did not do an internal examination but after prodding her in a few places and standing back for a good assessment, his comment was conclusive. 'No', he didn't think she was, and he added, 'with a neck like that essentially produced by male hormones, I don't think she will ever reproduce!'

Well that sounded conclusive enough but nature cannot be taken for granted so we hung on in hope. The gestation period reached its full period of time and then it became a full year. After a further 3 weeks and two more days we gave up.

Just at that same time our mare Carmen was expecting a foal. She was one of our foundation Shire mares and there was no doubt about her foaling prospects. Heavy in foal she had displayed all the usual signals. Her teats had waxed up and her pelvic arch had slackened. This usually means the foal is imminent. Earlier in the day in question, I had met up with a local young man called Tony Wray. He was a former Household Cavalryman and had asked me if we had a horse he could ride. I had laughed – 'definitely,' I said, 'a very fat mare called Dusty – come over after tea and I will introduce you.'

He was as good as his word.

'I'll tell you what Tony,' I said, 'just take her round the track past Rigg Hall and on to Plane Tree – just to try her out. I have booked her in at the Farrier for a set of shoes in the morning and you can ride her down there.'

On his return it seemed that some of the farmers and particularly one old horseman, had joked about Dusty.

'No, definitely not in foal but she would do well at the fat end if you send her down to the market.' Well that was that. Tony put her in one of the stalls in the converted cow byre (now the shop). 'I'll see you in the morning,' he said.

I was up most of that night and Carmen had given birth to her foal at about 4 am. After dressing the foal's navel and giving the mare a feed, it was breaking daylight. It was then I remembered Dusty. 'Better give her a small feed,' I had spoken out loud, 'She doesn't need it but it will be a little treat.'

I opened the top door and looked into the stalls where Dusty was tied up – 'What on earth!' Pushing open the bottom half of the door I was inside like a flash. Switching on the single small lightbulb, I took in the scene that met my eyes in amazement. A cord was stretched from Dusty for what must have been a couple of yards. It didn't appear to be broken and the end disappeared under a tressle we used as a saddle rack.

I feared the worst, it had got to be some sort of abortion – well Dusty didn't seem worried, she was still stood quietly tied up. This was to develop into a quite remarkable situation and this was only the beginning. Peering into the darkness under the rack, I could see a small object. It felt quite cold and very wet. At that point I thought my worst fears founded – a foal, possibly born alive but now dead. What a thing to happen and what a terrible waste – if only we had known. I was feeling very sad about the whole affair and blaming myself. At that moment I felt some movement in my hand – all was not lost.

Reaching under with both arms I carefully lifted this very small and wet bundle and drew it towards me. I could feel it shaking.

With just a few urgent strides I had it in the shelter of the hay barn and was rubbing it vigorously with a small wisp. Definitely alive but not yet kicking. I covered it over and went into the house for some warm towels – we just happened to have an old Aga at that time. It was magic – the response was immediate and the kicking not long afterwards! Dusty, I have got to add, was totally unconcerned and still stood quietly – a very reluctant mum.

She had no sign of an udder or in fact any milk – I thought about the words the Vet had spoken and the male hormones. It took ages for her to produce milk but we knew the foal must have its colostrum. After plastering on a good coating of fresh butter and sugar mix around her teats the foal eventually persuaded Dusty to let the milk down. What a relief it was. It was indeed a miracle foal and it was a bigger miracle it survived. If Tony hadn't wanted to ride she would have probably dropped the foal in the field and walked away from it. We would not have even known.

We called the foal Jagger – as Mick Jagger. He seems to be a survivor.

CHAPTER NINETEEN
Going too far

To put this whole story in perspective we have to go back to the year 1975 and a year that took me to The Great Yorkshire Show with a yearling filly called Princess.

It had all started with the purchase of this young horse from a farm just outside a small town in Lancashire. A lovely and rewarding experience I shall never forget. It was Monday 28th April. I had made the journey to the farm with a Land Rover and trailer — just in case! As I remember the farm it was situated fairly high up in the Pennines and I imagine it could be pretty bleak in winter.

They were very nice people and I enjoyed their warm hospitality and Lancashire frankness. I suspected the lady of the house wasn't really too eager to see the horse go. She was obviously very attached to it.

We seemed to talk for hours but I don't remember much haggling about the price — a little bit of banter perhaps. Eventually we all shook hands and I was now the proud new owner.

We now had to persuade our yet unnamed yearling into my aged single axle Rice horse trailer. Fortunately she was used to being tied in a stall so with a few strategic moves and a bit of persuasion — food I think — in she went.

It was pouring with rain and as grey as slate. I was beginning to wish that we hadn't talked quite so long. The drive back to Scarborough was horrendous. It was lashing down as I made the M62 intersection and pulled on to the motorway. The wistful face of the lady at the farm still stuck in my mind — a touch of sadness.

By now I was in the thick of it. Rain pouring down, heavy spray from goods vehicles and a general feeling of claustrophobic gloom — it was like driving through a nightmare. It got darker, and suddenly I was numbed by my own thoughts — no trailer lights! Oh heck! — for want of a better adjective that's printable. I pressed

... and a bit of persuasion —
food I think!

harder on the accelerator but I knew I wasn't going to make it before lighting up time.

Suddenly a new and more pressing thought slowly dawned upon my mental horizon — The trailer — it had no glass in the frame of the small front window. Without hesitation I signalled and pulled on to the hard shoulder. This was an emergency.

I looked in through the frame and I could have cried. This young filly was saturated, all the driving rain and spray had been thrust towards the front of the trailer and had found its mark. She was wet and shivering. Quickly I rummaged in the back of the Land Rover and by a stroke of good fortune found a large piece of canvas sheet. I quickly rolled it up and stuffed it into the window frame. 'Hang on, beautiful' I said to the filly — 'I will soon have you home'.

This set-back spurred me on and I shrugged off the grey mantle — let's get back to Staintondale I said to myself. I decided to leave the motorway at Tadcaster and get across the A1 — bit quieter I thought — especially with my lights problem. What a journey — It seemed like crossing the Atlantic.

Once we got off the M62 I stopped and climbed into the trailer. The young horse was fine now and had warmed up. On we went crossing a few minor roads until we eventually joined the A64. Relief wasn't in it. I had been more concerned about my lovely newly purchased young filly than I was about producing my vehicle documents at the local Police Station.

Home at last. Our interesting stone flagged Souvenir Shop was at that time the cow byre and that was to be home for this special young lady at least for the night. I unloaded her down the ramp and led her into the middle standing.

A good rub down with a straw wisp and a feed of bran and corn and she would be as good as new.

I carried in a couple of bales of straw and made her a deep bed. An overstuffed hay net was my final offering, together with a full water bucket. It was a very tired young animal that eventually hit the sack that night, and that was only the horse.

The next morning I awoke with a feeling of sheer exuberance. What a wonderful find, I couldn't believe my good luck. I got dressed quickly and rushed out to the cow byre.

The filly greeted me with a sharp whinny as I stood proudly looking her over. 'You're lovely' I said 'I shall call you Princess.'

An overstuffed hay net was my final offering.

Late that day as promised I rang the previous owners. 'Yes we got home safely in spite of everything' and then, 'Yes she's fine and no problems.' Then came the next question. 'What are you going to call her?' 'Well', I said 'I am going to call her Princess because of her lovely nature and good looks.' There was a silence and then a wistful voice said 'I'm pleased — that's what I was going to call her!' ...

As a comparative newcomer to Shire Horses and with even less experience of the show ring I decided Princess was worth showing off if nothing else.

At that time there was a Shire Breeder in Staintondale who was helped by his enthusiastic if sometimes outspoken Son in Law. I decided to take Princess round for an opinion.

'You've been amongst Showmen for that one' said the older man. 'Nice little filly' echoed his companion.

'Is thi goin to show 'er?'

Praise indeed and I knew it was frank and genuine.

'Tek' er ti Yorkshire' he answered his own question in a strong local dialect. 'I'll 'elp thi' and — she'll need a bit o schoolin an a set of bevils.'

Why not I thought — start at the top!

My new adviser, Victor, was as good as his word. He came round

Hang on, I'll get behind her with a whip.

and taught me the basics of showing technique.

He took up a judging position.

'Right now, walk her away from me in a straight line and then turn her inwards towards you and walk her back towards me. Make her walk on — tickle her with your whip!'

We did this a few times and then:-

'Not bad, keep her at it though and keep her head up. Now we are going to try the trotting out. This time make her trot and make her look lively and pick her feet up.'

It wasn't too good — 'Hang on. I'll get behind her with the whip — she's got to show herself better than that.' The response was amazing, she started to use her hocks and went really well. 'Keep that up every day for an hour or so and she'll soon get the hang of it, your job is to make sure she impresses the judges. You'll need a set o bevils.'

I looked puzzled 'Bevel shoes — she'll need to be shod,' he said 'Go and see Blacksmith at Cloughton.'

I was lucky, the village Blacksmith, Edgar, was a heavy horse enthusiast and although regretfully passed away now, in his years of smithying, had shod more than his share of cart horses. His eyes seemed to light up when I told him what I wanted. 'Young Shire 'oss eh?' He paused for thought 'Bring her down, let's have a look.'

I almost flew back to Staintondale, hooked the trailer on and back I went.

His wealth of knowledge was his stock in trade, he cast an admiring glance over Princess. 'Good Shire feet' he said 'Plenty of depth at the heel!' He continued 'Yorkshire Show eh? Well I know a man who will look her over for you. Hang on I'll ring and see if he's in.'

Such enthusiasm and goodwill really impressed me — what a friend to know.

Within minutes his 'man' appeared. A man who is still around as

I write this book and among many of the names I would like to mention. For reasons that will eventually take shape this book is for the most part 'No Names, no pack drill!

This man stood back to make his assessment. He moved forward and ran his hand slowly down the cannon bone to the coronet pressing down hard.

'Will she pick her feet up?' he enquired, at the same time proceeding to do just that. 'Not bad feet', he said 'She'll look better shod.' He stood back. 'Walk her round a bit.' His eyes explored every contour. 'Yes' he said 'She'll show all right and she's big enough.'

The Blacksmith spoke, 'Right bring her down on Thursday night about seven — it's oer warm in't day time at the moment for shoeing them things.'

I duly arrived at the forge and led the horse inside. Again I was to be impressed. There on the anvil was a set of perfectly made, hand forged bevel shoes — and without so much of a rough measurement being taken. This was the work of a master craftsman. To this day I still have two of those shoes.

My new adviser was now looking towards the great day, 'When you get to the Showground you will need somebody to plait her up and do her tail. I have a mate who works for Bernie Hopgrove — go and see him and tell him I sent you.'

Plaiting up and bobbing tails were a foreign language to me — it sounded very complicated. The Bernie Hopgrove is a fictitious name and on arrival at the Showground with my youngest daughter Anita it became even more so, because the man in question wasn't there and neither was his 'man'. My heart sank into my boots 'What on earth do we do?' This was the Great Yorkshire Show and not the village fete. But help was at hand.

A man sat outside one of the stables in the heavy horse section. He had watched our arrival on what was the eve of the first day of the show. I think having my young daughter with me helped, people seem to get into conversation easier. He called across. It was 'Hi there bonnie lad' and 'How are you pet' to Anita. I recognised the Geordie influence and the warmth and hospitality of his tone of voice. It turned out he was very much a Yorkshireman! However . . .

We walked towards him. 'And what are you showing?' His enthusiastic chatter drew us towards him like a magnet. He was a small dapper little man with twinkling eyes. I explained our predicament after telling him about our yearling filly Princess. He told us his name was Frankie Walker.

'No problem', he said 'I will come round to the box at 7 a.m. and plait her up and put you right. He smiled 'Is this young lassie showing her — she ought to be, Judges will tek to her!'

Late that evening we met two other very helpful men from my native Derbyshire and they immediately took to Anita. One of them later became a good friend and in spite of my Derbyshire origins insisted on calling me 'Ilkley Moor bah tat'. His name was Iain Yates.

It was a wonderful introduction and put my mind at ease. We were taken to the fodder yard, water supply and all the other areas we needed to know. A big showground can be a nightmare to newcomers and especially one who hasn't shown before.

The great day dawned and we were up long before sunrise. Our friend and guardian angel kept his word to the second. Not only did he plait Princess up but he also showed us how to show off the feather on her front feet.

'I'll walk down to the main ring with you when it's time.' It was all very re-assuring.

Now we were walking to our destiny. A number card hung around Princess's neck and she looked resplendent in her plait and flights.

I couldn't believe the overwhelming public interest in these heavy horse classes. It was nothing short of besotted adulation. We had a job even getting into the ring. 'If this support' I mused 'could be channelled into a business enterprise it would be a runaway success.' I was in business myself and very much aware of the values of public interest from a publicity point of view. 'Shire Horses are a magnet', I concluded.

It was a small class and we were up against the country's and county's top professionals. Princess by name, Princess by nature was a model of behaviour.

We were a well placed fourth and for a first attempt we were delighted. As I walked proudly out of the ring, Anita rushed towards me — 'She was super', she said, 'Ought to have won!'

A man suddenly appeared from nowhere, he leaned heavily against me almost losing his balance. I smiled, he had been enjoying his day. There was a distinctive aroma of malt liquor. His

Princess was a model of behaviour.

speech was slurred, 'Sheez not daft that filly', pause for concentration, 'Sheez not daft but sheez just gone too far!!'

It slowly dawned what he was trying to say. Princess had more than her share of white markings (I shall wisely leave it at that) 'But' he leaned speaking with some effort and occasionally losing his balance, 'I know a good Stallion that'll just suit her — ish mine!'

That Stallion turned out to be Carr Coming King, and the man's name? Well let's just say that although I didn't use his Stallion we became good friends and had a few sociable drinks together.

As I write this book, as many visitors will know, we still have Princess who is now 19 years old. She blessed us with our own Premium Stallion Mascot, which she foaled in 1980.

CHAPTER TWENTY
Pioneer or eccentric entrepreneur

I had returned from the Yorkshire Show with some brand new thoughts. First and foremost I think was the rather poor prospects for breeding Shire horses. The oil scarcity problem seemed to have receded, people had accepted the higher prices that were originally going to bankrupt the Western World and more important, self sufficiency with horse power was becoming no more than a forlorn hope.

Oh yes, the showing species still did well from a price point of view but these accounted for a very small percentage. There is no such thing as an average price for a Shire Horse — call it what you will. It is either good or bad.

It seemed that private motoring will survive and that means tourism and visitors to the area.

By now I had got really hooked on Shire horses and I had been looking seriously at my inadequate buildings and stables. The yard was a mess. An assortment of scrappy implements from the horse era and nowhere to renovate them.

Slowly a plan began to emerge from the debris in my mind.

What about some nice new stalls — tailor made and purpose built for these big horses. Even our new yearling had had to stoop to get into our cow byre. And — my enthusiasm gathered pace — an adjoining building to restore and finally house all this equipment. And then the yard — still the original old muddy fold yard. What about concrete with a man made stone sett pattern?

I knew a man who could do it — it was me!

That same day I measured up the area in between the stone buildings and the hay barn (now Video Studio). I carefully drew up a plan and decided exactly what could be fitted into it.

By now I had a lovely mental picture — it is the scene our visitors see everyday. In this mental picture I saw people — all the

I knew a man who could do it — it was me!

faces I had seen at the Great Yorkshire Show. The same lovely faces, young and old alike. Faces filled with nostalgia and thoughts of happy days of youth. I saw faces filled with admiration and wonder. Small children standing back in amazement but each and every one in love with a Shire Horse. I saw fulfilment in my picture, and a great deal of pleasure to be shared. To do what I wanted to do was going to need capital and although I had a small business I was struggling financially and cash was at a premium.

Well nothing else for it, I shall have to go and sell my idea to a bank — they usually have money.

In 1975 it was not easy. The main question asked was 'can you service the loan?' This means — how much does your enterprise earn and can it afford to borrow? For a new enterprise needing funds for development it was a non-starter.

'Oh yes, quite a good idea Mr. Jenkins but .... Shire Horses as an attraction — well, er, you are obviously an enthusiast but, er, are there many like you?'

I thought I was an enthusiastic and confident talker on the subject. I oozed with nostalgia and buttercup meadows, granny's pegged rugs and mangles. They were not impressed. With my spirits flagging I had one final thrust. I telephoned for an appointment at a Yorkshire Bank — there, said it! The Manager's name was Mr. Flowers.

but ... Shire Horses as an attraction?

113

He listened carefully and was very interested. "You have a unique idea there and I think the plan well thought out and a viable proposition. It may take you a while to get established but I am sure you will succeed. From this bank's point of view, to secure any sort of loan I would require satisfactory balance sheets of any previous business and of course the transfer of your account. Whether we manage finally to help you is of course up to you but I wish you well and I shall keep an eye out for your progress."

At that time my balance sheets wouldn't have impressed anybody and the thought of rushing into my own bank shouting "That's it! I shall transfer my overdraft elsewhere" (reminiscent of Tony Hancock) would have brought only one reaction — 'Good'.

It was now 1976 and things were beginning to look better. Whatever happened now I had made my mind up. I was going to do it and fund it myself over a period. At that time planning permission was not required for certain farm buildings and so from that point of view I could make a start.

What I was concerned about was spending a lot of money over a fairly long period and then having problems when I decided my enterprise was sufficiently developed to open to the public.

I wrote to the National Parks Officer to clarify the position. This was the reply dated 13th September 1976.

Dear Sir,

Shire Horse Centre and Farm Park Staintondale

I refer to your letter dated 2nd September 1976 and your site meeting with my assistant Mr. Elm in connection with the above proposal.

It would appear that in the first place you are to run the holding as an agricultural unit and as such no planning permission will be required.

I would suggest, therefore, that when you are in a position to discuss definite alterations to running of the unit, you contact my assistant Mr. Elm.

Yours faithfully,
National Park Officer

It was a reassuring letter or so I thought. Now with my plan in operation I would make a start.

First job was to clear the area. It was a ramshackle scene. Two old hen huts, a wooden turkey verandah and the remnants of a wood and corrugated iron building about on its last legs. I had been told

114

it was the old Threshing shed and had originally housed a barn thresher which was fed by taking a couple of tin sheets from the roof. The machine was then fed from the top.

One lovely story from the 1930's. The farm man had gone to the house to get the men's wages for half a day's threshing. Miss Dawson came to the door 'Now William' she said 'how much for the men?' 'Well I'm afraid its three shillings each Miss Dawson.' (15p) 'Three shillings! Whatever is the world coming to!' Ah well, inflation and all that.

Once we had a clearance, levelling began and a lot of the stone used for building the dry stone wall on the yard was excavated from the foundations of the new building.

When the trenches were out, the strip concrete foundations were in and I began building. With my previous building experience and knowledge I was able to order a full load of Tilcon hollow building blocks. I specified an hydraulic off loader. Quality blocks, in quantity at the right price. That driver made history. In 1976 I think it was the largest vehicle to negotiate the lane and the bridge over the beck. He had to shunt to get round. Then there was the ten foot gate almost set in a pond — most times it was. It's hard to believe now, but for fifteen years we put up with a permanently blocked pond overflow that flooded the road in wintertime and made it impossible to go out without wellingtons. Things got even worse later on, but more of that later.

These drivers were always cheerful — 'your moat was a bit of a problem, there wasn't room to get past the vehicle without falling in it!' He had to shut the gate. 'It's not my moat' I said, 'Only wish it were, I could do something about it.' He meticulously unloaded the blocks all carefully stacked beside the footings. 'Well at least you got them here' I said and thrust a pound note in his hand. I won't bore you with the building work but it was the start of the making of a dream.

Once finished, new concrete floors were laid and the stables decorated. I choose original old fashioned shades of dark red and green.

Talk about Five Star accommodation — the horses were very suspicious at first. We even had to spread a bit of horse manure around.

I reckon this to be the biggest D.I.Y. self build kit ever, and that was only the start.

'Your moat was a bit of a problem.'

Now to clear the yard of some of the clutter. The most awkward of these rusting relics was a turn of the century McCormick self-tie binder in near scrap condition.

It just happened that my son Glenn was off work through injury after a motorcycle accident. He was, like me, really a mechanic by trade and useful with his hands. We dragged the machine into our new posh work area and looked it over. All the sheet metalwork was in tatters. After careful examination we decided a new bed (metal floor to platform) new guards and a new band box would have to be made.

The self-tie binders created havoc on their arrival, as thousands of farm workers engaged in scything and sickling saw them as a threat to jobs. They really were a revolution. The mechanical corn reaper had been bad enough but this was a threat to a gang of field workers. They were around for well over fifty years.

Anyway, back to work on the binder. Surprising though it may seem it didn't take too long. I think painting it was the worst job.

We really went to town, and an old friend of mine George Watson of Sneaton even made a brand new set of spindles for the reel.

We are more than fortunate still to have some of his generation around. When the last old fashioned farrier and wheelwright has

116

passed on, rural communities will be a poorer place. They will be skills lost forever. The binder is now in its new quarters and the band box even has a supply of genuine oiled binder band! The binder pole is in the roof above and all it requires to drive it is a three horsepower team.

That is the story of one item out of many. We have a lot to do yet but we were on our way.

CHAPTER TWENTYONE
Blowing up the wind

A very funny incident happened in March 1976. It was the sale at Kirkbymoorside at 12 noon of the entire contents of a Blacksmiths Shop and Smithy. A sad event really, but not without a touch of romantic aura. These were the years of my future destiny, and collecting all the pieces of rural memorabilia I needed took me into some remarkable situations. They say every picture tells a story, well I have got to say that there is a story to practically every piece of yester-year that we have in our colourful collection. Putting and piecing it together and embarking on painstaking restoration work took me nine whole years. Life was pretty uneventful from a domestic point of view, our elderly neighbour who incidentally owned the pond, still kept a few cows but they were never a problem. In wintertime they were in and the gate the driver had the problem with, was left open. Back to the events of the day.

Quite a few of us had decided to attend the sale for various reasons — two of the local blacksmiths' sons and their apprentice were amongst the crowd and obviously a lot of local people and what we call curiosity seekers.

We had decided to go early and have a look round and then go for a pint at a local hostelry. Duncan the apprentice wanted a farrier's tool box and tools — there were several.

I wanted anything that was reasonably priced that would lend itself to my project. We had our few drinks and returning in excellent humour waited for the Auctioneer's bell to commence the sale. It started quietly as most auctions do, each waiting for another to start the bidding and then hopefully coming in on the act.

Some of the larger items and less interesting pieces went pretty cheap. I bought a job lot of hammers of every description. As many as I could carry. Every one to tell its tale with shafts sculptured with the blacksmith's hands. Thumb holes and palm grips, all were

He walked round and round the box.

there. It got to the tool boxes — there were several.

'Can I see three pounds?', said a hopeful Auctioneer. 'Two' said somebody. 'Three' came from the back. 'Four' 'Five' 'Six' I pricked my ears up at this amazing response. It did not stop 'Ten' 'Eleven' 'Twelve' — 'Fifteen'. We looked round at the bidders — they didn't look like Blacksmiths. I think the final price was about thirty pounds and that set the going rate. This was 1976 and we couldn't believe it.

At this point Alan our local blacksmith who now does a variety of wrought iron work, walked forward into what was a man made selling ring. A circle in fact. He walked round and round the box with mock expression of looking for something.

'Can I help you'. said the Auctioneer.

'Yis', my blacksmith friend retorted, 'I was lookin for t'hoss — thought it were included in't price'. There was uproar, bystanders were just about falling on the floor with mirth. It took a few minutes for order to be restored and several people had joined our group in conversation. It had been realised that our colleagues were blacksmiths and this in itself created interest.

One rather elegant lady who was obviously a follower of the Barbara Woodhouse animal programmes — do you remember 'Sit't'? approached us.

119

Looking at my friend's brother who was the farrier, she enquired. 'Tell me' she said, 'Is it true that if you breathe up a horse's nostrils you can talk to it?'

There was no flicker of hesitation in his reply 'Missus' he said, 'It would be as effective as resuscitation through the rectum!' I have got to add that he didn't put it quite this eloquently.

You are wondering who bought the tool boxes? It turned out afterwards that they were from different local authorities setting up craft museums and had open cheques. They got run up (a trick played on people by bidding against them and then dropping out). Well, serve them right. I didn't attend many auctions after that, the writing was on the wall. Between Antique dealers and local authorities what chance did one have?

It is not my intention to dwell too long on collecting old implements. It would be very boring. Suffice to say that I have travelled miles and tried to make our collection an interesting one. You could say that the most boring of all was driving back from Altrincham in Cheshire on the M62 with a horse plough on a trailer.

Talking about antiques there is another interesting story that is worth recording.

Always on the look out for items of interest in local newspapers the following heading caught my eye. 'Small Museum to Close.' I read on — it was a small private collection of local domestic and farming items which had been run by a village Blacksmith at Hunmanby. It did not pay its way and the owner was considering ways of disposing of it. The article went on to say that the owner was engaged in a lot of Ecclesiastical wrought iron work and was also interested in vintage motorcycles. At the time I was the proud owner of a 1958 Triumph Speed Twin. Well, what was I waiting for? I needed exhibits, and sacrifices have to be made. I didn't have spare cash to buy with anyway.

I rang up with my proposition. An agreed amount of museum pieces as a straight swop for my bike. After a look at the bike and examining the situation it was agreed. In fact we got a good deal because the owner said we could have anything that he didn't wish to keep or anything that hadn't been loaned.

I was luckily able to call upon my sons and son-in-law to help move some of these items — there were even some battered old horse implements stored in a field.

What a marvellous start. It was a miracle really because my wife

Ann with almost the view of some bank managers had said 'It's all very well Tony but I think you will need something else beside Shire Horses. Some of the wives might be more interested in some old domestic items.'

She got her wish, and using what we already had as a base, (I tell visitors our unwanted wedding presents), we managed to put together our interesting cottage museum. For some of the items that have either been loaned to us or given can I take this opportunity to say thank you to the donors. One item is a beautiful Christening gown.

In 1978 I bought the old Ruston Proctor Threshing machine. It was from a farm sale held at Scalby High Mill in September. It belonged to a man called Pickering and the whole amusing incident has already been described in my previous book 'At a price that's very nice'. Threshers are bulky things and usually stood outside and were well sheeted down. Well, ours survived this for a year or two but a machine that age (it was made in 1890) starts to deteriorate rapidly if not properly protected from the elements.

In the early 1980's I decided to build it a home. Again with the help of my sons and son in law Rob, we built the shed it now stands in. Using all second-hand and re-claimed materials we assembled the leg sections and top frame. Then using our tractor front end loader which, by adding a length of telegraph pole we managed to make into a crane. Glenn did the driving and perched the five angled steel roof trusses on top of the poles with infinite precision.

Another marvellous D.I.Y. building which I designed from materials on hand and built (what do they say?) on the cheap. Well I have a talented family and some talented friends and this is reflected in our achievements.

The only building we had when we came, apart from the small range of stone buildings, was the old pole hay barn, now reclad and refurbished as the Video Studio.

My wonderful constant daily satisfaction is to walk round in the evening and count the years in terms of renovated buildings, vehicles and implements, carefully planned and low profile new buildings, tidy yards and walls, attractive fences. There has not been a minute wasted.

CHAPTER TWENTY TWO
Make a wish

It is time to depart from the past and move to life at Eastside Farm once we had settled in and finally decided on our future plans.

The following pages are dedicated to two personal experiences actually producing the foals, or rather helping nature to. I am going to start with the birth of Nobby because he is the oldest of the farm bred horses we still have. Our farm character.

To give you some idea of how long ago that was, Princess his mother is now eighteen. She gave birth to Nobby when she was three.

The morning he was born was a bright sunny day in May 1977. I am very lucky, my memory is both long and colourful. Signs are quite apparent when foaling is imminent especially within twenty four hours of giving birth. We note the udder and development of the teats. We look for a slackening of the bone on either side of the tail which allows the vulva to open up, and sometimes after a waxy substance appears on the teat itself milk will actually run. Foaling is nigh. How nigh depends on the mare herself. After breeding horses for seventeen years you learn all about their funny little ways and very secretive nature. A horse has the ability to withhold the foaling action until she thinks the time and place safe and suitable.

Princess, probably the sweetest and kindest natured horse we have, is no exception. I had been keeping Princess in overnight for two or three nights and I knew the foal was ready to make its debut into the world. What is important especially with young horses, is that you are present if possible at the birth, just in case of complications. Horses like humans need exercise, so each day out she went for a wander round the field, whilst I kept a careful watch on developments.

On the morning in question she was turned out as usual. I had looked her over and I just couldn't believe she could hold on to the foal much longer. All the signs were there.

I led Princess to the field nearest the farm on the new approach road. We call it the horses field from way back when we arrived at Eastside with a horse and a pony called Dusty and Smokey. However back to the present. I walked slowly back to the farmyard. It was a lovely morning, to be enjoyed.

Once on the yard I turned and looked back. Visitors to the farm have sat in this very yard and heard this story as I explain exactly which field I mean. Princess was walking round, making a small circle and making it smaller each round. Then she slowly crumpled her knees and dropped down. At the same time rolling slowly over and stretching her head and neck.

It's happening out in the bright sunshine. What a perfect setting. What do I do. Fly in for a camera or keep a careful watch on developments. I chose the latter. This was magic in the making, the creation of a new life. And I was witness to it.

They say you should make a wish when you see a new born foal. This was more than making a wish, this was previous wishes and dreams once again all coming true.

I saw the foal's head appear and come up off the ground. I saw this movement tear the membrane (placenta) and the foal's head shake as it cleared its nostrils. What a sight to behold.

Then, suddenly and without warning, instead of Princess laying and resting a few seconds before the final push and completing the delivery, she stood up.

I couldn't believe my eyes. Now I was running. Running down the track as fast as I could make it. What on earth was Princess playing at.

At the field gate I quickly climbed over and took in the situation. Princess was walking away with the foal suspended by his haunches, front legs and head dangling and nose nearly touching the ground.

My midwifery applications have been wide and varied but this was new. I quickly got behind the mare and simultaneously gathered up, foal, membrane, tail the lot!

Princess, who I suspect was totally baffled by her sudden change in status, just carried on walking.

My thoughts raced through my mind. I hope she's not going to keep this up for long - half a foal weighs, the best of fifty pounds, plus the extras!

I need not have worried. Princess only walked on for a few yards when the compelling forces of nature and possibly because she was

Half a foal weighs the best part of fifty pounds

aware that help was at hand, she carefully got down.

The contractions started immediately, accompanied by inhalation of air through flared nostrils and loud groans. She was pushing hard now. I grabbed the foal's forelegs and pulled. A look of wide eyed wander - came over the face of our new arrival. He seemed to express more than wide eyes curiosity at this human intervention. Another push, another pull and this well developed and heavily boned foal made his debut into the big world.

Princess lay her head down, a rest was necessary after all the effort. There was no rush, all was well. I pulled our yet unnamed foal round to the mare's head. The umbilical cord as yet, still attached it was eyeball to eyeball. A sigh of relief all round as they saw each other for the first time. Nature is truly wonderful. A mare is usually quite happy to stay down for quite some time but of course like all young beings the foal was anxious to be up.

The next stage is really comical because young horses are all legs. The legs of a young foal at birth are nearly as long as they are at maturity. The standing up process is more than difficult as each attempt seems to become even worse that the first. They seem to be able to collapse in every conceivable direction - endways, sideways, backways, you name it. But as nature intended, getting stronger with every attempt.

Finally on four legs, they stand rocking precariously looking for a bit of help from Mum. You do not intervene at this stage as it is important that the foal makes the effort unassisted. Now of course it is different, the foal desperately needs a drink and guiding it in the right direction whilst helping it to stay on its feet does help.

The foal will probably weight around 50 kilos at birth so it is not always an easy task. On several of these occasions I have finished up on the ground with the foal on top of me or vice versa!

Out in a field among buttercups and daisies, it was a pleasure to be alive that lovely May morning.

Oh yes, Nobby. The name actually bestowed upon him by some visitors' children staying in our caravan was 'Nobbly Knees'. They were impressed with his great bone structure and knee joints (wrist in fact). The name eventually became 'Nobbly' and finally Nobby. His bone and substance is still very apparent. One of the real old fashioned sort that should have been given the status of 'rare breed'. Unfortunately it has been left too late. The great bone and prolific feather has given way to the present modern version of a Shire Horse.

Make a wish

126

CHAPTER TWENTY THREE
A large acquisition

During my quest for horse drawn implements and vehicles I had usually stumbled unwittingly into some amusing incident or situation. Looking back I think collectively they would fill a book by themselves. Anyway let us not get too carried away, one book at a time.

We were nearing the end of the 1970s and by now I had built the new stables and the adjoining building. Primarily the building was intended for restoration work and later for storage of the finished implements. The yard, previously a quagmire of mud had become a dumping ground for new acquisitions. "Looks like a scrap yard," my wife had commented, "One of these days when you're away on one of your Rugby trips we shall have a sale and get rid!"

Shirley our eldest daughter agreed, "It's an eyesore, goodness knows what people think when they call to see us." I just laughed, "One of these days," I countered "I shall have all that lot restored."

Well, most of my observations and predictions had now become reality. The yard was cleared and concreted and the buildings now house some shining examples of farming memorabilia. I was beginning to realise my ambitions.

Today I was off to a local farm sale. A veritable Aladdin's cave to someone like me. It was to be held at Scalby High Mill which at the time was owned by a man called Pickering.

"And don't go buying any more big, scrappy looking rubbish to clutter the yard up again." Ann had made this comment at breakfast just before our two sons Glenn and David had left for school. I saw them grinning. Young lads have no feeling for the past anyway. The future is all important to them.

The Sale itself was a revelation. Rows of old horse ploughs, scrufflers, harrows, small tools. Two Threshing machines and a collection of stationary engines were only a small part of the live and dead farming stock on offer.

I would have loved to buy the lot but funds were limited and I soon found that I was competing with one particular man, who seemed determined to do just what I could only think about. I had told my wife that I was only going to buy a horse plough and at the time I meant it. My bidding rival didn't give me chance. I didn't even get one. When I did bid, I got ran up so I wisely gave him the benefit of the doubt. It cost him a few extra quid so I had to be satisfied with that.

My initial enthusiasm for this sale was now giving way to disappointment. I felt robbed.

The Auctioneer had now started selling in another area. It looked like an orchard and I could see what looked like a large removal van thing on four great iron wheels being the subject of the attention. I looked at the trees and wondered how they got it in! Perhaps the trees grew round it, I mused. It was in fact a Ruston Proctor Thresher or finishing machine. "A real collectors piece," said the auctioneer addressing the crowd. "It's that all right," I thought, "Must be a hundred years old." I was right too, the auctioneers went on "Delivered into Scarborough 1890," he said "Where do you want to be."

Curiosity got the better, I moved closer. He asked for a start of a hundred pounds. I thought it might make a thousand.

One dour faced man in the crowd said "Fifty". It was a start.

"Can I see sixty," the auctioneer looked round. Well here was my chance to at least put in a bid and then I could clear off. It would make more than I wanted to pay.

Did I want it anyway? - Ann's morning comment still fresh in my mind.

"Sixty," I put my hand up and then walked on. It was not my intention to get drawn into making more bids. You could be bidding against a corn bin for all you know! I was only twenty yards or so away when a great roar rang out. "Tony Jenks!"

"Oh heck," again I couldn't believe it, "Not mine, not for sixty quid and I thought my bid was frivolous." I walked back, "Jenkins," I called out, "Staintondale."

The Auctioneer's Clerk made a note against the lot number. It was now mine.

"Well" I thought. "I may as well go and have a look at it." Talk about sight unseen!

A dumping ground for new acquisitions

My worst fears were soon realised. It was pretty obvious that the trees had in fact grown round it and they were not young trees. Walking round this monster I could see that the wheels were well and truly sunk into the ground. The question in my mind raised more problems. How do I get it out? Do I cut down the trees.

What does it weigh, and then the big final question, how the devil do I get it home? No wonder it was cheap, I concluded. They must have seen me coming.

By now several eager looking youngish men were round the Thresher and then round me. One said "I'm glad its staying in the area, it's lived here all its life you know and it doesn't want to be going way," he continues, "Where are you from, Staintondale, that's not far up the road. Do you need a hand to get it out?" I looked up, not my guardian angel again. My prayers were   certainly being answered.

He looked round. "The easy way would be to pull it backwards up that bank."

"Is that possible," I said looking doubtful. It was a steep grass incline leading into another field. "I've a four wheel drive tractor, it'll pull her up there."

At that point my new found friend took over. "There'll be a drawbar for it round here somewhere, probably in one of these sheds." Walking towards them - "We'll need a couple of spades and a shovel. Dig these wheels out." As if by magic, sure enough the drawbar was found. Not just the drawbar but the elevator. "You'll need this, look after it, it would take some replacing." The item in question was like a heavy leather belt about twelve feet long with like little metal buckets rivetted on.

The rest of this bunch of obvious enthusiasts started to dig down to reveal the bottom half of the wheels, "Hope old man Pickering kept her well oiled up," shouted one. "She won't have been moved for a while." It was the understatement of all understatements.

At last we were ready.

"Right," said Dave after we had fixed the drawbar. "I am going to pull it backwards up that bank and you are going to steer it with that drawbar at the back end" (really the front of the machine). "If," he went on "It rocks over and smashes itself to pieces in the process, don't blame me. It's a bit of rough ground is this and she wasn't built with suspension units".

A great laugh went up - well there was no other way. Live a little

130

Wheels well and truly sunk in the ground

dangerously. He climbed onto the tractor, I grabbed the drawbar. Would the wheels go round was the question on everybody's lips.

We moved off. A great cheer went up and round went the wheels. So far so good. Dave wasn't joking about the ground or the suspension. This one hundred year old machine swayed and shuddered as we slowly started up the bank.

I could see what he meant about smashing to bits. The old girl was creaking and groaning like a ship in a gale but she held together. We made the top. What a relief.

Dave climbed out of the cab, "Shall I carry on and take her home?" he asked.

"What. You mean pull it along the road?" I couldn't hide my reservations.

"Oh, she'll make it. She'll have travelled hundreds of miles will this old lass and on some pretty poor roads."

"You're on, let's go. I'll drive slowly in front with the Landrover. Shouldn't we have somebody walking though - waving a red flag?"

Out of the yard we went, along the lane and finally on to the road. The noise of the iron wheels on the metalled surface of the road was shattering. It could be heard coming for miles. The old machine swayed, shook, moaned and groaned but no bits fell off. We looked like getting it home in one piece.

We clanked and banged through Burniston and on to Cloughton. Cars pulled up, people came out of their houses, 'What was it, an early missile launcher. What a racket. And moving at about four miles an hour it seemed an eternity just to cover the few miles we had travelled

But on we went. Out of Cloughton we now headed up Newlands towards Staintondale. I felt a lot easier now away from the traffic. If she fell to bits we could at least pick them up without getting run over!

Up over Hayburn Wyke top and down towards Emmersons hill. I was following behind now, still couldn't believe nothing was going to drop off. Then the first sight of trouble.

Smoke was pouring from the iron hub of the offside rear wheel. I overtook Dave and flagged him down.

"We've go a wheel on fire," I said.

Dave laughed out loud, "Hardly" he grinned, "They're iron, lack of oil in the hub, she's dried out."

We pulled over into a convenient layby.

"I'll slip down to Roger Carrs at the station and get some - won't be

We now headed up Newlands

two minutes." I drove off.

Soon returning I was pouring oil through the oil hole just as the school bus went past. It didn't register at the time but we had been noticed.

Hub filled up we carried on. Now without a problem and not far to go.

Back at the farm Glenn our youngest son had walked in the house looking quite smug and secretive. He was trying not to smile. Ann caught his expression. "What's tickling you," she said suspiciously. "Nothing," he looked down. "Come on Glenn, you know something - have you seen your Dad." It was too much. Glenn laughed out loud.

"Where is he and what's he been buying?" At this Glenn collapsed in a heap on the floor with mirth, "I don't know Mum - but it's ever so big!"

To bring this story to an end I have to mention that I persuaded Dave to stop his tractor and the newly purchased machine, in an area where it could be readily turned round.

"Just in case you have to take it back," I joked, "I'll just go and get permission to land it first!"

.

CHAPTER TWENTY FOUR
A Smuggler's tale

According to our deeds the new farmhouse at East Side had been built in 1814 by one Robert Mead. He had purchased the holding from the overseer of the Freeholders, William Mainforth. He owned Rigg Hall at the time and East Side had previously been part of that property. The actual purchase had taken place towards the end of the Eighteenth Century and again the deeds clearly show the importance of the Staintondale freeholds and how the manorial rights were handed down and jealously protected. Because Eastside had been part of Rigg Hall the rights, gifts and rewards were carefully written in.

Wrecks, commons, water and minerals being predominant, not forgetting Turbury (the cutting of peat for fuel). At this point, rather than relate to earlier history I am going to refer to one incident that led to a book being published called 'The Gentlemen go by.' It is the intriguing story of a murder trial and the events leading up to it. The accused was a man called William Mead and the victim James Law.

Piecing together revelations recorded from the trial and having some personal knowledge gained by researching our Deeds and other historical documents, I have been able to speculate on my own version of events. It can only be speculation and it is entirely without prejudice.

Smuggling at the time of the Nineteenth Century was pretty rife on this sparsely populated stretch of coastline. The rewards were high and the risk minimal. One thing however, and I have got to say, almost inevitable element, was to destroy it the greed of man and stark unashamed jealousy, not uncommon in small, close communities.

I have got to refer back to Eastside Farm because this is where my interest lies and more than that because William Mead was the son of Robert Mead who built the farm, produce of his first marriage. To understand the situation you have got to visualise the geographical

The contraband was brought in by longboat

position of these farms relative to the coastline and very much relative to the detection of activity by the Coastguards. All are sheltered, fairly isolated and almost inaccessible except by horseback. We are talking of a time 200 years ago.

The contraband was brought in by rowing boat vessels anchored off the coast, I suspect on moonless cloudy nights and signalled in by lanterns.

It is said a tunnel existed between the undercliff and a point just inland. These men, all farmers, had located a tunnel (possibly a worked out smallseam of coal) and dug a shaft down to it. All very convenient and undetectable.

Smuggling had been going on and meetings held at local markets or fairs (the cattle market today). The meetings were primarily to arrange for the transportation of the contraband and for its ultimate destination and disposal. It is hard to believe just how far a pony and trap could travel in the darkness and dead of night, and on a regular basis. The roads were only tracks over rough moorland but the ponies knew every inch of the route.

On the night of the shooting incident James Law together with some friends and henchmen were riding back in the early hours of the morning, returning from the previous days market. They had been drinking at The Talbot Inn in Scarborough until 1.00 a.m. and were noisily making their way back to Staintondale. James Law lived at New Hall Farm at the junction of the road leading down the Dale. Since the coming of the railway it has become known as Bridge Farm.

It was Thursday 14th February 1823. As they approached Burniston village the noisy conversation had probably turned to their smuggling activities and possibly William (Billy) Mead. His cottage was now only a few yards in front. The mounted entourage stopped outside the house.

What probably started as reasonably good humoured taunting and remonstration, soon developed into an ugly scene of pre-meditated vengeance. James now suspected Bill Mead of informing on some of their activities.

It got noisier and more beligerent and Bill Mead could now be seen in the upstairs bedroom. What went through his mind is again idle speculation but let us put ourselves in his position. A gang of revengeful men, again possibly the worse for drink but certainly whose intentions looked ominous.

Glass shattered as the pistols flashed

Bill Mead retired out of sight afraid for life and limb. Was this to be a lynching. Leaving nothing to chance he reappeared at the window, a pistol in each hand. Glass shattered as the pistols flashed. James now slumped forward, the bullet had found its mark.

Friends pulled him from the horse and he was carried into a nearby house..

It is not clear exactly what happened next but evidence showed that Bill Mead and some of his friends left the house and set off for Whitby. They broke their journey at Eastside Farm, no doubt to see Robert Mead, his father.

After a delay of a few days an investigator was sent from York to look into the felony. (No village Bobby in those days!) It resulted with Billy Mead being apprehended and charged with murder.

A trial lasting several weeks ensued, making National headlines. It was held at York Crown Court and attracted masses of people, some standing in the streets outside a packed Courtroom. Eventually a guilty verdict was pronounced and Mead was sentenced to a jail sentence in York Castle. Years later (legend has it) he was released and eventually deported to Australia after pleading guilty to stealing cattle. I read this last bit of information in a local newspaper not so many years ago.

Some of the contraband is reputed to have been transported from Eastside Farm over the moor to Pickering. One interesting little revelation from the book describes how one night contraband was being taken by pony and cart over the moors to Pickering. No doubt acting on a tip off, the Coastguards pounced. All right said the man leading the pony, "You got me fair and square, I will go with you to the Police Station."

The officers had already examined the contents of the cart and were quite cock a hoop about their conquest. They were in high spirits as they joked with the driver. "We knew of your little game. It was just a matter of time."

Little known to the Customs men the man they thought was alone, had an accomplice. He had thrown himself into the heather when they were accosted. Now he quietly and deliberately walked behind the cart and very careful not to make a sound, he systematically unloaded the cart and hid the contents by the roadside.

Arriving at Kirby Police Station the gleeful Customs men seized on the cart. Their triumphant moment arrived. You can imagine their spontaneous and furious reaction when they found the cart empty.

There was no disguising their anger as they vented outrage at the driver, "What, where, how - why you!!", one officer nearly exploding. Looking as innocent as a new born baby the driver spoke, "I know nowt," was his only comment.

CHAPTER TWENTY FIVE
Developments

By 1982, after extensive restoration by ourselves, the family had leased Rigg Hall Farm just a few hundred yards to the North of us and linked by a track known as Riggs Lane. At one time it was owned by the Overseer of the Freeholders, Robert Mainforth.

Our elder daughter Shirley and her husband Rob, together with David our eldest son and his wife Liz having divided the house into two, had moved in with their respective families.

We had planned a shared enterprise to make the running of our eventual Shire Horse Farm a family affair.

One of the first jobs was to clear the lane of badly overgrown thorn bushes and brambles and open it out for a vehicle. This we did and the then National Park Ranger organised some employment training scheme labour and fenced it along one side to prevent grazing cattle from eroding the hedgebank further, and restricting the width.

The idea was to make a clear access for our eventual visitors and partly protect walkers from livestock.

At that same time the elderly neighbours of ours who owned the land, had decided to retire from their small farming activities and rent the land to a tenant.

It soon became obvious that so far as we were concerned things were going to take a turn for the worse. Within weeks a bull appeared on the lane. It just happened at that same time that we got a visit from the Park Uplands Management Scheme organiser. He had come to examine the work and said he thought some attempt should be made eventually to rebuild the old wall. He spotted the bull — 'What's that doing on this road?'

I must admit by any stretch of the imagination I wasn't happy with it either, whatever type of bull it may be. My daughter who was expecting a baby had a toddler and a young daughter just starting school — she had to walk her through this lane pushing a buggy.

'I will look into the bull question' said the Parks Officer, 'leave it with me.' He was as good as his word, the bull got moved, thank goodness, but more was to come. Times were changing and so was our quiet existence.

It was a great help having the family close by and our lovely grand-children. Although I have to be fair and say having them and us! living so close together did create a few prob-lems. Nevertheless problems apart we

She had to walk through this lane pushing a buggy.

would welcome them all back tomorrow. Shirley our daughter and family are now all living in New Zealand.

Back to the present. At about this time we were busily engaged carrying out a two phase tree planting scheme designed by the North York Moors National Park Landscape Architect. It was part of a voluntary scheme set up to encourage the planting of more trees in the area. From our point of view it was to help enhance our future development plans and also to act on a suggestion by the Parks Officer's assistant, that trees would provide screening for cars being parked. I thought that was good forward thinking.

Well time was moving on and it was fast becoming a not how but when situation. Did we have enough to offer the public, did we have

142

the layout attractive enough and above all could we offer good value for money?

In fact, were we ready to open our doors and how much should we charge. I decided to consult with the National Park and the people who were engaged in development and promotion.

A meeting was soon arranged and three of the Parks Officers came to the farm to offer expert advice — two of them I have already mentioned and had met, and one, the Park Promotions Officer I had not. They were very enthusiastic and helpful and looked round our displays and collection with great interest. In fact I think they were impressed. During the ensuing discussion it was suggested what a wonderful demonstration unit this would make.

I was more than pleased, this was the encouragement that I had been waiting for. 'Well' I said, 'When do we open and are we quite ready?'

The answer was spontaneous, 'Open as soon as you like, you have plenty of interest in your static displays and of course your horses — they will be a tremendous attraction.' The next question was how much shall we charge.

'Well what did you have in mind?', said one.

'One pound for adults and 50p for children I thought.'

They were all agreed that was quite a modest amount and certainly acceptable. Well that was that, a great step in the right direction and the next move was up to me. They wished me the best of luck and again offered any help they could give and went on their way.

I was excited and a bit nervous. This was decision time and I had got to make it work. Well there was no rush. I believe a successful business is only established through creating a good first impression. People have got to go away happy and satisfied. They have got to feel that they have had good value for money, will tell their friends, and more than that, come back again.

I decided it was finishing touches time and the time for a little breathing space and the right opportunity. Opportunities in my view present themselves but you have to grab them.

A friend of mine had got me interested in competition ploughing with the horses. He did the ploughing and I provided the horses, Princess and Nobby and the plough. We had travelled around with them quite a lot and had been featured several times in a black and white photographic souvenirs book. The book was produced to illustrate a day at a very popular annual event 'The Festival of the Plough', held at Epworth, Nr. Doncaster.

This was the Winter of 1983/84. Quite apart from our ploughing activities my mind was now on final preparations. This included trimming hedges, tidying up ditches and some new fencing. Things were going to plan.

The opportunity I had been waiting for came in the shape of a telephone call both unexpected and unpredicted. 'Would you like to join the Committee of the World Ploughing Match horse section?'

I have described this event in a previous book so I won't bore you with details. Suffice to say it was about fundraising and I was being invited to help. You can probably guess the rest — I offered to organise an open day here at the farm and give all profits to the sponsorship fund. The various thank you certificates now hang in our Coffee Shop.

It was a great success, it created a lot of interest and above all it gave me the springboard I needed to get this venture off the ground. I decided Spring 1985. Unfortunately the day although not spoilt, was marred by events on the road and the field adjoining our farm through which the road passes.

Apparently our tenant neighbour was less than happy either about the event, or the fact that people were crossing his rented land. Several people whom I know well, were accosted en route and told to turn back and others were rudely spoken to. Worse was to come, a herd of bullocks suddenly appeared, let in from another field; they were stampeding round followed by a pick-up truck. The road in question is a County Highway and, for centuries, part of what was known as the old Parish Road. Although designated as a green lane, it was once the main and only access to this farm and others. From my own research it was used regularly as the LNER delivery route for their delivery van from Staintondale Station. There should have been no argument as to its status. It goes without saying that I complained to both the owner of the land and to the National Parks Officer. As an avid listener to BBC Radio Four's programme 'Face the Facts' presented by John Waite, I realise how easy it is to be branded as a trouble-maker. In any event how many people can face the facts or even want to? Needless to say I got no replies but did I expect any?

I was determined that these or any other events were not going to deter me from developing my small farm. 'A concept and an ideal.' — Although that wonderful compliment and description was yet many years ahead. The future or the anticipation of the future spurred me on. Giving pleasure gives pleasure, and the thought of running a viable business out of both a hobby and an obsession was enough to shut out some of the discomfort.

The elderly neighbours no longer farmed. The cows had now gone, no longer taken in for the winter and the filthy, muddy field access gate was firmly shut. On a dark winter's night it was to be avoided except by necessity. The elderly neighbours had previously agreed to a cattle grid but that arrangement had been slammed shut as firmly as the gate!

Laugh and the world laughs with you — cry and you cry alone — nothing was going to get me down. Let us look at the lighter side of life. By now we had attended the World Ploughing Match at Horncastle in Lincolnshire. We were placed somewhere in the middle out of a field of thirty or so. It must have rated as the wettest ploughing match ever. Our farming visitors still talk about it!

As that coming winter drew nearer so did the following Spring. We finally opened to the public on Spring Bank Holiday Monday 1985. What a wonderful and rewarding experience. The visitors loved it and we loved our visitors — What nice people and such enthusiasm! It was amazing really because looking back we didn't have such a lot to offer.

It was not so much working what we had to do round the visitors, it was simply working the visitors round what we were doing!

They watched us schooling young horses, putting harnesses on for the first time, and even Graz (Graziella) riding our Shire Horse Stallion round the field. No patio chairs, PA system or demonstrations in those days. No programme, no video studio but a lot of warmth even on a cold day.

We had no signposts to guide the visitors here, it needed a map and a compass to find us, but find us they did. They talked about us to their friends and they brought them to see us. And they are still coming back.

Our success story was born and thriving. I was ecstatic. I called 1985 My Year.

CHAPTER TWENTY SIX
Of dogs, pans and thruffers

As solid as a rock! What a marvellous reassuring ring those few words have. Something to cling on to, something to trust and something to stand the test of time.

It effectively describes one man and his workmanship. A man who, over the years has left his name literally, written in stone all over Staintondale and beyond.

The original old stone buildings which now form the centrepiece of this enterprise, were built in the early nineteenth century and possibly long before. Not many people realise this, but they are basically dry stone walls built from stone with only one square face. The strength of the walls lies in the construction, which was very important. It involved bonding all joints by carefully selecting every piece. There were also pieces called 'Thruffers' referred to in the title, which bonded the inner and outer skin together.

A stone wall is constructed, not just built, and a good stone mason knows exactly where its strength and weakness lies. I have written this chapter about Des, because he has left his trademark well and truly on our buildings. They are there to be admired now, and for posterity. He also taught me a lot about pride in your job and certain building skills that are a thing of the past. Above all he taught me something about stone. He told me that when he started building, and it was nearly all stone buildings at that time, that he worked six days under tarpaulins cutting and dressing stone and six days building. In his early days he said builders were builders. The stone and the timber was on the site and everything was made from it. I rang him because he had been recommended and I was soon to learn why. I told him what I wanted. 'Well now let's see, I shall be at so and so's until next Wednesday and then I have half a day at Cloughton. I have my regulars you see, have to work their little jobs in between. Then there's emergencies'. A pause for thought. 'Can you pick me up at the bus stop at the end of your lane a week on Friday morning, ten past seven?' And then, 'Oh could you get some sand and cement?'

At that time he didn't have his own transport. He carried his tools in his bag and his skills and experience in his head and his hands. It was a laugh from the start that day, he had a marvellous sense of humour and an explanation for everything.

I have never taken to anybody so readily, he called a spade a spade and everything else a bustard! Well, something like that. Work, he was a colossus among men! It seemed to me at that time, that he could be mixing a barrowful of plaster with a shovel in one hand, and plastering a wall with a trowel in the other. Many people will remember this description of him because that is just how he was.

I have been involved in building work for a very long time now, so these comments are from experience and well deserved. 'Right', as they used to say on the building site' Are we having a start?'

The first job we looked at was a broken stone lintel over the barn door. It had the inscription upon it 'R & M 1814'. One Robert Mead no less, head of the Mead family when the 'New' farmhouse was built.

It was cracked right through, and had allowed the stone work above it to slip and push forward.

'Water' said Des looking up at the gutter. 'If these buildings had proper spouts on, the water wouldn't have washed all the mortar out of the joints (pointing) and caused the stone to move' he went on 'No point in repairing these buildings unless you are going to fit new spouting'. When he said things like that, he said it with such conviction, it was advice you ignored at your peril.

At that moment a wasp emerged from the crack in the lintel — followed by another. Des was suddenly more concerned about the appearance of the wasps than he was about gutters. 'That job will have to wait until you get rid of those Kami Kazi (Japanese suicide pilots) Bustards!!' He explained 'There will be a nest full of them Bustards in that wall — thousands of 'em. Get the little Bustards out'. I laughed 'How?' I said, 'Smoke 'em out, burn 'em out, but there is no way we can take that wall out, until they are gone. That nest could be a yard long. What else is on the agenda?'

'Well', I said' I have got some ambitious plans for the creation of a blacksmith's shop, and the old low doorway cart shed would

147

be ideal' I paused 'Well except for the fact that it is very unstable, and the stonework above the old wooden door lintel is bulging out'. 'Let's have a look at that then' said Des. Again he looked up at the verges. 'Same problem!' he commented 'Water's run down the front, it's got into the stonework and then saturated that old beam — be a bit of old ship's timber that!' he went on 'It never dried out properly and that's done the damage — the beam's rotted'. He ran his eyes along and above and then examined the inside. 'The pan (wood wall plate) running along the wall is all bowed out with the wall and rotten too, by the look of it. We shall have to prop those rafters and take it out!' Again a pause whilst he took in the whole situation. 'The whole lot right down to door top level, will have to come down!' 'Whew', I said contemplating a lot of work. 'It can be done' said Des, 'But we shall need a bit of scaffolding'.

My mind was working well at this point and the realisation of creating something I had always wanted, suddenly occurred to me. 'Could you build an archway into it?' I spoke a bit hesitantly because I didn't want to put this man off doing the job.

'Well we would call that a segment, you couldn't really get a full archway in there, but yes I could do it'.

My eyes shone 'That's marvellous. It would really give my blacksmith's shop some character'.

'You will have to make a profile', said our by-now master craftsman (well, in my eyes already) 'Can you do that?'

'No problem at all'. I couldn't wait to get started.

'I'll just have a look at the other walls to make sure we have a stable building before we start pulling down. Don't want the whole lot collapsing on our heads'. He walked round the back of the buildings with the eye of an expert.

"Problem there" he said, `Can you see how badly the back wall has been pushed out? That's because the roof hasn't been tied in and it's pushed the walls apart'.

'What can we do about that?' I enquired.

'Buttress' came the reply 'We build a purpose built buttress against the back wall and stabilise it. It won't go any further'.

I breathed a sigh of relief. It all sounded too good to be true. 'Right, for a start, we shall need to dig out and put a solid foundation in. There will be a lot of weight and pressure, so we don't want any movement'.

I helped in this first operation and after witnessing the type of stone and heavy flagstones selected for this job, I mentally thought it would need an earthquake to move that lot. In fact the more I got to know Des the more I realised that it would take more than a simple earthquake — more on the lines of a nuclear explosion!

The work progressed well and I spent the day carrying stone. It is hard for some people to imagine this, but a seven foot high buttress with a four foot base and something like two foot thick, would take several tons of stone.

Each piece was laid with precision and at intervals bonded into the wall. At last a large piece was accurately cut for the top. Des trowelled on a bed of mortar, 'There, that'll just fit in there'. He dropped it into place — perfect. After pointing (flushing) all the joints he stood back 'That'll never move', he said. 'Not unless somebody drops a bomb', I thought; 'and even then, we could shelter under it'.

That out of the way we turned our attention to the front. By now I had been and hired some scaffolding and we erected that first, Des was as good at taking down as he was at building.

Armed with a long cold steel chisel and his four pound lumphammer he set about it. His forearms were a give-away for the physical effort his work demanded, and he lifted the heavy stones off effortlessly.

'Here catch hold of this' he would say now and again as the scaffold buckled under the weight.

'I'd better lift some down' I said and proceeded to do just that, before the weight did some damage. 'Just stack it all inside the building, we don't want it getting wet'. I laboured away enjoying every minute, as the two of us set about putting the world to rights.

There was a laugh every few minutes as well, as we each swapped a yarn or two. His stories of building in his apprentice days fascinated me — far removed from all the tools and equipment found on a modern building site of today. 'It was all plumb-lines and plumbobs then' said Des. 'No fancy plumb-rules'. (Vertical spirit levels).

I don't want to bore my readers with too much technical detail, but the springing of an arch is a marvellous feat, and one that has been known to man for thousands of years. It is done with a profile or form and this is set in position and built over.

Each segment which forms the arch support is carefully cut and

It's got to last out the building, said Des.

set out on the profile. The stone selected, Des explained, must be hard and weather resistant. 'You don't want soft sandstone that's going to weather and flake away — it's got to last out the building'.

Each piece of segment was certainly hard. I could hear the ring of the steel chisel as it occasionally deflected from the cut. They looked marvellous just set out in dry form, and the centre key stone, the crowning glory.

Des explained, 'You see the strength of an arch is in the segments and the fact that they are being pushed together by the weight of stone above. The keystone is tapered and of course this means wedge shape. It effectively wedges the segments against each other'. Even now in its dry stone wall form (without mortar) you could have removed the wood profile and it would have stayed in place.

The lovely colours of different stone types are very evident in the arched stone of our Blacksmith's shop. There are shades of blue, red and grey and the brown tints of iron ore, which give away the secrets of its metal content.

By now as the days had gone by I had spent some time and got rid of the wasps nest — no need to make too much of that episode, but like my builder friend I was very relieved to see the back of them. Now we could set to work replacing the broken Mead lintel.

This man's confidence in the skills of his craftsmen predecessors never ceased to impress me.

'All about cantilevers' he had said, 'Have you got an iron bar and a prop about 8 feet long?' He went on. 'I'm going to pin the wall whilst we take out that lintel, by supporting one important stone with the bar and prop'.

He knew exactly which stone, and within the space of a few minutes we put his cantilever theory to the test. I was amazed. No modern Acrow props and screw jacking system, no complicated

150

scaffold. Nothing more than one steel bar and prop and a wealth of knowledge and know how.

Again we are talking about supporting two to three tons of stone. The broken lintel removed, the wall was carefully rebuilt with a plain stone lintel and pointed to match in with the existing wall.

The inscribed Robert Mead lintel had to have a home, broken or not, and the opportunity to find it one came not too long afterwards. It is now proudly displayed built into the front of another old cart shed, by this time the area we call our 'Farm hand tool collection'.

This weathered and age-damaged front gable was also under threat of collapse and again, Des to the rescue. 'They want preserving really', he had said at the time of its removal. 'Anything with a date on it!' Well here was the perfect site. A south facing aspect at the front end of a building which is clearly in view to visitors.

I tell the Mead story of the smuggling and the murder trial on a fairly regular basis throughout the summer. We are proud to own Eastside Farm and proud of the previous owners and its colourful history. Life is a sort of circle and each piece is a segment of that circle. This story is very much a chapter of my life really, and could be described as an instalment of one's autobiography. To preserve and protect the past has given me a lot of pleasure, and to people like my builder friend, it must have given a tremendous amount of satisfaction. I commend it to posterity.

O yes Dogs! I almost missed this bit of my title. These were timber wall ties really, and when a building was up to the square — that is all four walls of equal height, the pans (wall plates) were laid in position. The dogs, (one at each corner) were laid over them and gable ends built up with the dogs built in. The ends of the dogs were then nailed or spiked into the pan and this prevented the apex roof pushing out the walls.

I wonder if these are the real subject of the expression 'A dog's life'. They certainly couldn't go far and even being chained to a wall would be better than being built into one!

As a footnote to this chapter I also have to credit the lovely stone Inglenook inside the house, to this true village craftsman.

CHAPTER TWENTY SEVEN
An Ominous visit

This book is about a planning dispute and of course the background to it. I have tried to describe it as accurately and truthfully as possible. It is not about too many laughs although it is not without its humorous side, but please read on. During our second year into our visitor attraction opening, a few problem areas began to emerge. One of them was of course the gated access already described. Now you have to get a good mental picture of this situation as it existed then, it is nothing like it now.

The gated country road ran across a field adjoining our property but the field did not belong to us. Access to both the field and the road was through a gate. Just inside there was a pond originally, and because of a constantly blocked overflow pipe the pond very often flooded.

At a later date the pond was fenced on both sides after being cleaned and a new overflow fitted. At the same time the gate was moved to a point further away from the pond.

This operation had happened at about the same time this chapter starts and was a blessing. After almost twenty years it seemed like an act of God. Thanks to North Yorkshire County Council.

At the other side of the field was another gate where the road continued on to our property. It was this area where the problem emerged. It was not a man made one. In the summertime when stock were grazing in the field, on a hot day they found shelter by the hedge and trees just outside our property. This in itself was not a problem but to visitors not used to cattle — and a lot are not, it was.

How to move them while opening the gate into our property and keep them clear whilst driving a vehicle through? Quite an ordeal for some people — they all look like bulls!

The answer was staring us in the face. I still had the heavy steel rails purchased for the other aborted plan. A cattle grid would solve the problem and make life easier for all concerned — that included us!

Again, no sooner a word than a deed. With the help of a local builder and a contribution from a tractor excavator we were in business. Concrete was laid, foundations built and hey presto in just one day it was installed. Magic!

Well not quite. It seems we had trespassed once again. what we had trespassed on this time is unclear but it again brought wrath and condemnation and the threat of legal action. Fortunately for us the NFU Regional Secretary was able to pour oil on troubled waters (or should I say turbulent) and bring sanity to bear.

Kipling my friend, 'If you can keep your head.

On the 26th of June 1986 we had a visitor. Up to this day things had been progressing quietly and we were trying to get on with our lives. The enterprise itself was going smoothly and I was feeling very happy. Our small attraction was going to work out and hopefully would become viable. It is not easy getting a business, so far off the beaten track, off the ground. As I said before visitors had to find us first.

There was an air of half expectancy when a different visitor arrived at the farm one day. I found it somewhat disturbing but I can't honestly say why. Some of us will remember telegrams and a telegraph lad on a bike; I can remember the anticipation that sometimes people spoke of, a kind of telepathy perhaps. This was a quietly spoken man. I would say slightly nervous, perhaps he expected a hostile reception.

'Can I have a word with you 'he said, 'perhaps we could go inside?' 'What have I done this time?' Although he didn't look a policeman, I was beginning to think I could get myself into trouble without trying.

The last similar experience to this, had been when a valuation officer had arrived from the Rating Office. He came in a classic white car which was obviously his pride and joy. I am going to relate this story first and then return to our mystery man.

He didn't leave me in doubt — just stuck his hand out, 'I'm the District Valuer', and produced his card. My heart sank. I have got to say that my heart is used to sinking, so much so it has life rafts slung across its bows.

My thoughts raced, 'Don't know about sinking hearts, if he

slap's some rates on this place it will sink the whole enterprise.' 'It hadn't made a bean yet.

This pleasant faced man, taking a sweeping glance round said, 'It has been brought to our notice that you are carrying on a business here and we do not appear to have received a valuation assessment'. I know full well what he meant but were there not mitigating circumstances? 'Well' I said 'We are only open on a limited basis and anyway most of these buildings are agricultural buildings and used for that purpose.' He smiled again. 'Well how limited and how agricultural?' I rather liked his manner.

Immediately I burst forth with my explanation. I told him about my original idea and the plan that put it into operation. I described the work and preparation and of course the breeding of the horses. At this point I emphasised the Ministry of Agriculture's recognition of the breeding of Heavy Horses and the fact we kept a licensed Stallion. Essential buildings and all that. I made a point about the road he had just slowly negotiated with his rather nice motor car. 'Take that road' I said, 'It is all right talking about rates but the road across that field is a County road and who maintains it? — Muggins!' I was getting into top gear. It was easy to talk about carrying on a business', I went on, 'But the cost of trying to maintain that road is a constant burden and I wouldn't care so much if it crossed our land.'

'I must admit', he said looking down at his polished shoes, 'I did wonder if I was on the right track'. I think he was referring to the mud and the cow pats but I had made a good point.

'More than that', I think I must have sounded almost pleading, 'For the amount of business we are doing any further pressure on overheads will see me off.'

'We are not in the business of killing off enterprise, shall we just look around?' he said quietly. With that I showed him round — well, talked him round would be a better description. I think my enthusiasm shone through because at the end of the tour he said, 'I have listened to your story and I am impressed. I seriously believe you are dedicated to what you do, in fact' he went on 'I don't think you really need the buildings or even the horse because with your enthusiasm, you could make your living telling your stories on a Public House car park.'

'Now he said 'I will get my tape and measure all the buildings and stables and make my assessment. In view of what you have told

He did not mention in what capacity.

me, and if you are prepared to let me have a copy of your current balance sheet, I promise you it will be a fair one! He got into his nice classic car and no doubt it was as reliable as his word. One of the old school and a very nice person indeed.

We return to the mystery man. I think the most disturbing thing about this visit, was that, although this caller eventually explained that he was from the National Park office he did not mention in what capacity. He was not particularly forthcoming and both of us (my wife was now present) found him a little bit inscrutable. Despite that, he had quite a pleasant manner.

He started to ask a few questions about the setting up of the enterprise and whom we had originally been in touch with. Also he wanted to know exactly what we did here and when we were open. I had nothing to hide and so I went thread through the needle about the whole situation as I saw it. Oh yes, planning permission had been mentioned but up to now it had been very vague, It was always 'it is thought', or 'In some areas'. 'Nobody', I said 'had ever been specific about which area, although I had pointed out on several occasions I had no objection to applying for change of use for the buildings on the yard. What I did object to, was having to apply for anything that would deprive us of our farm status and turn us into a commercial visitor attraction only'. I had made the point, when is a field not a field?.

What a pity somebody didn't just turn up with a set of planning application forms at the time and offer some advice and assistance on exactly what was required and how the formal application should be made.

Our visitor listened with interest and made a few notes. 'I don't suppose you have any correspondence or copies of anything previously discussed?'

Now it was our turn. My wife left the room and appeared minutes later with a complete file. As an ex-solicitor's clerk, she had it all at her fingertips. It was all there. The correspondence, the reference to site meetings, the help and encouragement, the tree planting schemes and above all the names of all National Park Officers previously involved.

He studied it all very carefully and surprise, surprise, 'Well you certainly seem to have done all the right things' he conceded. Then a remark which stuck the knife in. 'Actually' he said, 'the reason for this visit was an anonymous letter. Somebody has written to say

156

you are using buildings for business use and not paying rates and you are making money charging admission and not declaring your income. In short, defrauding the Inland Revenue'.

We simultaneously exploded!

'Do you mean you have to take notice of mischief making of the worst kind — poisonous anonymous letters?' 'I am afraid so', he said 'They are followed up in exactly the same way as any other complaint we receive.' At least we now knew we had an enemy, unpleasant though that may be. 'Anyway' said the visitor. 'I shall be on my way. Thank you for being so co-operative. I have made a note of all relevant information and I shall now go and follow it up. You will be hearing from me shortly.' When he had gone Ann and I looked at each other. 'What was he then?' I said. Ann considered for a while and answered 'Well I should think he is either a solicitor, or,' laughing, 'A National Park Secret Service Agent!

On the 20th August, nearly two months later we received a letter as promised. It confirmed all that we had said as correct and also that he wanted to confirm planning consent would be needed if we were to open more than twenty eight days in total in any calendar year. He told me to consult his colleague (named) if I wanted to discuss it further.

He also in the letter described our enterprise as a most interesting, educational and tourism resource. Well I concluded we are nearly at the end of our season. I will decide on my future plans and do as he had suggested — discuss it further and find out just where planning consent was needed.

In fact I was contacted by a Parks Officer who visited me on 23rd April 1987. I received a letter from him on the 8th May of that year, but again I found it vague with regard to determining the area or areas in need of planning consent. I have mentioned how easily this could have been resolved at that time, with the simple act of helping to fill in a few forms on site. It is also interesting to note that at that time there was to be no objection from the Area Surveyor with regard to the road and the subsequent high financial cost to me would have been avoided.

CHAPTER TWENTY EIGHT
Cool clear water

There are some amusing situations that are not associated with horses, well not directly, but incidents brought about by our diversification to Tourism - Visitors.

One summer afternoon the first year we were open, Graz and myself were spending some time schooling our stallion Mascot. I should explain that Graz, or Graziella to give her full name, was my first assistant and a tremendous help towards setting up this enterprise and certainly a treasure so far as handling young horses went. She stayed for three years.

On this particular day, although it was not one of our open days, a car appeared coming along the track. Half expecting it to be a visitor calling to enquire about something or other, I handed Mascot over to Graz and went over.

It was an officer from the public health department wanting some information about our tea room and the volume of trade. 'How many cups of tea do you serve'? was one question. I must admit I was a bit annoyed at the interruption in the first place, but less than pleased at what I regarded as trivial. At the time the level of trade was such that on a poor day it was possibly no more than half a dozen cups.

'The point is', said the officer, Now you are actually using spring water for public consumption, it will need to be tested.' Well it is', said I boldly, 'Every year by your department'. 'Ah, but this is different, E.E.C. regulations.' I think I almost exploded 'Six cups of tea - E.E.C. regulations!' The man looked worried, I went on 'Have you any idea of the amount of paperwork printed, published and destroyed every single day by the E.E.C.? Hundreds of tons of nonsense and gobbledeguck!'

I calmed down. He was a nice bloke and only doing his job. He explained that more stringent tests would be needed to check the water and analyse it for mineral content and heavy metals -'Well to protect people's health.'

It seemed ridiculous to me, after all as I pointed out, in almost twenty years we had entertained friends and guests from all over the world - most commented on the sweetness and purity of the water. More than that, a previous owner of this property called Dawson lived to be over a hundred and his son nearly as long. Not much wrong with the water I said - can only be improved with a drop of whiskey. We had a laugh.

It was finally agreed that he would return at a later date with some equipment and containers! 'The water', he said 'Must be tested at source.' After he left I looked at Graz (pronounced Gratz)' Heavens, if he comes back as things are at the moment in the corner of that field, we shall be lucky to find the spring let alone the water'.

I had a mental picture of nettles, thistles, couch grass and what we call general rubbish growing rampant and completely obliterating our source of succulence.

In fact the urgent state of my mind prompted us to put Mascot in the stable and almost run the uphill two hundred yards to investigate. 'Suppose he comes back tomorrow', I gasped as we covered the ground like a couple of stags. My fears were well founded-what asight greeted us! 'Right Graz', I said - The big purge - let's get this lot sorted out.

It was a mess. The bit of wire fencing round the concrete collection tank had been almost demolished by the big horses reaching over it. At the same time it looked as if a foot had been caught in the wire mesh and literally tore it apart.

We used the tractor to pull what remained of the fence clear of the wilderness. The grass and weeds had grown into the mesh and held it like the tentacles of a giant octopus.

Once the fencing was clear we set about the greenery with slashers and scythe until the concrete top of the tank was clear. We raked it off and set to with a pair of garden shears!

It looked marvellous - a little lawned area carefully tendered it only needed a bowl of flowers and it would look like a shrine!

We erected a new bit of fence and topped it with barbed wire to keep the horses clear 'That should do the trick', I told Graz 'Now we are ready for inspection.'

But August ran into September and we closed for the season. October came and went but nobody came.

'Ah well Graz, at least it's tidy, now we shall have to keep it so. One

159

day somebody will turn up.' It was a very dry Autumn that year - very dry, and as we approached December and Christmas we were beginning to wonder what the winter had in store. I think that nature has an uncanny way of balancing itself and its seasons.

One day in mid December early in the evening my wife said -'You haven't left a tap running outside have you, the kitchen tap is only dribbling - the pressure's gone. Odd I thought, why now? A tap 'on' outside would have shown itself sooner. I probably should explain that with the nominal pressure of a small head of water, our taps will only respond as single units. Turn one 'on' outside and the water stops inside.

After years of living with a spring supply you learn never to take it for granted. There is always this nagging thought 'What if the spring dries upT

This was on my mind as I took a lamp and went out to inspect all taps, troughs and ballcocks for evidence of a problem - all was OK. So now we had a problem, but it would have to wait until morning. It has been very dry though I thought as I climbed into bed that night. The next morning Graz arrived for work as usual and we set off to investigate - back again to the shrine and I think I said a little prayer.

We got a big iron bar, jammed a spade into the joint between the two concrete slabs and slowly levered the removable one off - it was reluctant to move after years of sleeping quietly beneath its blanket of algia and moss. It gradually slid off -so far. We peered into the murky interior - I could have kicked myself for not bringing a lamp.

Graz shot off for one whilst I went to inspect the spring head itself. I found the level to be below the collection tube. Once we had the lamp the true state of things inside were revealed. What an amazing sight - well at least the water must be good, good enough for a whole family of frogs to be living in there and using ledges on the side as spring boards for their own private swimming pool.

Simultaneously the same thought dawned on us - our eyes met 'Sample at source?' You shouldn't laugh!

In the bottom of this pretty miserable looking reservoir a few inches of water stared up at us. Jeremy Fisher and his family seemed to revel in it. Down the side, a very modest trickle, spluttering and spitting emerged from the inlet pipe - well at least it was still running!

'What we need to do' I told Graz 'Is to stop off the outlet, measure the dimensions of the tank to calculate the capacity and then we can

Once we had the lamp the true state of things inside were revealed.

determine the rate of flow in. This would then tell us whether we had sufficient water being delivered for our needs and if so why was it empty - possibly a leak?'

Finding a leak on the 200 yards length of old pipe hadn't been too difficult in the past - we usually determined the exact route of the pipe by sighting in a few sticks and then paddled along the route looking for a squelchy bit - well feeling for one really.

Today was not our lucky day. As we hastily made a bung to stop off the outlet pipe it started to rain! It got worse. As we measured length, width and depth for our capacity calculations it started to pour down. 'Let's get the thing covered up before the rain fills it for us', I said. 'Some hope of finding a wet squelchy bit now!'.

With the information we needed all recorded, we set off for the farm -'Give it an hour', I said 'And we can go back and take a reading'- (How many gallons had flowed in measured in inches).

We had calculated the tank held 160 gallons - our total storage capacity and now, as the truth dawned, it was obviously totally inadequate for the visitors' consumption let alone stock. It was easy to relate this to a few flushes of the loo.

Once again at this point I shall leave you with the picture.

It turned out that the flow of water, although hesitant, was adequate at the time (no visitors) that there was a serious leak which was obviously losing us more water than the spring was providing. But more important that the storage system was not just totally inadequate, it was also clearly unacceptable.

We never found the leak - at least not just then. Nature was indeed balancing the shortfall. It rained and it rained and it rained. Miraculously the supply recovered as the ground got sodden and the wet clay and soil gradually sealed off our by now quite undetectable leak-water was running everywhere!

This story also has a happy ending and I have to mention this, as you probably enjoyed your nice cup of tea or coffee.

Another D.I.Y. job has been completed. With the help of my son David who just happens to be a plumber plus a few friends, we put in a whole new system of vented storage and supply piping.

Such was the professionalism of this job. When at last the Public Health Officer came to do the inspection and water analysis he was impressed.

'One of the best I have seen', he commented!

CHAPTER TWENTY NINE
The Bombshell

The purpose of this book is to examine our planning problem in retrospect. Everything, they say, is easier with hindsight. We now return to the plot and looking again at the background, and the disturbing influences that led to our many months of harassment and trauma. This enterprise had settled down to almost a routine and enjoyable situation. There had been a few incidents but turning the other cheek and an occasional symbolic gesture — if you know what I mean — had proved effective.

Our problem now was visitor numbers. We were running at a loss and struggling. How do you get visitors interested and more important, how do you make sure they find you?

Looking at the funny side, although I am not sure the visitors found it funny, we actually had some people drive all the way from Hornsea to visit us. After driving round the area for two hours, they trundled all the way back to the Tourist Information Centre at Hornsea to complain they couldn't find us.

Signs were what we needed but where and how? I decided to take the initiative and a gamble. The A171 was close by — our nearest main road. My plan was simple and effective. I would make a few signs, have them professionally painted in brown and white and erect them myself. I would then write to the County Surveyor and ask for deemed consent (something I had read about) to allow them as temporary signs pending an application for a more permanent arrangement. So far so good, as I effectively put plan A into operation. (The world loves a trier!) Well it certainly helped, and encouraged by the fact I had received no response to my letter I felt rather smug.

It lasted throughout the whole of that first season and as promised in my letter to the County Surveyor, I dutifully removed them at the end of September.

Painted in brown and white and erect them myself.

Unknown to me there was a stirring in the bushes. I had been rumbled. But by who? The following Spring I again erected my 'Temporary Signs' and at the same time sought the help of N.Y.C.C. Traffic Signs Department for either a form or procedural advice. I had written a letter.

Before a reply was received other events were unfolding. A telephone call from a neighbour brought bad news. He had sighted a gang of N.Y.C.C. workmen with a small truck removing and taking away my·signs. I was furious (again) and after all my diplomacy and overtures.

A friend of mine who had an ear to the ground, told me where they might be, and whom I should contact. It did not take me long to follow this information through.

I was less than polite. 'Do you realise those signs are temporary and with assumed deemed consent.' Better be careful I thought. 'And more than that, they were expensive signs and I shall hold you responsible for damage!' He listened, so I pushed on, 'I have written to County Hall for permission pending a formal application — you had no right to remove them!' He turned out to be a very nice man and I think he sympathised.

'I will return them to you personally and I can assure you there is no damage.' He added confidentially 'One of your neighbours is making trouble for you every time you put a sign up, we get anonymous telephone calls. In fact', he went on 'We had one this morning to say that you had clagged one to a road signpost.' Well here was a clue, who would use a word like 'clagged?'

He was as good as his word and later that day he returned the signs to me. My assumption was correct, he was a nice bloke and it was reassuring to know that there are human faces behind a lot of bureaucracy.

As proof of my integrity, I quote a reference from a reply card dated 16th November 1988. The card read 'Thank you for your communication which shall receive attention, as and when staff resources permit.' It was of course the reply to my letter regarding permanent traffic signs and the necessary procedural advice.

Was it a joke? I decided to telephone and find out.

Again I made contact with a human being — another helpful person who explained all. 'Oh it meant what it said, in fact at this moment in time we are really struggling staff wise.'

I was amazed 'So we just have to wait do we?', I said 'How long before the situation changes?' 'Could be weeks', he replied and then 'What was it about?'

He listened intently to my account of events, I think we even managed a laugh.

'As I see it you don't really have a problem. All you need is a supportive letter from the Yorkshire and Humberside Tourist Board confirming you are a member, and of course that you are a bona fide visitor attraction. If you accompany that with a plan of where you already had the signs, we will do the rest.'

I really couldn't believe my ears. It was the Eighteenth of November and my birthday. 'You have made my day, my year, and the rest of my life. In fact you have set a precedent, because this is the first really helpful local authority department I have experienced.'

It was not to last. My euphoria was to be torpedoed once more.

Weeks went by and I heard nothing. I had submitted a compelling and supporting letter from YHTB together with a plan almost immediately, but now it was another new year, and another new season approaching. We desperately needed those signs. I decided to telephone and ask for my friend in court. It was a rather subdued voice that eventually answered.

'Not good news I'm afraid. You need some help'. The last bit sounded ominous. 'Do you know a County Councillor who would support you?' There was a brief silence. 'I can't really say any more than that — sorry but your application met total opposition. I wish you the best of luck.'

How many roads must a man walk down? another song as always, sprang to my mind. Well I thought inwardly 'As many roads as it takes, I am not giving up.'

The ideal Councillor I thought, had got to be someone with a vested interest in the management of Yorkshire and Humberside Tourist board and also, in the County Council. I knew exactly who. I wrote him a letter. I had chosen the right person and a detailed enquiry into the full circumstances was instigated. It was not to my advantage and bearing in mind various comments, perhaps, I should have taken action at the time.

The reply I received referred to — surprise, surprise 'Planning approval and road signs — or the unauthorised use of!'

Well it was fair comment to a point, but only to a point. I was still in the dark as to exactly what needed planning consent. And since the last official visit by a planning officer I had heard nothing.

My recollection of the last visit was one of grave concern about the County Road which served our property. The track across the field. I had applied to the Countryside Commission for some help towards maintenance, only to be referred back to the National Park Authority, who had been unable to help.

More than that, in 1987 I had contributed to the Countryside Commission's Countryside Review Panel with my own views and objectives. This was for European Year of the Environment and a subsequent publication, 'New Opportunities for the Countryside.' Needless to say it was about roads and access, and I expressed the view very strongly that I should be getting some help maintaining this County Road. To start with, it was not on my property and yet I had maintained it for almost eighteen years at that time.

The incredible amount of deterioration during the winter by monster agricultural vehicles was devastating. These were vehicles sometimes many times the weight of a motor car and almost twice as wide. And again nothing to do with our enterprise.

You may well wonder what all this is leading up to? Well it is really quite simple. I had told the planner on his last visit that if the County were prepared to do something about the road, then I would consider looking at the planning issue.

'What is the point', I had said 'In encouraging development here when all we get is complaints about the track across that field (County Road) not to mention hostility from the tenant of the land. I must add that both tenant and owner had refused point blank by letter, to help with maintenance. Did they even want us using it? Well certainly the hostility was to continue as the following paragraphs will reveal.

1989 was a Summer of Sunshine. A recorded figure of 83 days when the temperature exceeded 70°F. This was against a national average of 52 days.

Well sunshine for some. But it seemed, for Staintondale Shire Horse Farm clouds were already gathering.

The season had started well and we were all in high spirits. Some of the signs had gone of course, but visitors were all ready coming back for repeat visits — and telling their friends. Our growth might be slow but it was encouraging.

My concern for this enterprise has been of a protective nature. I had no wish to either destroy or even threaten our lovely environment. We have lived here now, as I write these chapters for twenty four years. This has been a lifelong commitment to perfection. A rose to grow, a rose to cherish.

You can imagine therefore, the effect of a telephone call from a Yorkshire Post newspaper reporter on Friday morning of June 9th — it was devastating.

My wife Ann had answered the telephone and a brief conversation ensued. I saw her face drain of colour. She handed it over to me 'It's a Yorkshire Post reporter'.

A voice spoke, 'Hi Tony it's Steve here, how are you?' It turned out that we had already been in contact a year or two previously. That is the good thing about Press relations they are always there and I have always been willing to co-operate. Publicity to me is vital for survival and a friend in the press is worth a lot.

None more so than now. The question hit me like a stone 'What are you going to do about the enforcement action being recommended to the North York Moors National Park Development Control Sub Committee?' he went on, 'I just mentioned it to your wife.' No wonder she turned pale. What was he talking about? At last I found my tongue 'What enforcement action?' 'Well', said my reporter friend 'Apparently you are operating without planning permission and your enterprise is causing problems.' 'Well that's news to me, what sort of problems?' 'You mean you know nothing about this order, or its consequences?' 'Nothing', I spoke with incredulity.

'Well here are a few things you should know. For starters I quote, they are saying that the farm is seriously detrimental to the character and appearance of the area. And also that the site is inappropriate for intensive tourism use!'

'Don't say any more', I said 'What a damned nerve.' 'Well what do you propose to do?' said the reporter. 'I'll tell you what I am going to do — fight them. It is just not on. This farm is a beautiful place, it has been described many times by visitors as idyllic. The buildings are compact and low profile and everything we do is in the best interests of conservation. So far as inappropriate goes, that's rubbish. Shire Horses and the countryside are this country's heritage. We encourage visitors to share this wonderful situation and from a youngster's point of view it is very educational!' I paused for breath. 'We have also inherited a wonderful history dating from the XIIth century. It concerns a Charter granted to the

Noble Order of the Knights of St. John of Jerusalem. It gave them the freehold of the Manor of Steynton in Blackamor together with other gifts and privileges. Not just for them, but for their heirs and successors forever. Pretty impressive stuff hey?'

I was in top gear by now 'Oh it's very real as recent records show. Pursuant to the Charter granted by King Stephen, the freeholders of the Dale could claim exemption from tithes tolls, and land tax. Also, by virtue of privileges granted by the old Charter, they could claim exemption from serving on juries at assizes or sessions. Robert Mainforth, who was overseer for many years, read the Charter to the Judge in Northallerton when jury men were called from Staintondale. This latter information is from the History, Topography and Directory of North Yorkshire published in 1890.'

Let Battle Commence!

'Sounds quite amazing', said the reporter who had listened fascinated. 'But where do you fit in?'

'I fit in very easily. We are probably one of the few remaining farms with deeds dating back to the Eighteenth century, and which include the manorial rights. As a Staintondale freeholder I shall use them in any way possible — might even don my armour and mount a Shire horse charger. Mind you it would have to be Mascot the Stallion in true Destrier fashion!'

'It's a good story', he said 'Look out for tomorrow's Yorkshire Post!'

An eighteen month planning battle was about to start, with all the relevant acrimony, trauma and at times distress. It was a battle to be won.

CHAPTER THIRTY
Crunch meeting

'Farmer Defends Tourist Venture' headed the report. It was the start of some very supportive press and television coverage that was almost to dominate local news for the next few months. I was very glad of it.

I have got to clarify one point though. I do not regard myself as a farmer even after twenty odd years of keeping various livestock. My career has been a business one, and this farm was purchased originally to start a riding stables.

A farmer is a man who cultivates the land and grows crops to both sell, and feed his livestock. I do not fit this category but I suppose to a Journalist a farmer is a man who lives on a farm. Ah well!

The meeting the report referred to came up the following Wednesday, the 14th June 1989. I did not attend, simply because I was not aware that I could have done so. I soon got very wise to procedure in the coming weeks, and I wonder how many other people are ignorant of their rights?

The following day under a banner headline 'Crunch Meeting on Horse Centre', I was able to read about it. It did not please me. If the evidence put forward as background by the planning officer was as reported, then it was either a fabrication of the facts or the lack of them.

They had stated that we had been inviting visitors since 1976 when in fact we hadn't opened until 1985 and that they hadn't heard from me since 1982.

My records and copy letters would clearly show that we had received visits and held serious discussions with planning officers in June 1986 and again in April 1987. Both I might add, inconclusive and neither of them suggesting the Draconian action now being proposed.

They had also stated, I quote 'lately there had been complaints

170

from the Parish Council, particularly concerning the narrow and steep access to the site.' I must confess this latter paragraph pleased me even less. Who were these people, who were complaining and why? We had been operating for four years without any hint of a problem, and certainly no reports of any accidents. Besides why not complain to me? I concluded other forces were at work — again.

It might be worth adding at this point that this area is becoming increasingly dependent on Tourism, and cars coming down that lane were a welcome sight to some people. The report concluded with a decision taken at the meeting that North Yorks Moors members were to visit the farm and meet Mr. Jenkins before deciding what action to take.

Well that meeting on site came the following month, and by now we had received some wonderful television coverage of the dispute. I had been interviewed live on our attractive stable yard, which was as usual a mass of summer colour, flowers and foliage. Our tubs and hanging baskets are the envy of our visitors and have won us endless awards. Add to this our very tidy and well maintained stone buildings and adjoining grass paddocks and you have a mental picture. The interviewer was asking questions. 'They say your enterprise is detrimental to the Environment. What do you say to that?'

I swept my eyes round in a panoramic gesture and pointed.

'Look around you,' I said. 'This is a beautiful place and we put endless time and energy into keeping it that way.'

The cameras took in every detail focussing on flower heads and greenery. The effect was a kaleidoscope of mellow stone and bright summer colour.

I think that question was suitably dealt with.

The final question. 'It's going to be a long battle then Mr. Jenkins?'

'It's going to be a long b——y battle,' I replied. Later I saw the piece on television, I could see why the presenter looked a bit startled. Still I meant it. They hadn't shown me much mercy.

The day of the meeting dawned and we had prepared for it. Although acrimony was possibly in my thoughts at no time during discussion did I let it show. Politeness and good humour costs nothing.

We had placed a bowl of lovely sweet peas on a table in the ladies toilet.

171

The meeting itself I regarded as an inquisition. I felt I was being tried for treason. My almost lifelong efforts were under threat and my well received and popular enterprise was being doubted. There has got to be a thread of Kiplings 'If' running through this story because it kept my head above water. I am going to quote a line or two I thought relevant.

'If you can trust yourself when all men doubt you, and make allowance for their doubting too.'
'Or being hated, don't give way to hating.

'It's going to be a long b----y battle.'

Or being lied about, don't deal in lies.'

The planner was again quoting his version of the background. I was biting my tongue. My adviser had said, 'Do not get involved in arguments, just listen.'

He (The Planner) was now talking about the access and especially the part of the County Road that was the infamous track across the field. To me he seemed to be implying that this was private property, and I was using it without authority. I could have been wrong.

He went on 'Mr. Jenkins has been demanding that the owners pay for the maintenance of the road.'

I could contain myself no longer. I found it so emotionally distressing that I broke down. I was choked up and found that in trying to defend myself, I was making a mess of the situation. Something I wanted to avoid. My adviser excused my predicament and took over.

What I had wanted to really say, was that this was a lie. Even more poison was being purported by forces unknown. What I had asked for, was a responsible arrangement to make other users of the road contribute to the maintenance. If they felt that any rent they paid the owners of the land put the responsibilities on the Landowner, then so be it. I had written a letter to this effect which was passed on to one of the tenants. It received an immediate rebuff.

I had felt very annoyed at the time because not only had I maintained the road over all the years, but in the early 1970's I had a contractor level it, stone it and then, I even hired a full size road roller from Scarborough Borough Council to make a first class job of compacting it.

In retrospect I now realise that I was making a rod for my own back. This was a County Road No. WY407G and maintainable at Public expense — facts I was not aware of all those years ago. The County Council were in fact opting out of their responsibilities.

One winter's day I had seen my efforts destroyed, as a shuttle of tractors and muckspreaders had turned the road into an unrecognisable quagmire. Mr. Planner you stuck a knife in me that day! The meeting continued and as Councillors looked round, I made an excuse to go and compose myself and then entertain my visitors.

It was July and quite busy. Each open day I give talks and demonstrations and today was no exception.

I knew we had a lot of supporters present and I wasn't going to let them down. The show must go on. Soon back to my usual good natured role as host, I quickly established contact and a very appreciative audience listened intently. Some of them I know, were all for giving these visiting Councillors a piece of their mind. In fairness I have got to say that quite a few were both sympathetic and supportive. Others were there either to pay lip service or line up in opposition. I was learning.

The site meeting dispersed and our day continued as normal. Several of the Councillors stayed on to look round our enterprise and seemingly enjoyed it. It would be fair to say that one or two of them were genuinely impressed and pledged their support. This I found very reassuring because I did realise the value of someone actually speaking on my behalf at the next meeting of the planning sub-committee. One comment made to me that day I did not like. It was to this effect 'Oh I think you will get approval eventually — but you will have to be seen getting your backside kicked!' Someone arrogant enough to ignore the distress and trauma that myself, my wife and staff were going through and stupid enough to think I would concede to being made a scapegoat — I think not.

It was another month now to the next meeting and this was to be held at the North York Moors National Park offices at the Old Vicarage Helmsley on Wednesday August 9th 1989. Support for this venture was now flooding in and many old campaigners were giving me the benefit of their experiences. It was pretty obvious that the park planners were not exactly flavour of the month.

With such wonderful and overwhelming public concern for the future of this enterprise I felt invincible. My strength was the appreciation and encouragement people gave me from all walks of life and all parts of the country.

In the next few months exciting events were to take place and the considerable interest this would provoke left me in no doubt about the outcome.

A bonus came in the shape of two other Councillors who contacted me. One rang to apologise for not being at the site meeting but wanted to come and see me. The other to send copy of letter addressed to the Chairman of the forthcoming meeting. It was very supportive and explained that this particular Councillor would be on holiday and unable to attend. Well at least we had friends in Court. I decided to strengthen my defences. There had been a lot of misunderstanding and doubt about the background to this development and I realised from the attitude of some people that they were not conversant with the facts.

To counteract this I decided to copy some of the relevant correspondence and send it to members of the committee prior to the meeting. The truth, the whole truth and nothing but the truth.

CHAPTER THIRTY ONE
Shires go marching in

What exactly did we have at our disposal that could create the biggest impact and draw attention to our plight. And how do we publicise our outrage and anger at what we considered to be Bureaucracy gone mad? These two questions had an obvious answer — It was big, it was heavy and it was impressive.

We planned our next move like a military operation — it was to be our *coup de grace*, well a blow for justice anyway. On the morning of the meeting we would take our plough pair Princess and Nobby to Helmsley. This mother and son team were very much part of our family and after all, their future was at stake too.

As luck would have it we had some friends staying with us from Batley and they were very enthusiastic supporters. We decided that the civilised way to approach this offensive was to have a pow wow — well we had a barbecue! We then planned our morning strategy. At the crack of dawn we would box the horses and head North for Helmsley.

Soon our plans were taking shape. The brass mounted plough gear was being burnished and the brasses polished — we would make an impression come what may. Sleep didn't seem all that important. My Senior Assistant Hilary and her willing helpers soon got caught up in the infectious enthusiasm. What an impressive show of defiance. It was hard work but the farm motto 'Nothing by halves' inspired the operation. Agincourt was to be re-enacted outside the precincts of Helmsley Castle.

As the glow of the charcoal faded and the last of the food consumed, our sights were on the morning and the job we had to do. It would soon be 6am.

It was a typical grey start to the day and we drove through a patch or two of rain. Well, did it matter, it was a grey day for us anyway — well was it? We were going to change all that! Our plans and timing

175

were on schedule. Princess and Nobby were all prepared and groomed and travelled comfortably in the trailer.

We arrived at Helmsley early and eagerly observed an almost empty car park — we could choose our best vantage point and it didn't take long. The trailer was backed into place — front facing the main road. After all this was a protest demonstration.

We carefully arranged the placards around our vehicle and trailer 'Save the Shire Farm' and, in the case of our horses 'It is our future that is at stake as well'.

Our friends started to get a petition going just as soon as people were about. It was amazing how many people had heard of us and indeed how many had actually visited the farm.

We didn't start to harness the horses — that was to come later. In the meantime they were stood side by side in the extra large trailer contentedly munching at their hay nets.

Time was steadily passing and everybody was in high spirits. The atmosphere was of great expectation and the ever increasing interest in our demonstration very rewarding. We felt the world was on our side.

At last the big moment came. Time to get the horses out and start to gear them up. We have a particularly interesting set of plough gears, the backbands were made in Scotland something over 100 years ago. These together with a gleaming pair of black highly polished collars with nickel hames created a feast for the eyes.

We carefully put it on the horses — collars first, then blinders (blinkers) and then backbands.

I should add that collars in this part of the country are called barfen's. A set of gleaming polished steel plough chains came next, followed by the coupling together of the horses.

A crowd had gathered as you can just imagine and one older man who had watched the proceedings with the eye of an expert, said 'An when you've got 'em yoked, you want to hang b . . . .y plough on and go 'an plough 'em up!'

At that moment a smiling friendly face appeared. It was the Councillor who had missed the site visit but had come to see me at the farm later. 'I have just bought the sugar lumps I promised'. It was a promise of unequivocal and long lasting support. Something I was to realise the value of later. It was not my original intention actually to drive the horses with the plough lines. For one thing they were not used to main roads and the volume of traffic and for

There was no one more proud than me that day.

another I did not wish to cause a traffic hazard. However, events like the support of the horse era gentleman and spurred on by my own confidence and determination, I decided I would if necessary, drive them right up to the door of the planning office.

I turned their heads towards our target 'Get up Nobby, c'mon Princess! 'I gave a click of my tongue and drove them on to the highway. We were on our way. There was no one more proud than me that day. The horses looked magnificent — just imagine the picture. Two majestic horses almost a perfect match. Feather washed out white and flowing like driven snow. The black highly polished leather a backdrop to the gleaming brasses and polished hames. What a memorable experience.

Hil and Sarah walked outside their heads for safety but the horses never faltered. You would have thought they worked in the middle of a busy main road all their lives.

People were stopping in their cars to offer encouragement. Shopkeepers were leaving their shops to come over and offer their support — even cash, would you believe? That day for a brief period, Helmsley came to a halt.

As we approached The Old Vicarage which was the N.Y.M.N.P. Headquarters we were besieged by what was later described as 'World Press'.

Television Crews, Camera-men, Journalists, Supporters — everybody. What a reception! I was told by one reporter that he had been to the offices to tell one particular planning officer what was going on outside and his colour had literally drained away.

Following this meeting lots of letters of support were coming from all over the country. Our press coverage had now reached the Nationals. A Daily Mail three quarter page article was headed, 'Farmer calls on Horse Power in fight for his Livelihood.' It was followed by a title heading 'How Princess and Nobby won the day in the Shires'. This was Thursday August 10th 1989. The reporter described the action — 'Two mighty shire horses clip-clopped into action yesterday to help their owner with a reprieve for his business!' It referred of course to our taking the horses to the planning meeting.

What a marvellous boost to our moral and our defences! It was

How Princess and Nobby won the day in the Shires.

178

later picked up and used by Horse and Hound as another victory for Horse Power.

The public loved it and the support flooded in. This was reinforced by more coverage on local television of the day at Helmsley.

The actual meeting, although described as a reprieve, to me seemed little more than a stay of execution. It had become increasingly obvious, that the underlying problem was our old adversary, the old Parish road which ran across our neighbours' field. However my trump card was still to play.

The Planning Officer had spelt it out. 'The access road to the farm itself was unsuitable in its present form and there was no land available to improve it.'

In other words they were not prepared to take steps under their statutory powers to provide for, either passing places or the widening of this country road WY 407G. One Councillor at the site meeting had voiced an opinion that they should and could. Was there even a solution to the problem? It is rather ironic because at the time it could easily have been overcome by a voluntary offer of allowing a couple of modest passing places on the field by the owners of the land.

The mood of the meeting itself was one of guarded optimism. Our friends in court were the councillors who vehemently supported what they described as an ideal low key development and just what the park needed.

The planners, visibly shaken by the amazing public support and events outside were anxious to make public that they thought a solution could be found.

I sat poker faced, my cards were still close to my chest.

The Chairman of the Committee eventually had recommended that the matter be adjourned for six months and that further talks should be arranged to try and find a solution. Well at least a breathing space, and I owe a debt of gratitude to several Councillors who fought hard for my survival. I should say, one in particular who gave an impressive interview on my behalf for a local television channel.

I felt very strongly that I was being deprived of my legal and established right of access. To this end, I even obtained a copy of the Enclosures Award. It was addressed to the several proprietors (Freeholders) of lands or other Hereditaments within the Township or Lordship of Staintondale. It was dated 3rd October 1829.

179

Downdale Road was set out and awarded a breadth of forty feet and it extended through allotments (land) to an ancient road leading down the Dale on the East of John Mainforth's old enclosure. The WY 407G! I have done my homework but the law is a ponderous thing and we are not going to live forever! Right now, I needed a road and within my grasp I thought I had the answer. Just a few years earlier I had purchased some land adjoining our property which was bordered by another section of this old County Highway. It would be possible, although expensive, to swallow my pride for the time being and look seriously at creating a brand new access road to the farm, something like 300 yards of soil excavation and new stone foundations. This was of course subject to approval by the planners, and satisfactory public and vehicle access rights being established. I was about to play my hand.

Time was slipping by now, and the season had ended as usual at the end of September. We only had six months, so I decided that I would take the initiative and start applying pressure to get the proposed talks under way. Needless to say (would you believe) and I am a prolific letter writer, it still took until November, but at last a meeting on site was arranged. There had been some adjustments to staff structuring at the National Parks Office. I had been informed of this, and I was looking to establish a good relationship from the onset.

The new planning officer duly arrived at the farm, this time it was a woman. I was not to be particularly disappointed, but I must admit an early remark about an inappropriate site, did put me on guard.

My attitude has never faltered. This is my life, it is my world and this development belongs here. The horses were practically all born here, and it is where they belong.

It is not some kind of amusement arcade that can be moved around and pitched somewhere for its best volume of customers — and cash. If making money were my only purpose in life, then as a businessman I could have thought of a million better sites.

Quality of life was the reason for my buying this farm in the first place and quality of life is my reason for fighting to hang on to it. And which is more, it is this quality that endears the public to it and what makes it so unique. They show respect and appreciation and we respond to their support.

CHAPTER THIRTY TWO
Onerous conditions lead to a blockade

Putting my prejudices behind me I had put forward my proposal for a new road. We had walked the fields overlooking the farm and the plan that I had suggested received a favourable response. The Planning Officer took the view that a new road, almost parallel to the established access was acceptable and would have less impact on the landscape. I agreed.

We discussed other aspects of the planning application and, for the very first time in over ten years somebody actually sat down with me and produced a set of forms. More than that, actually explained planning procedure and paved the way for open discussion on which areas were involved. I was impressed. Passing places were mentioned on Downdale Road but certainly with no particular emphasis. It was thought, (convenient phrase), that Highways wouldn't be asking too much! The main access point would be subject to the Surveyor's report, and safety would be a consideration. I thought that sounded reasonable.

The retrospective application would be submitted in January and subject to approval, the Surveyor's report and conditions would follow in due course.

I did wonder why the latter couldn't have been submitted to me for approval before the meeting. After all I was footing the bill! At the meeting there was an air of relief — was this much publicised and possibly embarrassing dispute about to end?

The Planner presented the case well. She referred to 471 letters of support — even to the extent of quoting very favourable comments from them and some criticism of planners! She also said that only one letter of objection had been received and it was from a neighbour of Mr Jenkins. She read it to the meeting. The Area Surveyor had not yet made a recommendation, but she thought he would be stipulating certain improvements to Downdale Road and the access point to our property off the road number WY407G. All of which we were to pay for. I am still at a loss to understand why this could not have been dealt with within the six month period recommended by the Chairman at the August meeting. The Planners then tried to impose a condition that approval be only granted to me personally and was not to be transferred. One Councillor stood up and said that was grossly unfair and said that at least my sons be named as successors. Another said that the sort of press publicity this case was attracting was making them a laughing stock.

In the event my business was seriously devalued by a stipulation that it could only stay in family ownership. I was there, and I listened to the report with calculated apprehension. Well it sounded fine but some of the conditions about to be imposed were vague on account of them being conspicuous by their absence — what would they amount to and how much would they cost? We had to wait and see. We were now into 1990 and another season was looming large.

I was starting this season with a new assistant and I was looking forward to something less traumatic. How wrong can you be?

Before we opened to the public the full conditions attached to the planning application arrived. We had won, to quote my adviser a 'Pyrrhic Victory'.

'Onerous' — one word fitted the situation. Was this the straw that broke the camel's back? I read and re-read. The cost was escalating before my eyes.

At almost sixty years of age I must admit I was calculating how long it would take to earn this sort of money, and more than that, was it really worth the effort?

'Oh well Kipling old lad' (with apologies) I quote, 'If you can make a heap of all your winnings and risk it on one turn of pitch and toss!' I intended to stay in business come what may, so a few more weeks of argument and objections were acceptable. I was not giving in now.

I wrote a strong letter of protest and set out my objections in no uncertain manner. My planning adviser observed 'It seems that they have decided that if they can't get you one way, they will get you another!'

Several weeks of discussion took place and of course by now, the cat was out of the bag. A new road was in the offing and it did not suit everybody. In fact people who had pledged support suddenly turned against us. People in our immediate vicinity as well. Why this sudden change of attitude? It began to smack of conspiracy, I found it disturbing. To me it seemed ominous. Somebody had loved to see us fight but hated to see us win.

Stopping the use by visitors of the County road across our neighbours field, would have effectively put us out of business.

Now we looked like surviving with our alternative access. There had already been one solicitor's letter saying that the proposal was ill advised and inappropriate and warning of the consequences. It had been rejected emphatically by all parties including the County Secretary as being irrelevant.

This was not to be the end of this matter and a closing of ranks became apparent. I have referred earlier to the purchase of this land which gave us another access to County road No. WY 407G. Although at the time of purchase and immediately afterwards thoughts of a new access road had been envisaged, but of course the cost was prohibitive. Having said that we had mown a strip right across it which had become known as 'Tony's landing strip' one summer.

The story continues and it is with unmitigated sadness that I have to record this next episode of developments closely associated with the planning dispute.

Throughout the entire period I had tried to conduct myself in a dignified manner. Our protests although effective had been by demonstration and not belligerent confrontation.

Many times I have been provoked and even lied about over certain issues, but to lose your temper is to lose the argument. Having lived here for over twenty years I had taken this village and most of the community to my heart.

It was now obvious that some small element was intent on poisoning this situation and it hurt.

On Wednesday 9th May 1990 the sound of heavy metallic clanking and banging could be heard. It was a summer's evening and still quite bright. I went round to the front of the house to see where this intrusion of noise was coming from. I did not have to look far. The County road which I have referred to previously, and which is known locally as 'The Stripe' was being posted on both sides. Alternate short and long heavy stakes were being driven into the ground with a mechanical post knocker. The width of the track was being restricted to a bare minimum and passing or re-passing of vehicles rendered impossible.

I was shell shocked. This was an attack from a very different angle and totally unexpected. The scene was one of being imprisoned in your own home, as this stockade like edifice took shape.

This lovely old ancient meadow was witnessing an act of aesthetic vandalism, and I was witnessing desperation of a kind I had not previously encountered. Why oh why, oh why? That night we found sleep difficult and so it was an early next morning, that found me seeking urgent legal advice.

Relief! To a point the law was very much on our side. It seemed that after living here for over twenty years we had an easement which gave us private rights to use any width of access we may find necessary along that County road.

If this could be proved to have been established for over forty years, then there was basically no action that could threaten it. I knew from my own records and from a History, Topography, and Directory of North Yorkshire dated May 1st 1890 that we could claim 100 YEARS! The advice I received was compelling — get the posts out and try not to cause any damage or disruption or a disturbance of the peace. If there looks like being any sort of nasty confrontation then you would be wise to call upon the services of a local Police constable.

The last bit sounded ominous — I hoped at least we could behave like civilised people. How to get them out was the immediate problem. It would not be easy.

I had an important site meeting that day. It was to include myself of course, the Planning Officer, the Area Surveyor, the County Secretary and my Architect. Big guns indeed. We walked the gauntlet between the posts, it was a bit like a scene from Custor's last stand.

It was also an embarrassing and daunting experience and one I shall never forget.

What went through my mind, was the timing of this unprecedented action. Was it sheer coincidence that this defiant display had occurred on this day, or? the plot thickens, had there been a leak? When nightmares occur in the day-time and we have had our share of those, logical thoughts give way to doubts and suspicions. I joked about a chainsaw but inside my stomach felt sick.

We were walking round the circuit as it were, to explore the possibility of a one way system. It had been suggested by the Area Surveyor. I was trying to make the point that I didn't care what they decided, but must I continue to pay for the maintenance of this old country road?

At the point of the proposed new access a detailed discussion took place.

One of the Surveyor's assistants had previously suggested the wall which partly surrounds an old stackyard, should be removed to widen the existing road towards this proposed new access. I had pointed out that it didn't belong to me and rather than getting involved in compulsory purchases (which he had suggested) could we reach a compromise?

It was this compromise which was now under discussion.

An agreement was reached. The new access road would be located 20 metres North of the South West corner of our property which coincided roughly with the existing access. In addition the Public Highway WY 407G had to be widened to 5 metres at my expense and subsequently surfaced. The road widening was to be carried out within the existing public highway, which included the verge.

The one way system was left as an option but it was later dropped. One way systems are fine whilst everybody is travelling in one direction. We did not have this much control on the old existing County Highway! Well so far so good, I was quite happy with this development and throughout, all discussions and suggestions had been amicable and friendly. This part of the conditions, although costly, I decided would improve our image. People paying admission expect a tidy approach road and first impressions count. I had great plans for it all ready. Wide grass verges, a line of trees and daffodil bulbs!

As time has gone by, we have created a very impressive driveway approach which has won us praise and admiration from many sources.

Well that was that. They were on their way, and I was left with the posts. They were a couple of foot at least, into the ground and we couldn't even move them fractionally. I telephoned all round locally for a J.C.B. but without success. What now? Suddenly I had an idea. Tractor hydraulics — the three point linkage. They could lift a ton or two.

With my young female assistant Jeanette, I drove across to the

Success and a spontaneous hooray!

first post. It was basically an old timber lifting technique using a short twisted chain.

I backed the tractor close up to the post with the transporter platform frame just touching. The chain was dropped over the post to the bottom and wound round the frame. Up we go. Well at first we didn't. Such was the effort needed to pull these posts from the hard ground, the tyres flattened at the base. We held our breath — a burst tyre or? And then slowly, the post started to emerge. Success, and a spontaneous hooray! We never counted the posts but you will see from the illustrations taken from actual photographs — there were a lot.

It took hours, but as time went by my capable assistant Jeanette got very adept with the chain and we made better progress. Our legal advisers had emphasised no damage so we were very careful. We then had to carry them all to the gate and neatly stack them.

As the last one had been pulled out, we had thrown it high into the air together with our hats! It was a defiant gesture and it hadn't gone unnoticed. Jungle drums were sounding and bush telegraph was winging its way.

I am not going to make capital out of the resulting response, but suffice to say there was one. It is only with regret, that I feel justified in recording my account of these events.

It was not the end of an attempt to block our use of this road, and shortly afterwards because this ploy had failed, the field was deep ploughed and laid over, away from the track. The result was a deep void along both sides. Possibly as effective as the posts, but the damage to the environment was incalculable. This was possibly the oldest meadow in Staintondale. There were no previous records of it ever having been ploughed, and we have no reason to believe it ever had.

The Easements created by the Mainforths and the Mead families for hundreds of years had been brought to an end.

Oh yes legal action was possible but that didn't undo the damage. And in any case it seemed so very futile. My new road was going to make a break with history. Robert Mead had purchased East Side Farm from the Mainforths of Rigg Hall in 1770. The stripe, was a stripe across a meadow then!

CHAPTER THIRTY THREE
Summer of discontent

The background to this enterprise as put forward by the planners was, to say the least, extraordinary. I quote item 2.1 'The use of this property as a Shire Horse visitor centre began in the 1970's on an occasional basis without the benefit of planning permission, but by 1982 the level of use was such that the owner was informed that planning permission was required and invited to submit an application.'

Not just extraordinary but quite remarkable. We did not open to the public in any shape or form, limited or otherwise until 1985!

One newspaper reporter told me 'You have already got their backs up (The Committee) with your outspoken comments.'

I must admit my attitude had been less than conciliatory. At that time I had been unable to distinguish friend from foe, and Planners and Planning Committees were to me one and the same thing.

Later I was to discover how wrong I was and how important it was to have the support of some Councillors.

We have now got to the stage when a section 278 agreement arrived through the post. It related to passing places.

Although as I have mentioned already I was aware some kind of passing places were required. I was not prepared for the specification that was to be demanded.

They were of standard Ministry of Transport Highway specification and I was required to submit the necessary plans drawn up by an architect. The responsibilities of carrying out such works was enormous. So far as a planning Committee goes and I do not intend these remarks as derogatory, they are something that just happens. They look harmless enough.

Alongside every highway there are what are known as main services. Mostly they run under the ground and include water, electricity, telephone and in some areas, gas.

It is up to the developer to establish the exact route and plan accordingly. It is time consuming and costly. More than that it can sometimes make excavation in certain areas almost impossible. With my previous building experience I was very well aware what I might be taking on. What we are really talking about, are road improvements usually carried out by civil engineering contractors or local authorities. They wanted me to arrange to carry out these works, take final responsibility and pay. The road in question is known as Downdale Road and it carries mainly local traffic and agricultural vehicles. Well, that was the case twenty four years ago.

From my excellent memory I can categorically state that at that time there were two Ford Anglias, one Transit van, one other car and my own, using Downdale Road. Plus of course a few small tractors in the shape of a Massey Ferguson 35, a grey Ferguson and an old Fordson Major. Add to this an occasional small cattle truck and you have the lot.

How very different in 1990. Well over a dozen privately owned vehicles, large and small delivery vehicles, endless tractor traffic, and not the small variety any more. Plus visitors and tourists of course and not all destined for a visit here.

One farm vehicle had been described by a visitor as of 'Frightening proportions' when met head on once, on this narrow lane.

I am not going to say that such vehicles have no place in rural situations such as this. They are part of the mechanised revolution that has swept agriculture into the 90's. What I am going to say is that it is this same revolution which has changed the nature of the requirement of rural roads.

Not only had the horse and cart gone, but the roads originally developed for them should be gone too.

The economy of the dale is now becoming increasingly dependent on traffic. Local traffic, holiday traffic and business traffic. Downdale Road was long overdue for improvement and yet it had taken my dispute to highlight the fact.

Well I thought, my argument was sound. The cost of these passing places, bearing in mind the unknown and unseen hazards was going to be high. Could be very high.

I weighed it up very carefully and decided a 50% contribution was fair. We open only five months a year and the road improvements would be an all year round benefit for the local community.

I would offer to pay for two of the proposed passing places and put myself at the mercy of the Committee -again. Well after all they had been reasonable and supportive so far. I thought I was getting to know the system.

I am now going to quote from a letter sent to Northern Echo in October 1989, in response to a report published by that Newspaper. It was sent to me by a helpful staunch supporter and sympathiser.

He had written. 'The report gives one the impression that both Hitler and Dick Turpin have come back from the dead and taken up residence at the Old Vicarage, Helmsley. One to say 'stand and deliver or else', the other to force the Shire man out of business. He went on to quote from The Local Government and Encyclopedia on Highway Law, C. Cook, Part IV 1980 Highway Acts:-

'It is the duty of road authorities to keep their public highways in a state fit to accommodate the ordinary traffic which passes or may be expected to pass along them. As the ordinary traffic expands or changes in character, so must the nature of the maintenance and repair alter, to suit the change.'

Well they probably thought, because this was described as a Shire Horse farm, that horse and carts were very much the order of the day. I am referring now of course to the planners and my dispute.

Anyway I was going to pursue my argument, and with

Horse and carts were very much the order of the day.

190

the responsibilities of Highways very much in my mind I wrote to the Area Surveyor. There was no relaxing of attitude, but a site meeting was arranged with one of his assistants. We were to survey the length of Downdale Road and look at the proposed locations.

I was not too happy about two of them. At this point I was quite prepared to discuss the passing places, but my strategy was then to question the degree (if any) of my responsibility to improve this road. The man in question was again very amicable and he agreed, that the proposals, in their present form would be difficult. He not only agreed to changes but made some useful suggestions. Now it was up to me. I had to get an architect to draw plans of the sections of road involved with details of each passing place. I had then to submit them for approval before work could commence.

I had still not signed the agreement and my attitude was getting less favourable.

Costs and more costs. Oh and I almost forgot, we had to pay for, and erect passing place signs.

Again I wrote the Surveyor. 'There are seven farms, several private houses, holiday cottages, a camping and caravan site and an engineering workshop all generating traffic. It is grossly unfair and unreasonable to expect me to pay for the whole of these road improvements.' At 10,000 visitors a year, in one week that was approximately 150 cars or only 6 cars an hour. Less sometimes than local traffic volume. He was unmoved. 'I shall be obliged to refer you back to the Planning Officer' was his only comment.

I tried endless times — even quoting a letter from a previous visit by a Planning Officer less than three years earlier when he had stated he had consulted Highways and they (at that time) had no objections to this development providing facilities were provided to turn vehicles, off the road. Again he was not impressed, 'Those were only off the cuff comments.'

I decided what we needed was a questionnaire in the form of a visitor's own survey of the access, and any problems they had encountered. We carried it out on 1,000 visitors over a peak period commencing Spring Bank Holiday 1990. (See Appendix II)

The results were enlightening. We asked three questions as follows:

1. Did you meet any other vehicle travelling in the opposite direction on your journey down the lane? (Downdale Road)
2. Did you have any problem or passing difficulty with any other vehicle on Downdale Road.

3.   In view of the narrow and winding access road do you think the enterprise worthwhile and should it be encouraged?

A space was left headed 'Comments.'

Visitors were invited to answer the questions honestly and of their own free will.

The results were as follows.

817 recorded no problems and out of these

465 made mostly very favourable comments.

26 recorded no problems but suggested minor improvements to the road, by the Local Authority. 42 had managed to misinterpret the questions and only

10 had any problem at all and again most only minor.

The rest were either taken away or picked up by children for recreational use!

The reason I am putting these facts together is to demonstrate the effort and hard work that went into our campaign.

It was not just about showmanship or bellicosity, it was about calculated research and a sound defence. Obviously the Shire Horse incident at Helmsley had highlighted what I considered to be heavy handed dictatorial action.

I have to say that the results of our survey are verifiable and now rest with Yorkshire and Humberside Tourist Board at York. They have subsequently been used for student research.

As commercial members of the board it is worth recording the excellent support we received from the Development Manager at that time. Also from the Director of Tourism and Amenities for Scarborough Borough Council.

The affair rumbled on and in an effort to enlighten the local population and other interested parties, Staintondale Parish Council called a public meeting at the Village Hall at 7.30 June 20th, 1990.

A Planning Officer and members of North Yorkshire County Council were present.

It could be described as a non event, with few pertinent questions and a lot of outright curiosity. One question stuck in my mind, or my throat! 'When were the passing places going to be provided?' Spoken quite loftily.

'Just as soon as Mr. Jenkins signs the agreement' came the reply.

Nobody thought to mention that the agreement had only just been sent to me. An agreement ensuing from the retrospective planning application in January!

Appendix II

Specimen comments on Traffic Survey form:

An entertaining and informative afternoon. Well worth encouraging especially one with so little impact on the environment.

●●●

We have visited Staintondale Shire Horse Farm for the last four years (including 1990) sometimes twice in one holiday. From memory we have never encountered any other traffic on the road to and from the farm. Only those who are really interested visit the farm, many people making return visits. It should be retained in its present form.

●●●

'Rural' nature of access road is part of the charm and realism of the place. Definitely worthwhile — awful shame if people (especially young people and children) didn't have the opportunity to see these traditional things. This is my second visit — and equally as enjoyable as my first. Access has been no problem. We are staying on a farm which uses the same access and there have been no problems in the entire week. Numbers visiting in the peak of the holiday season appear to be relatively small and therefore traffic problems are unlikely to be created. This is especially so, as the centre operates on a 'timetable' basis and therefore traffic is likely to be travelling in the same direction at any given time. As an ex Police Officer I found no difficulty, no traffic hazard and no congestion whilst approaching this worthwhile enterprise.

●●●

We think everything here is just right. Natural and beautiful. We found no difficulty at all getting down here. Extremely enjoyable.

●●●

Well worth the journey — you expect winding roads in the countryside and drive accordingly. Half of its charm is the delightful

CHAPTER THIRTY FOUR
The nutcrackers

This was the all important meeting. The planners were going to recommend that the retrospective application be refused and that the County Secretary be authorised to commence enforcement proceedings against us. In other words, after all the effort and negotiations they were still prepared to close me down.

It was October 10th 1990 at the Parks headquarters, Helmsley. By now I was an old hand at facing such threats and I had already acquired an agenda from County Hall. The notes about the background were still unchanged. They were misleading and inaccurate. This time I decided to take action.

Another paragraph headed 'Conclusion' also caught my eye. It stated that I found the Committee's requirements 'unreasonable and unacceptable.' This was nonsense and taken totally out of context. On the contrary I had found quite a few Councillors sympathetic and some very supportive and helpful.

What these remarks had been aimed at was the road improvements in the shape of passing places on Downdale Road.

I accepted that there was a degree of responsibility but how much was a degree?

You will have gathered from my last paragraph that I was less than happy about the whole affair. I was also worried about the cost. Again I wrote to all Councillors on the development control sub-committee prior to the meeting. (See Appendix I)

My objections to certain conditions were carefully set out, and I explained my reasons for them. I also set out a projected cost, and also the job losses that would result if I was closed down. My opinion at the meeting was that the 'Conclusion' 2.4 paragraph had got to them first! Well a possibility. I sat and listened to the planners presentation with critical interest.

It was mainly about the discussions, but I did notice a slight shift of emphasis on the passing places. Paragraph 2.5 (extract) 'was aware, that such passing places were likely to be required.' Generally though it was a fair assessment, and my co-operation and help towards trying to reach agreements on other issues was mentioned. But, now the big but! 'Mr. Jenkins will only sign an agreement he thinks fair and reasonable. He considers that the road carries an ever increasing amount of local traffic with increasingly large agricultural vehicles and considers he should only therefore have to pay for two out of the four passing places.'

'Hear, hear!' I felt like shouting, but of course you are not allowed to speak.

I waited anxiously for a response from the floor. What about my impassioned plea. Did nobody share my viewpoint? Had anybody even read my letter. Would the enforcement action be pursued? One Councillor stood up. 'Mr. Chairman', he said 'Don't you think that we are taking a sledgehammer to crack a nut? Surely if Mr. Jenkins is prepared to pay for two passing places and his budget is stretched, can we not ask him to pay for the other two spaced over the next couple of years?'

In the meantime another Councillor had made a late entry, and had glanced at what I assumed was my letter. I am not going to quote what he said because I am sure it was meant as a light-hearted remark. But I got the impression it implied that this planning applicant was a Nut that should be cracked. He then went on 'The four thousand pounds that Mr. Jenkins is saying that he is committed to, is only a bond — a surety. He doesn't have to pay it at this moment in time.'

Well at least my letter had been read. In it I had listed the cost of these conditions and what I already had spent on a new road. With the fencing, tree planting and landscaping, plus the passing places, it ran into thousands of pounds. I didn't believe my small enterprise could stand it. At 10,000 visitors a season it was nothing. Less than the weekly intake at some major attractions.

There was a slight lull in proceedings. I think the next question was on several Councillor's lips and waiting to be asked.

'Could we have the last amount explained' said someone. 'And how a figure of four thousand pounds was arrived at?'

Everybody was looking towards the Planning Officer. The Planning Officer was looking towards the County Secretary. 'Could you explain to the meeting?'

There was at this point, just a hint of conferring between official heads, seemingly in agreement. 'Well', said the Secretary 'It appears that this is the estimated cost of four passing places, and the amount referred to, is the amount Mr. Jenkins would have to pay if for one reason or another he couldn't or didn't carry out the work. In other words 'in default' of the agreement. The County Council would then do them and Mr. Jenkins would pay the bond to cover the cost!

I couldn't believe my ears. Knowing glances were exchanged between various people. My estimate in my letter to the Councillors had been more than double that. In fact if any problems had been encountered with the main services I had referred to, or unstable embankments, just one of them could have cost the amount they were talking about.

Leaning over to my wife, I whispered, 'At that price let them carry out the work. Come on let's go home and put a cheque in the post today.'

In the meantime the meeting had decided to accept the proposal put forward by the first motion. We were followed outside by eager reporters and two Councillors.

I reaffirmed my next move 'It's a cheque in the post today, the dispute is over.'

One of the Councillors spoke 'And don't delay — do it. We don't want you bringing anything back here!' The other one laughed. There was relief and hugs all round. It had been an eighteen month struggle and at times an ordeal.

The reporters closed in looking for the report in tomorrow's newspapers.

The jubilation was evident, the relief rather more personal.

Next day it was 'Victory for Shire Horse Farm' and 'A Jubilant Tony Jenkins etc etc.'

It brought telephone calls, letters and cards from many people.

I owe a debt of gratitude to a lot of special people not least my planning adviser, courtesy of R.D.C. There are many, many more, it would not be courteous to mention just some of the names or of various associations but thanks to you all.

It seemed our personal traumas were at an end. In November 1990 we received our green coloured planning approval certificate, and for a few days the relief was indescribable.

There was more trouble waiting in the wings. Just a few more

Victory for Shire Horse Farm.

days after celebrating our success, two ominous looking envelopes arrived in our post box.

Two County Court summons — one for each of us. Do you remember the irrelevant solicitor's letter earlier in the book?

This was not the end of our problems, it was only the end of the beginning.

It is now nearing the end of 1993 and litigation still continues.

Well Kipling, I am still filling the unforgiving minute (again with apologies) and hopefully my sixty seconds of distance run, will give me some reward.

I consider that I shall have earned it!. If I allowed this book to end on anything other than a happy note, I should have failed in my belief in old fashioned values.

In spite of our personal distress at what we consider to be, totally unjustified legal action, a silver lining emerged from the darker clouds. In July 1993 for our contribution towards (would you believe?) successfully integrating Tourism with the Environment, we won a Yorkshire and Humberside Tourist Board 'White Rose Award.'

More than that, we were also nominated by an independent panel for 'England for Excellence.' The ultimate accolade we still strive for.

Appendix I

This is a copy of the letter which I sent to every member of the committee, together with extracts from the survey of a thousand visitors to the Farm.

October 1990

Dear County Councillor,

In the event of my small rural enterprise coming before the North York Moors Planning Committee again, I offer the following observations.

Without this diversification, my small 50 acre farm is totally unviable. I have worked long and hard for fifteen years to create what many believe to be the best small rural attraction in the NYMNP. Our recent survey of over 1000 visitors here confirms this (samples enclosed). The survey also shows quite clearly that neither access problems or passing difficulties were encountered. I am asking for nothing more than fair play. Not favours, not financial support, just fair play. There are seven farms served by Downdale Road, an agricultural and marine engineering shop, a caravan site, plus other domestic and holiday cottages.

Highways are asking for four passing places constructed to their specifications, all at my expense. I did not learn of this until after the meeting in January, when these conditions were imposed. In fact, the detailed agreement and plan did not arrive until June. It added up to a staggering commitment approaching £20,000, including a bond amount of £4,600!

I have offered to bear the cost of two passing places as a gesture of goodwill in line with the degree of my responsibility, and I have written to Mr A Burns explaining my position. In addition to this of course, there is my offer of the provision of a new farm road, which incidentally I have now implemented at a cost of around £4000. We are only a small seasonal enterprise. I have no wish to go bankrupt along with a lot of other small businesses now struggling. More than that, seven seasonal jobs go with me.

I sincerely hope County Councillors will share my anxiety and not withdraw support.

Yours sincerely, Tony Jenkins

CHAPTER THIRTY FIVE
Had we shot a robin

In the closing lines of the previous chapter I referred to the end of the beginning. The beginning of the end was to be as elusive as the peace of mind that we hoped would accompany our eventual victory.

The irrelevant letter of January 1990 followed by the summons in November of that year was the prelude to over three years of distress and trauma. A law suit brought about for no apparent reason but one that was to cost us dearly.

The plaintiff's case was supported by a legal aid certificate. It was also made much worse by the fact that they were also close neighbours and had been personal friends for over twenty years.

Other elements were now to add to our problems. In December a terrible storm blew up which woke us in the early hours. The wind was screaming and every timber beam and rafter shook and shuddered. Outside heavy bangs and thumps interspersed with the sounds of wind blown objects being dispatched with a force that was frightening filled the air. I peered out of the windows in to a black night. It sounded as if the whole farm was being ripped apart. What hand of darkness was this? The cold grey dawn slowly made its presence felt. Sleep had been impossible so I had sat there just waiting while my imagination ran riot.

I tried to reassure myself that it was probably not as bad as it sounded but I really did fear the worst. The wind was still screaming and inside this old house with its two foot thick walls it seemed a haven. I felt very grateful for that. Outside it was very different. Wild was an understatement. I slowly got dressed and mentally urged the daylight on. Were the horses safe, had they been hit by some of the flying debris? Had we any pantiles left on and what other devastating damage had occurred and how much more was to come? We could only wait and see. With plenty of weather protection zipped and buttoned I took the handlamp and ventured forth. In the shelter of the farm courtyard it didn't seem too bad because the wind was pretty well a straight Northerly.

Once away from this shelter and as daylight slowly filtered through the dark I was suddenly caught up in what seemed like a whirlwind. Metal sheets were flapping on building roofs and the sound of tearing timber and crashing structures filled the air. It sounded like something from a hurricane scene in a film.

I suddenly thought about the rabbits of all things, they were all housed in the pets corner which was sited in the large open fronted barn which also accommodates all our carts and waggons.

Hanging on to my hat and struggling to keep my feet I set off down the track. I hadn't gone far before some of the devastated scene began to unfold. Pieces of corrugated Perspex sheet were blowing everywhere and all around me as darkness gave way to dawn, I could see broken pantiles, torn off guttering and debris, everywhere. What a mess.

The wind was relentless as I passed the barn where we keep the Thresher. All the roof lights had been ripped out and litter was scattered everywhere. Worse was to come. I turned into the paddock and realised just how bad things were. The wind was being tunnelled through the natural cutting linking us to Rigg Hall and coming straight in off the North Sea. It had struck a corner of what we were still calling the new building and smashed into it with all the force of a typhoon.

The scene which now met my eyes was one of total devastation. There was no respite either. Eighteen foot lengths of corrugated steel sheets were being torn off the roof and sent flying through the air like a pack of playing cards. I watched in horror — we had ten horses living out in the surrounding fields and these sheets could have sliced into a horse with the ease of a butcher's cleaver.

They were taking off and landing way out of sight into the gloomy daybreak. Gloomy was the situation. What did I say about my sinking heart?

I remembered the purpose of my mission — The Rabbits.

Now I really did have a problem, the risk to life and limbs was now graphically apparent. The section of roof immediately over the rabbits had gone, and more was under threat. I made my way round to this area keeping in the shelter of the hay barn. This was the epicentre of this destructive storm. Fortunately the hay barn was full of hay so it was well ballasted and secure. Once round this I was staring into the full force of the gale.

Across the back of the pets corner two horizontal 7" x 2" baulks of timber with vertical steel cladding were bending like an archer's bow. Any minute it looked like something was about to give. In front of this corner section, still on their respective benches stood a variety of rabbit hutches with their residents inside. The only thing to do was to wait for a lull in the wind, rush in and grab a hutch and run like the clappers well something like that.

I stood poised — here we go — number one! It was like some kind of crazy relay race but this was not a game. Seven times I made this mercy dash and seven times later the rabbits were safely housed within the shelter of the next door hay barn. By now of course there was plenty of light and I could see the full extent and radius of the damage.

The roofing sheets were distributed over five fields some struck vertically in the ground, I shuddered. Better go and check the horses. With great difficulty I started along the track. One eye out for flying object and one for a sighting of the horses. I now knew what our friends in America suffered at the hands of a Tornado and this was just a cyclonic wind. Just!

The wind was hostile and frenzied and I was well aware of my predicament. At the time although I was not to know, it had taken the slate roof off Rigg Hall just one hundred and fifty yards to the North of us. My son, daughter in law and children were virtually prisoners. Trapped inside by flying roof tiles!

I found my way to a point where the underground culvert across the gravelled car park area runs into the ditch. A corrugated roofing sheet was buried deep into the hedgebank it had severed every stem and basal shoot at ground level and left a gaping hole.

The wind behind me now, I carried on down the track. Roofing nails and washers were strewn everywhere and shattered pieces of perspex roof light glistened in the grass verges. What a cleanup operation was in store. By now I could see clearly across the fields and what a sight met my eyes. Roofing sheets smashed, purlins and timber lay everywhere. It had blown far beyond our boundary and into the field where our original access crossed.

My assistant didn't arrive until 9am. What a shock she would get. I was down as far as Mascot's field now and the horses had seen me. Mascot came flying down his field, hooves kicking up great divots of mud. The wind stirs horses up and seems to make them nervous. Today was no exception and it was still with ecstatic relief that I watched them rearing and plunging with no visible signs of injury. Wonderful. I think they did their equivalent of a war dance just to let me know all was well. As I glanced along what had been a newly constructed stock wire fence, I could see a section that had been severed by a wind born flying missile in the form of a steel roofing sheet.

Slowly I returned to the farm. Although the horses were safe I must admit that I felt pretty miserable. This was the destruction of my pride and joy, our lovely new open fronted pole barn. So much admired and so useful on wet days to entertain our visitors. I consoled myself at least it was insured.

The salvage operation was both hard and arduous. These eighteen foot sheets were heavy and in their buckled state unwieldy. Shattered and splintered timber, endless amounts of nails and washers, debris of all sorts. It all had to be cleared.

I should add that this building was nearly a hundred foot long and thirty three-feet wide. There was a lot of roof! Armed with a petrol driven Stihl saw and a large trailer we set about it. Sheets had to be cut for transportation and whole sections of roof dismantled. It took us several days. There was an extensive insurance claim form to complete and some immediate roof repairs to be carried out. These applied to the small range of stone buildings on the yard. We were given the go ahead on these.

I was told to get estimates for the larger roof previously described, but that didn't present any real problems. Well, not until we submitted them that is.

You will all have heard of small print. To cut a long and, complicated story short it led to a visit by a firm of loss adjusters. It seems their job is to see that the insurance company pays out as little as possible and that you don't have as much of the insurance protection wrapped round you as you thought you had! 'Well Mr J. it seems, judging from the roof estimates that your building was under insured' the voice of you know who.

'That's ridiculous, I insured the building only two years ago for a sum agreed with the company'.

'Ah but inflation'.

'I don't know about inflation', I felt like exploding. I followed up:'If the company had made any suggestion at renewal time I would have listened. The house is index linked why not a similar scheme on farm buildings?'

'On a self build scheme using part reclaimed materials actual replacement value is sometimes difficult'. He said that he would see what he could do and make a written offer. I knew I was saying goodbye to watching roofing contractors put a new roof on. Another large D.I.Y. kit in the shape of Tony Jenkins and his able assistant loomed large. Never mind we did it, and it looked none the worse. We had a few hairy moments though. Once when we were up on this roof in some sort of force eight wind, the ladder blew down. We were stranded on the roof.

Before the roof had been reinstated as it were, another body blow struck. Severe weather and snow in February 1991 brought even more problems. What a sad and miserable sight it made. A building stripped of its roof hung in tatters and its once proud contents were now exposed to the pitiless elements.

My lovely restored vehicles looked lost and forlorn. I wanted to rush in, clean off the snow and wet and take them into the house. The way a child would gather up its toys. Kipling, my adopted mentor had a line to suit my predicament, 'If you can see the things you gave your life to broken'.

A bit melodramatic even for me I suppose, but it suited the situation. This period was probably the most traumatic of our lives. It had included a Christmas when we should have been celebrating our planning victory and instead we were beginning to feel like outcasts. The summons had prompted a telephone call to County Hall. After all the claim for trespass and damage had been motivated by the planning conditions imposed upon us. We were advised to see a Solicitor.

Don't ever get involved in legal litigation. It is a minefield. We were to discover the complexities and its pitfalls to our cost.

Only one local man inspired me to keep my head above water that, Christmas. Unfortunately he has now prematurely passed away. He was a former Rugby playing colleague who worked for the Duchy of Lancaster. I had gone down to get our Christmas tree. 'Roy' I said 'you have restored my faith in human nature'.

At the onset we were warned of the serious disadvantages of fighting a legal aided claim. We were never going to win.

Just about coincident with the Winter storms another shot across the bows was delivered. A second letter from the same source of solicitor, this time with what was later described at trial as a ransom demand. It was for a host of miscellaneous demands but not least for five thousand pounds and their costs. I saw it as frivolous and unjustified. It wasn't some kind of nightmare was it? We had bought the land now being used for the new access road in good faith from our neighbours and now it seemed they were either going to stop us using it or hold us to ransom. It posed another serious threat of closure and once more we had to fight.

CHAPTER THIRTY SIX
We raise the world's water table

Those of you who had read my first book will remember a chapter called 'Cool Clear Water' and a line that read 'Have you left a tap turned on outside?'

Nobody could have imagined that this same question would be asked again several years on. It was! At about 10pm on Tuesday, 13th August, 1991. Ann was just about to make a cup of tea. It had been a lovely sunny day and an extremely busy one at that. She turned on the tap — no water!

'Have you left a tap on outside?' I couldn't believe my ears. Shot a robin, I think we must have run over a black cat as well.

'Well I suppose it's possible', I said. I knew the girls had been filling water troughs.

Again I grabbed a handlamp and went out to do the rounds. There hadn't been any indication of the spring slowing down so I was a little bit optimistic. I should explain to other readers that this farm is served by a spring supply — we have no mains water.

I checked all outside taps and troughs and then climbed up into the loft. My optimism was misguided. There were no taps on but equally there was no water. The tanks were empty.

It was now the proverbial trudge up the field, a several hundred yard trek in the dark using the lamp. As I approached the site of the storage tanks I stopped to listen. It is possible under normal circumstances to hear the sound of water trickling in. All was silent. With untypical pessimism I screwed off the plastic manhole cover and shone the lamp inside the tank. It was empty.

Tomorrow was the peak day of our season and we could not open without water. No sleep tonight either and that was also a fact.

It is not until you have experienced a situation that you actually realise the implications. This applies particularly to water. Imagine a good old fashioned hot summer's day and twelve thirsty horses for starters. Add to that a hundred plus visitors all wanting a cup of tea — and worse, wanting to use the loo!

Well suffice to say we had to get some and as soon as possible. Just as soon as I got back in the house I grabbed the telephone. I knew a man who might have some ideas — his name was John Brand.

Luckily for me a rescue plan was put together. It involved two local firms who between them worked wonders. Our next big problem was stopping visitors making the journey down the lane and not deterring them from returning the following day. I put together a desperate message and made a big sign 'Closed Today for Emergency Repairs'. That same morning a 3,000 gallon tanker and tractor unit belonging to Ray Owen wound its way down our lane and made its way slowly and cautiously across our fields — well over twenty tons in total. We need not have worried, the ground was rock hard. A succession of dry summers and the lack of snow and heavy rain had stripped the land of moisture and the water table was at an all time low. Even the old stoned hedgebanks were collapsing as the soil turned to dust.

1991 generally hadn't been a bad year for us so far as visitors were concerned. I think the press and television publicity over the planning dispute had certainly boosted interest in our enterprise. In addition of course, the ending of the gulf war had brought more business from people who would otherwise have been abroad. The last thing we wanted was a crisis such as a water problem.

Our spring was still rising but slowly, so each day a trek up the field to top up the storage tanks from the tanker. At this moment in time the legal dispute was taking a back seat but was ominously still there. Other more pressing problems and thoughts filled my mind. What if the spring failure was permanent and what if the hole in the ozone layer was causing the problem — worse, suppose we didn't get much snow again this winter? We could not run a business or indeed much else without water and the nearest mains water was over a mile away. A mile as the crow flies but on the other side of what now appeared to be hostile territory. It might just as well have been a million miles. I shrugged it off, it didn't bear thinking about.

August ran into September quite quickly and soon the demand on our water supply started to subside. This was only due to the gradual decrease in visitor numbers. The weather had been excellent warm, sunny and very pleasant.

On Tuesday 3rd September we attended a ceremony at Rudding Park to receive our commendation in the Yorkshire and Humberside Tourist Board White Rose Awards. Proof that rather than being detrimental to the environment we had shown that it was possible successfully to integrate one with the other! This was something that I intended to pursue with relish.

Well at least some good news and justifiable celebration. We had a wonderful and enthusiastic staff and the award was well deserved. The season ended on a sunny day on September 26th. There had been no rain for two months.

In spite of all the problems, 1991 had been an eventful year and the Tourism and Environment Award had opened up new horizons. Plans had been laid for a whole farm conservation scheme which was both idealistic and ambitious. From my own point of view it was going to be the realisation of a dream. Reality in the meantime struck back. We received a letter from our Solicitor to say that a site meeting had been arranged with the other side for Monday December 9th. It turned out to be something of a non event and the vagueness of both legal representatives struck me forcibly.

One question by the opposition's man infuriated me 'Has there been a recent search made on the status of this lane?' I was blazing. This from people who had taken out a summons and accepted legal aid on the strength of supposedly sound facts and substantial evidence. Quietly and to myself I determined to approach the plaintiffs personally after this meeting and show them our conveyance deed and copies of recent searches which we had in our possession. I still did not believe they even had a case.

It was not an easy thing for me to do when the time came but I steeled myself. After all we had been close friends and any effort to salvage something was well worthwhile.

I carefully prepared the relevant documents which their solicitor had requested sight of. Our neighbours were to have a preview. I telephoned first and explained my proposal which was to try and convince them that we had acted in good faith and that the County Council had authorised the roadworks insisting that the road was a public highway. It was a claim that according to our conveyance was indisputable.

Our neighbours were receptive and willing to see the documents. I took them round. It was December and Christmas was looming large. I couldn't think of a better time to try for some reconciliation.

They seemed quite relieved that at least I was trying to sort things out and listened carefully to all I had to say. It was made clear that my visit was without prejudice and only an attempt to give them a clear picture of the situation and the events leading up to it. The documents I explained in detail and one in particular that was a copy of a search to the local authority made by their Solicitor for a transaction for themselves. It clearly stated that the road was a public highway maintainable at public expense.

At the end of this in depth discussion it was agreed that the dispute must end. We were both to make immediate contact with our solicitors and tell them a solution must be found. I walked on air as I got into my car. It was a wonderful feeling and I couldn't wait to get home to tell my wife. Christmas would be Christmas this year and my parting comment to our neighbours was that it was wonderful to be talking again. I meant it.

That Christmas we had decided to hold a couple of Sunday Open Days which we described as an experience of an old fashioned Christmas. They were to be in aid of Scarborough branch of Save the Children. They were an amazing success. Members of the branch volunteered to help and a plan was carefully prepared. It included a very lifelike nativity scene set in the stables using full size models and a beautifully decorated coffee shop and a huge Christmas tree.

The old Edwardian wall post box could be used for letters to Santa and I was to be the man himself. We had a full outfit complete with beard and a few Yo, oh ohs would complete the picture.

Christmas carols were a must so I also elected to strum these on my guitar and lead the carols. It was an unmitigated success and the children loved it. You can imagine the picture — lots of happy smiling children sat round a beautifully decorated Christmas tree singing carols with Santa. Wonderful.

Christmas fare was on offer, Turkey Soup and Sandwiches, Mince Pies with Brandy Butter, Christmas Cake and Hot Chestnuts. A real old fashioned Christmas.

We have a lovely old but restored horse drawn sleigh and in the absence of reindeer (oh dear, no deer, no), we stood two Shetland ponies in front and loaded it with Christmas parcels. It was a truly marvellous event and one that was to be repeated. More than that I was happy doing it. My heart was lighter and hopefully it would remain that way. I was to send a very important letter to my solicitor and I couldn't wait. This particular Christmas brought even more glad tidings. It brought a visit from John Taylor, an old neighbour who just happened to be in the water bore hole business — we were about to raise the world's water table!

CHAPTER THIRTY SEVEN
A year of many mantles

There is one striking feature about this farm and that has been its progressive and varied projects. Every year I find myself dreaming up some new scheme or additional facility and not least of these was the rebuilding and cladding of the old pole hay barn. Wet and cold weather was a problem and we had to have a covered area to get visitors inside. I had decided a studio type room with a small stage and seating would serve a dual purpose. It could be used as an educational facility and a video projection studio. We could show our own videos or possibly purchase a suitable one to use. I could also use my big screen and slide projector for talks of my own.

As usual a trip to a reclaimed timber yard came first. The materials are sound, available and reasonably priced. I drew up a plan for the conversion and carefully took off the quantity of materials. It was a lorry load.

We had just got this lot off loaded and neatly stacked and sheeted when I had a visitor — our local insurance manager. He was at the farm to re-schedule the farm buildings and contents insurance. Another way of saying higher premiums. It was amazing really because after the round of inspection he came in the house for a chat.

'I don't honestly think that the company will be too happy keeping cover on that old hay barn out there.' He looked towards me for comment.

I grinned, 'Fear not', I said 'That great pile of timber under the blue plastic sheet, is for exactly that purpose. We are going fully to renovate it'. I explained exactly what I had in mind and a little gleam seemed to shine from his gaze. 'Better come and have a look when it's done. You will obviously need increased and extended cover on something like that.'

211

Running parallel with this, the plan was being prepared for our whole farm conservation project. Something that seemed almost daunting in its magnitude but so worthy and important to me and this property. I determined that we should go for it. The work was to include creating a wildlife pond, regenerating all the ancient hedgerows, and planting yards and yards of new ones, planting a small broadleaved amenity woodland and rebuilding what seemed like miles of drystone walling. What a wonderful achievement to aim for. As you can imagine my mind and hands were full. Never a dull moment. I think all these things kept me so occupied that I managed to push the legal dispute to the back of my mind but it wasn't going to stay there. I think I was of the opinion that no news is good news. I actually thought that my visit to our neighbours was possibly leading towards a settlement. Perhaps they had decided to drop the proceedings. Alas my hopes and dreams were shattered. On the 25th March 1992 we received a letter from our Solicitor. It said that in spite of the deeds and documents which included the searches, that the opposition had seen and copied, they were still pressuring us to proceed towards trial.

So much for my December visit and Christmas goodwill. Well it wasn't Christmas now and my feelings about goodwill to all men had gone with the tinsel and melted with the snow. Our solicitors were still pointing to the legal aid certificate that our neighbours had secured and warning me of the dire consequences of not trying to reach a settlement. Apparently I was effectively in a 'no win' situation.

Well with apologies to Rudyard Kipling again, this is the bit when you do make a heap of all your winnings and risk it on one turn of pitch and toss. I would fight this injustice if it cost me every penny. Blackmail I would not tolerate and being held to ransom is something I did not intend living with. Needless to say I wrote a very very strong letter back.

For a bit of light relief let us return to the divine experience of drilling a bore hole! If I said that my very good friend and previous neighbour John was a wild version lookalike and larger-than-life David Bellamy then I wouldn't be far wrong. You, the reader would have a very good mental picture of this wonderful man and we can all enjoy sharing the experience.

If you remember seeing pictures of nuclear missiles and their mobile launching platforms, that is what this rig looked like as it crossed the field along what I have previously referred to as the stripe. On the tracked prime mover, pipe in mouth and laughing all over his face sat the man himself. His effortless and casual precision amazed me — he could have been driving a garden tractor. 'Hi Jenki' he yelled above the roar of this massive diesel compressor, 'I'll just take her through the gate and on to the lane'. I watched in amazement. He steered this complicated contraption of goodness knows what length through a ten foot gate opening with less than inches to spare. That was only the arrival of the machine. The events that followed are very worthy of a story.

This man knew his job. He was here as a mate and a friend and I had every confidence in his ability. He walked into our orchard and found spaces between trees. Looking at me he said 'Where's your septic tank and soil pipe?' I nodded towards the house 'Down across there', I said, pointing. He looked down at the ground between his feet, 'Right, we will go down here.'

This decision, made without the slightest hesitation heralded the start of a very rewarding experience and in more ways than one. You can go without food for days on end but you cannot survive many without water. At that time our very future depended on it.

The machine and its rig now had to be manoeuvred through the gate into the orchard and the drill and gantry erected. I was fascinated and intrigued. John joked, 'How far above sea level are you?' Realising immediately what he meant I said 'Three hundred foot so make sure you strike water before that depth — we can get salt-water from the sea!'

Now we watched as the whole rig was assembled. What a sight to behold and what an unlikely structure to be standing so loftily among the apple and pear trees. John spoke again 'There'll be a lot of muck you know — dust'll be everywhere. It will cover these trees and t'house as well I wouldn't wonder'.

This was something I hadn't thought about but I didn't have long to wait to see his words come true. The first fifty feet or so wasn't too bad, soft going in fact and I was told that this was unusually deep for unstable ground. It would need casing. Then we hit the rock. "That's better" said this curly haired and bearded figure, 'We need to get into rock'. By now the dust was rising in clouds and the green leaves and blossom of the fruit trees began to turn white. This was only the start, we had a long way to go.

You have got to picture the scene at this point. It was priceless.

This heavy mantle of stone dust was descending at a rate of knots. The curly hair and beard were also by now white with it. His shirt almost unbuttoned to the waist was full of it. It hung over his belt like a pack horse's carrier bags. In his mouth stuck his pipe and the bowl was full of it. Even the pocket in his shirt hung forward full to overflowing. He stood there at the controls of this powerful throbbing machinery completely oblivious and totally engrossed in his quest for water. He

You have got to picture the scene at this point.

looked as if he would be the first to need it. He was watching closely the spoil being thrown up by the drill. Suddenly he reached down and picked up a handful. 'That's better Jenki — water bearing gravel — we are getting there'.

He said we were down about a hundred feet and by now I was getting excited. It was a truly wonderful experience. Suddenly we saw the gravel getting wetter and the excitement was exhilarating. 'Will there be a gusher' I said 'Well I'll soon make you one' came the reply. 'We blow compressed air down and the water comes up — and we shall soon be able to do it'. I couldn't wait. When the water started to emerge it was pure ecstasy. I could hardly believe it. At this point I had to leave the proceedings to attend to other things.

Only a few minutes later the mobile phone rang and our intrepid

214

diviner had left the rig to answer it. I could see he looked thoughtful as he left his van so I called over, 'Everything all right?' It was not the answer I wanted. 'Not exactly' he said, 'We've lost the water. Come and have a listen it just sounds like somebody's pulled out the bath plug!'

I was knocked for six and I think it showed. 'Oh heck, that's terrible. What do we do?' There was not a moment's hesitation in his reply. With typical and supreme optimism bordering on the casual, he simply said, 'Don't worry we'll catch up with it again — just go deeper'. I found his manner very reassuring. He knew his job and I was quite happy to take his word.

At something over one hundred and fifty feet we struck again and this time for real. We could hear from the surface the magic sound of babbling running water.

'There's two underground streams down there Jenki. One running into the other and enough to push up a gusher. Go and get your camera'.

What a moment, this time I couldn't hide my excitement or my pleasure. I thought I would explode. These are life's incredible experiences and must be recorded. This was the ultimate in cool, clear water, and at this depth its purity was a forgone conclusion.

We leave this happy situation to pick up the parallel because we have got to return to the conservation plan. Part of this plan was the creation of a wildlife pond, and the difficulty now facing us was the fact that it was intended to be filled with the original farm spring overflow. Alas it was no longer overflowing.

Well the plan must go ahead and my mind was filled with a remark I had heard about two moorland farmers who had built a sheep dip. One had said to the other 'What are we going to fill it with?' The other had replied 'God'll fill it!' Well I felt about the same but I couldn't help some serious reservations. I couldn't think of a worse sight than an empty basin of earth just growing weeds. We had started the pond excavation just after we closed in September of that year. It was ideal dry conditions for the work of a 4 WD J.C.B. excavator but not ideal for the time when we needed to fill it. I had estimated at least eighty thousand gallons.

You are hardly going to believe this next bit. In October we decided to take a short break at the Manor House at Ingleby Greenhow in a self catering apartment. It was about thirty miles to the north of us. On the second morning of our visit, Ann called me to the bedroom window. 'Just come and look out here'.

I almost said, 'Do I need to?' I was enjoying a no-work-today-slow-to-gain-consciousness morning. I suspected it must be a peacock on the lawn or some other exotic species. With reluctance I dragged myself out of bed and across to the window. I blinked, blinked again and pinched myself. Our car, other cars, the lawn and the courtyard were white over with snow! And it was still coming down like goosefeathers. 'I can't believe this', I said to Ann, 'Just can't believe it.

What a week to choose for a holiday. It snowed, it rained, it sleeted and then it rained again. Heavy, incessant, persistent and wet!! Field corners were flooded, stretches of road stood in water and everywhere was soaked. I looked upwards, 'Well good job it's a pond and not just a sheep-dip!'

We drove home that Saturday, most of the route over the North York Moors. When at last we started to drop down towards Ravenscar the full effect of the rain was evident all the way. Water stood in huge puddles by roadside and low lying areas of fields were flooded.

We eventually turned off the A171 and headed for our destination. Again I could hardly wait. As we drove along towards the Shepherds Arms I looked towards the coast. There was a pond in nearly every field.

There is a name for this particular law when you have just sunk a borehole but I wasn't complaining. We arrived home to find our pond happily completed and its overflow discharging water in the ditch at an estimated several thousand gallons an hour. Had it not been for the flood overspill the pressure would have washed the banks away. Ah well, the water table was very low!

CHAPTER THIRTY EIGHT
Perge sed caute

A Spring conference of North Yorkshire Farming and Wildlife advisers group led me to a chance meeting with Doctor Malcolm Bell a man whose forthright manner and single mindedness I had long admired. He was associate adviser with a law firm recognised by FWAG. Was this the opportunity I had been waiting for? Could he advise me on what positive steps I might take to dent the confidence of the opposition and what exactly did he think of such a situation? It was after all a result of planning conditions imposed upon us and why should we be burdened with such crippling costs.

After the meeting which was held here on 30th March 1993 I had a quiet word. 'Well yes, certainly I could look at the background and some of the documents. From what you have told me it seems grossly unfair that you should have to capitulate just because of a legal aid certificate. Leave it with me a few days and I will contact you.'

He was as good as his word and in April an appointment was made for us to visit his office and together with a legal adviser they would give us their frank opinion.

We were not disappointed. After a lengthy discussion and examination of a massive file of documents which we had in our possession it was decided that we should get copies of certain documents from our own solicitors. I

The Jenkins family motto —
'Go on but cautiously'.

217

in my innocence could see nothing wrong in this. After all they were pushing me to settle on economic grounds and I was looking for an economic fight. Who could convince me of the best solution?

I have got to say at this point that the Jenkins family motto is 'Perge sed caute' meaning 'Go on but cautiously'.

Well I wanted to bear this in mind but on the other hand the family crest is a battle axe! Without going into details I have got to record that seeking advice elsewhere did not suit everybody and we soon found ourselves transferring the brief. Understandable I suppose but I wanted advice that I wanted to hear. After all it was me that had to live with my conscience when I had sacrificed my principles.

At this point further counsel advice was sought and how very re-assuring and stimulating it turned out to be. "Of course there is a risk of losing. In legal matters there always is, but you have all the evidence and supportive documents in your favour. It is a merce-nary affair and without the support of legal aid it would not have been pursued." He recommended that a second application be made to the legal aid board without delay. The certificate in his opinion should be discharged.

I must mention here in fairness that upon my own insistence, our previous solicitor had made a similar request. They in fact put together an excellent written submission which was rejected.

The same position was upheld. It was now a collision course with destiny. Expert evidence would possibly be needed and witnesses would be vital. I took this very seriously. No stone had to be left unturned and anything that could give a clear picture including maps and photographs would be help. I decided to start with Highways at County Hall. The definitive map. A booklet entitled 'Rights of Way Act 1990' had specifically stated that the routes shown on this map were absolute and final. They were legal and binding. I took my assistant with me and I asked to see it. The clerk was very helpful and to our delight it showed everything we wanted to know. More than that we were given a copy of the road schedule in Staintondale which was conclusive. We came back in high spirits — one to us anyway!

I do not intend to bore anybody to death by quoting blow by blow details of the period leading up to the trial. Our counsel had prepared a request for further and better particulars of the Plaintiff's claim and some interrogatories. He felt it was important to pin down the detail of this claim.

Our solicitor pursuing Counsel advice had pointed out to the legal aid board in the one last try to get the Plaintiff's legal aid certificates discharged, that this was a cynical and pointless piece of litigation which nobody in his right mind who was paying his own costs would contemplate.

He had not held out much hope in this direction and so the rejection I mentioned earlier came as no surprise. We had of course made a final plea to the plaintiff's solicitor to consult again with his clients, who of course were still our neighbours, and see if they were prepared to consider a reasonable settlement. It brought nothing more than a rebuff in that they were still seeking five thousand pounds to settle the case plus their costs. They also said it was a pity that we hadn't paid this amount earlier when their costs would have been lower.

I mentally thought about the family motto, 'Go on but cautiously' and decided to throw the caution bit to the wind. A settlement now was out of the question and a battle axe seemed a very appropriate symbol.

The rest of the Summer of 1993 was tempered by the pleasure we had all shared in preparing for and winning the Yorkshire and Humberside White Rose award for Tourism and the Environment. Our wonderful and enthusiastic staff worked so very hard and deserved a large share of the credit.

This farm in itself is idyllic. It is set in beautiful countryside on the North York Moors National Park coastline. It is south facing and set in a mass of summer colour and foliage.

We could never hope to compete with what nature had provided but with our carefully planned conservation work we had certainly enhanced a beautiful situation.

In November we flew to New Zealand and I seriously believe had we not done so, one or both of us would have cracked under the strain. Once our season ended in September it became impossible not to eat, sleep and think anything other than the impending court case. It was both traumatic and distressing and the strain of almost three years of it was beginning to tell. The New Zealand trip itself was a wonderful wonderful adventure and although we were very sad when our elder daughter and family had emigrated there in 1992, it gave us this heaven sent opportunity to get far away and visit them for Christmas.

It is very hard to contemplate travelling this awe inspiring distance and especially flying at speeds of 600 miles an hour. Just try to relate this to a twenty seven hour flight and you begin to get it in perspective. It is a long, long way!

We had decided to travel down to Gatwick Airport by train and stay in that vicinity overnight. This was to give us the opportunity to visit an old cousin of my mother's whom we called Auntie May. She is amazing and at ninety years of age was just about as excited about this trip as we were, 'And just send me some postcards, it's supposed to be a wonderful country.' She was right but it was the people of New Zealand that impressed us the most. Shirley had commented on this, 'They are so very nice Mum and they don't moan all the time. They are smashing.'

Our journey was an experience in itself and although there is a stopover at Los Angeles, it is still a long and tedious flight. We flew via America with Air New Zealand and the attention and service from the cabin staff was first class. This is a great help especially on a flight of this duration. We landed finally at Auckland Airport in wonderful warm sunshine. We had left Scarborough on a typical wintery November day and landed in Summer!

It was so funny to see the Airport all beautifully decked out and decorated for Christmas. They had huge Christmas trees and Reindeers and sleighs everywhere but this was early summer wasn't it? What a mind boggling contrast. Going from Winter to Summer in two days is one thing but a Summer Christmas is just not on!

We were then to take an internal domestic flight to Rotorua where our Daughter lives. A bit like catching a bus really and it really did have a driver and conductor — well that's how it came across.

There were only about six of us on the plane and the pilot sat at the controls just in front of us. It was only a short flight but the one steward personally made us a cup of coffee and brought us magazines to read.

This was our introduction to the lovely people of New Zealand who ask you how you are before they ask you what you want.

We touched down at tiny Rotarua Airport — in a quite tiny plane.

Shirley, our son in law Rob and the children were there to meet us — they were watching from a small balcony. At first they didn't realise that it was our plane. They were expecting something much bigger. And then the waving, the smiling and the hugging. Yes it was Christmas and what a wonderful one at that. Our cares and worries were a million miles away.

CHAPTER THIRTY NINE
Wrecking rights

'Several wrecks of considerable value having at different times been drove ashore within the Royalty of Staintondale which doubtless were the property of those who were Lords of that Royalty', I quote from an account of all the charters, deeds and public records copied by request of the freeholders by one Lionel Charlton, a teacher of Mathematics at Whitby. The copies were made in 1776.

The account taken from Bundle 3 went on 'Great disputes and animosities arose in the days of Oliver Cromwell, which of the freeholders of that Manor were or were not the real Lords?'

It seemed proof of purchase lay with Christopher Beckwith and John Beswick but not before long and tedious legal action was pursued. The two freeholders I have mentioned made a deed of covenance of the Royalty to a William Bowes, William Worfolk, Henry Brough and James Harrison to hold in trust for all the other freeholders that 'hold land within the Manor of Staintondale'.

It was contested by a man called Gregory Hay. He considered himself the just Heir of all the Royalties and in the year 1655 for the sum of Eighty Pounds sold the Manor to his cousin William Hay who possessed a small tenement at the lower end of the Dale adjoining Hayburn Beck (spelt Heyburn). He was a tanner. The other freeholders considering themselves aggrieved filed a bill in Chancery against Gregory Hay and William Hay.

It was a fascinating case which I have read and re-read and Lionel Charlton seemed in doubt as to the truth even after the freeholders won the case. I have heard it said and very recently that a case is only as good as the last witness!

I would dearly love to pursue more of the legal complexities and contentious issued outlined over several centuries in these documents, but I have to conclude by saying that the calm tranquillity of this lovely dale belies a turbulent past.

I must quote just a few lines from this long account for the benefit of the legal minded.

'The freeholders made a reply to this answer and the two Hays rejoined to their reply, but all these things produced nothing. It was ordered by my Lord Chancellor that a number of interrogatories should be drawn up, a commission held and the deposition of witnesses taken on both sides, to make the truth of the matters now in dispute, more fully and plainly appear.' It goes on 'Proceedings went forward with great spirit on both sides.'

Ah well, somebody else has been down this road we tread, albeit in 1662 and I suspect the verdict then was possibly worth a 'back hander'. We now return to the present because I must relate some of this colourful past to our life at Eastside Farm and also to a previous owner.

The lovely old cow byre and the adjoining original stable which is now the Cafe and Shop was fully restored in 1988/89. It is a building rich in atmosphere and when we first came here I found it always to feel a cool and calm place. A haven of peace. Sometimes in the early evening when I do the rounds of locking up, I can just sit in this part that was the stable, and soak up the calmness of this special atmosphere. The Dawson family had lived here from 1931 and had kept a few cows as well as other livestock. Before the coming of electricity in the late fifties, oil lamps were used in both the house and buildings. In fact the lamp hooks are still evident inside the house.

On occasions when power cuts have been prolonged in winter time, we have had to resort to the use of an oil lamp. Its soft silent glow complemented by a log burning fire is a wonderful experience in itself.

In the farm buildings lamp holes were sometimes built into the walls and one such hole is provided in what is now the blacksmith's shop. We use it to house a loudspeaker for our P.A. system.

When the Dawsons lived here, one of the sister's jobs during the darker nights was to get the cows into the cow byre and have the oil lamp lit. Another sister who was a nurse I believe, went by train to work from Staintondale Station. It meant a walk across the fields every day along the route our visitors now walk for pleasure. When this particular sister arrived home it was her job to milk the cows.

When we bought the farm the cow byre was still functional. It had standings for four to five cows divided by original wooden partitions. In fact in the 1970s when self sufficiency was beginning to look like something of a necessity, we had a few dark brown Jersey cows which we hand milked and even made rich golden yellow butter.

When we first opened to the public in 1985, only this same cow byre was used as a tea room and small gift shop. It was quite funny really because we decided we would leave the raised standings and divisions in, to create a feature. This meant that because some of the tables were in this raised area, it meant a step up. Now everybody didn't see this step in spite of warning notices. It became a 'Two cups of tea please' and then after turning to sit down 'Oops! er would you mind filling the cups again please?'

I must explain that the counter ran the other way then, across the right hand gable end.

By 1988 the enterprise had developed sufficiently to necessitate some improvements. I applied to the Rural Development Commission for a grant to restore the small range of stone buildings we are talking about.

The roof was in a terrible state and the walls not much better. Sagging ridge stones showed that the walls were slowly being pushed outwards. Well this time luck was on our side and a small grant was made available to renovate this building and extend the cafe.

We started on November 18th 1988 and what a morning to choose. It had snowed overnight and the red clay pantiles were white over.

Undaunted, a young local chap Graham Steel and myself made a start. Two scaffold towers were erected and we commenced the laborious job of stripping off several hundred snow capped roof tiles.

'Just hope it doesn't snow again and stop the job', I said. I was also thinking what a time of year it was to be doing it, but we needed to be open for next summer. We progressed favourably, my assistant was an excellent worker.

After the tiles came the slate lats and lime plaster. What a filthy miserable job. The dirt and lime dust was everywhere. We were covered from head to toe.

Once this layer was removed the rafters were exposed and we had hoped that some might be saved. We were to be disappointed, they were all woodworm infested and rotten with damp and age. We decided the lot must go and also the pans (wall plates) as well. Off with the lot!

We were several days into this work by now, and believe it or not it had neither snowed nor rained. Now we had the square of the building to examine — the walls. At this point I had a minor brainwave. We could stabilise these old walls by pouring a mixture of wettish sharp sand and cement down the cavities. This was quite quickly accomplished and we could get straight on with the new roof structure.

It was important to retain the original principles and pegged purlins. You don't talk about sympathetic restoration and use what are known as wood engineering and purpose made trusses. I shall not go on with a detailed account of all this work. The finished product is there to be seen and one I am proud of.

What is of interest is the level of the cafe extension floor. It now runs about two thirds of the way up the original stable doorway that you see from the outside. That was the difference in floor levels. And suffice to say that the old stable originally had a loft. The loft level was the beam end you see sawn off and a small wood spoked wheel mounted on it.

At least it gave us a hole to fill with all the debris taken from the roof and stone from the hole we cut through the wall. The breaking through bit, another Des masterpiece but that's another story. We got the whole lot finished and flagged by January 26th 1989, Ann's birthday. And without her knowing, planned and presented her with a surprise birthday party inside this very building.

The chapter is called Wrecking Rights and Timber. Well I have to mention here that for centuries along this coast, not only did the wrecks give up their lucrative cargo, they also provided superb timber of oak and pitch pine for the building and repair of these farms and outbuildings. We have some wonderful stout oak beams in the roof of our house. Timber so hard you cannot easily drive a nail in. There is evidence of these timbers in all our buildings but one piece in particular is a feature in the shop.

It is a sailing ship beam from the stem of the vessel and the draught marks are in Roman numerals. Possibly sixteenth century, who knows? Anyway there it is and it forms one of the main principles in the centre of the back half of the roof.

So there you have it. The stone for the building came from local stone quarries and not least the cliffs. The timber was provided by

225

the graveyard of wooden hulled sailing ships wrecked along the coast. And the money? Well take your pick. We have heard of the wrecking rights and the considerable value of these vessels. We have heard of the smuggling and the consequences of that. We have not heard too much about farming but we have heard some of these people described in court as the Gentlemen farmers of Staintondale, and the riding to hounds.

With apologies to Rudyard Kipling a line from his 'Smugglers Song' 'And watch the wall, my darling, while the gentlemen go by!'

CHAPTER FORTY
Bombed out of court

We were up early on the morning of the trial, in fact we booked an alarm call with British Telecom. Something that seemed ridiculous at the time but today we had a train to catch. Ann had discovered that trains into Hull ran from Driffield on a regular basis. It would save the hassle of facing a lot of traffic in Hull and also avoid having to worry about parking. We had been told to arrive early at the Court so that we could meet our Barrister and be briefed on procedure. The case had been set down for trial at Kingston upon Hull County Court for March 22nd, 23rd and 24th 1994. Today was the first day.

We drove along our new farm road to the point where we had to stop and Ann opened the gate. I drove slowly through on to what was in fact the disputed area and waited for her to get back in the car.

Consciously I looked towards our neighbours' cottage 'Were they as worried and concerned as I was?' My thoughts led me to looking over the access we had created and I thought how tidy and attractive it looked. Soon the daffodils would be blooming and the new trees bursting their buds.

I resolved it was worth fighting for. This access and the lovely new road to the farm with its wide verges and trees was a dream come true. We had battled with prejudice and unreasonable attitudes for years. This was my road.

We set off for Driffield and talked about anything but the trial. I was trying to appear nonchalant and unruffled but Ann looked ill. She was as white as a ghost and under a great deal of stress. And it showed. Underneath my assumed blandness I was working hard to keep my head. Something I fervently believe in.

Looking back over the last three years I think I was wondering whether for Ann's sake I should have tried to settle. She is not equipped to handle arguments or disagreement and I knew she was having a hard time. We had convinced ourselves that win or lose it was only money but if someone's health is at stake it is a very different ball game. Anyway too late now, let us hope that justice would be done and we could get on with the rest of our lives.

I think it was my own Father who told me that you could hang for your principles. It looked like I was going to lay mine on the line.

We arrived at Driffield well ahead of schedule and sat in the car going through the morning mail. Some very good news amongst it from Yorkshire and Humberside Tourist Board Tourism Advisory Service. It was for some proposed budget accommodation here at the farm. I have got to say that it was very favourable and this really pleased me.

The deserted platform at Driffield Station was quite a shock. My memories were of bustling platforms and busy porters. Today it was a pay train — a one man band. Never mind it is still rather special travelling by train. Something quite reassuring and relaxing.

We arrived in Hull and took a taxi to the Courthouse. Our destiny and possibly the destiny of the farm would be at stake over the next three days. We really were facing triumph or disaster and the legal process is slow moving.

The staff at this impressive Court building were very pleasant. They were efficient, courteous and helpful and we soon found ourselves in this modern complex having a cup of coffee. It was all very civilised. Soon our solicitor arrived who duly introduced us to our Counsel. He too was very nice — and, er, very young I thought inwardly. Or was it me coming to grips with my age. Prior to this I had a word with my old adversary who had been the area surveyor at the time of the planning dispute. He was there as an expert witness together with his assistant whom I had also previously dealt with. Expert was the word, his evidence was a masterstroke as we shall hear later. We were just about to be ushered into court when there was a rather large hiccup. Quite amazing and quite unprecedented I would imagine. Well for the particular reasons you are going to read.

It seemed that the judge selected to hear the case had already heard about us and the Shire Horse Farm. Apparently his wife and her Mother had visited the farm and gone home so impressed they had talked about nothing else.

This particular judge having listened to all this, felt that he could not conduct or give judgment in the trial with total impartiality. He felt that his personal knowledge would make this difficult. For this reason he had elected to stand down and another judge had to be summoned. That put an end to the start of the morning's proceedings. The trial would now start at 2.30 p.m.

Our two friends and previous neighbours had now arrived and a wonderful light-hearted exchange of greetings relieved the pressure. They were our sunshine that day. We decided that we would see the sights of Hull and then have lunch together.

At 2.20 p.m. we returned to the Court and were duly seated in the awesome surroundings of the Court room. A bit like a church really. Well this was a day of judgment. The first day of the trial is the opportunity of the Plaintiffs to give clear and compelling evidence to show good reason for their grievance. They have to try and convince the judge of their assumed legal rights and claims. Four witnesses were called, one of the plaintiff's being the chief witness on their side.

One question was put to both the plaintiff and his brother. I could not understand the significance of this question, nor of the response it brought. Was it properly understood? They were asked who had negotiated the sale and was it through an agent. Both said through their agent. The plain truth of the matter was that I was approached by the plaintiff's brother one day whilst cutting grass in one of our fields. He asked me why I had shown no interest in a block of land adjoining my property which they had put on the open market. I replied that I was not prepared to enter blind negotiations by bidding against something that had no ceiling. Matching one bid against another in other words, and knowing because our water supply sprung from this very block of land I had to secure it.

It was a gamble I had taken but it had worked. Against this background I agreed that I would talk to their agent with a view to establishing a fair value. It was then agreed that I should meet the two brothers personally and jointly and agree an acceptable price that we could shake hands on. It was a private meeting and it took place in the yard on their property. From this meeting and subsequent agreement the sale of the land was duly completed. This land had other attractive benefits, it would give us the opportunity to create a private farm road sometime in the future. For almost twenty years we had struggled with the problems of an access road not on our property but for many years solely maintained by ourselves. It had caused aggravation, confrontation and animosity.

I was previous in my assumption here and you are now reading about what it did bring. Even more aggravation, confrontation and animosity.

The two main witnesses were in turn cross examined by our Counsel. His manner with them was to say the least, charming and even at times beguiling. They said everything he wanted to hear them say.

"Oh yes we fenced the field from the road. Well folk kept leaving the gate open. Oh yes I can remember the road at the time it was rough and they were driving on the field. Well the fence stopped all that, they had to stick to the road. Well yes we left a bit of room for combines and things, they would have damaged the fence."

Our Counsel was purring.

"Well of course you did, you didn't want to be rounding up straying cattle. Of course you wouldn't want people driving on your grass pasture — you made them stick to the road. Naturally you left some space at the side. You didn't want your fence damaged did you? Of course not."

They fell willingly and eagerly as Counsel smiled back at them. Now he said 'Does the name F. Bloggs mean anything to you?' 'Oh yes he was our grandad', came the reply. 'Parish Councillor I believe?' 'Oh yes, that's the same man', confirmed the witness. I wonder if you can help me here? I have a document which was part of the survey carried out by the Parish Council in 1951. It was conducted by North Yorkshire County Council'. Our Counsel went on, 'It was with regard to several roads in the area and included the road in question. With regard to this particular road the question was, 'Is this road a public highway maintainable at public expense?' The answer given is yes and the document is signed F. Bloggs — would that be the same man?' Counsel paused. If gloating was within this man's make up it didn't show. He just kept smiling. 'Well yes that would be him!'

In a T.V. drama it would be followed with 'I rest my case'. This was real life drama and I wanted to applaud. I heard Counsel tell our solicitor afterwards that they would never have a better day and I was in full support of that statement. Together with our two friends and our legal representatives we were in high spirits. Gleeful would be a good word. I was feeling grateful as well because I realised a lot of hard work had gone into the preparation of our defence. Not

I wonder if you can help me here . . . ?

least the former Area Surveyor and I referred to his masterstroke earlier — it was the signed document. Our Counsel had earned my admiration too. His presentation was first class.

Day two dawned and found us in good spirits. Ann's colour had returned to near normal and today on our journey we openly discussed the merits of the case. In the event it turned out to be both an ordeal and a cliff-hanger and not quite what we thought.

It was now our turn to give evidence and our Counsel had held conference and explained what the procedure would be. Looking at me he said 'And you — you must not stray from the issue. The issue is the status of the road and not the rights or wrongs of this action. Keep your answers short and as brief as possible.' He obviously knew my limitations but I was also very aware also of my inclination to get carried away by my own personal viewpoint. The reason perhaps why I write these books.

At last I took the witness stand and found myself taking the oath. Their Counsel started questioning by showing a series of photographs. They clearly showed some parts of the road no longer in regular use but they were not areas I was conversant with. This caused me some concern because I found questions on these difficult to answer.

He eventually got to the point of the new access and I think he was confused by the original requirement of County Council and the compromise made because of some difficulty over land not in our possession. He seemed to be implying that I had not properly carried out the planning conditions imposed. He also seemed to be suggesting that I had not informed the plaintiffs of my intended new access.

I was getting very confused and felt that I was making a mess of something I should have found easy. When he again pursued the question of not fully implementing the conditions and widening the road for the length specified, I was choked.

The length required had included a sign belonging to our neighbours who at the time of the site meeting, I still regarded as friends. It would have meant removing this sign and the grass area it stood on and surfacing that piece as well. I had made the point about this friendship to the surveyor and asked, 'Can't I just skirt round that bit?'

Now they were accusing me of opting out of my responsibilities as well as taking this distressing legal action against us. It was just too much I just broke down. They were our friends ...

After a short time the questioning continued. 'It was not very neighbourly of you not to inform my clients of your intentions now was it?'

Well here again I should have jumped in with both feet and said 'Well it wasn't very neighbourly of them to sell us this land knowing why we wanted it and then taking legal action to try and stop us using it!' He also said that we had received the summons before the planning approval certificate which was not the case.

I wanted to argue and I wanted to explode. This wasn't the situation at all and I felt frustrated. Twice I had gone round to these neighbours and twice I had written and made overtures to try and end the dispute. Now it seemed I was being accused of hostility and it hurt. Well bearing in mind my Barrister's briefing and with Kipling still my mentor I decided that the bit that says 'And yet not look too good nor talk too wise' had to be me that morning. The case continued and our friend and previous neighbour took the stand. His evidence was clear and forthright. He knew the road to be a public highway and he had purchased his farm on that basis. He was in no doubt and he still had records to prove it.

North Yorkshire County Council witness was excellent. Indeed both the former Area Surveyor and his assistant were very effective. The witness in the senior position produced evidence and reference from 1929 onwards and maps from long before. His *coup de grace* came in the shape of the document I have previously described, and an attempt by opposition Counsel to discount it, was met with blow for blow moves a master chess player would relish. I should think he left the court in no doubt. Then followed the submission by our Counsel and he was very professional in this also. He cited a case Minton v Ramage and took it through to conclusion. It sounded a watertight and comparable submission. He left the opposition with the burden of proof. Their barrister then stood up and began speaking, he seemed to cite every case in the book that might or might not be relevant. Was this a confusion tactic or was this really such a unique and questionable situation? I was beginning to wonder myself.

His closing remarks left me feeling angry and disillusioned. 'My clients are looking for something fairly substantial in the way of damages. This land is off course a valuable piece of land'.

He was talking about the 7sq metres or thereabouts that had once formed part of the verge and were now part of the road.

'When I say value' he went on 'I am not talking about a price relative to the value of the land but the value relative to this successful commercial development. It could be described as a ransom strip!'

I was livid. Yes that summed it up, we were being held to ransom and were in a situation which I had referred to in correspondence with my solicitor as blackmail. That is why I was in court today. I had refused to pay. The judge then came to his summing up and said that he would proceed without delay and give judgment. What a relief. The nightmare was to end one way or another. He slowly and deliberately went through the background to the dispute and outlined the evidence given on both sides. Then he thanked those who had given such clear and conclusive evidence. It was all very correct and formal with no hint of partiality. I would describe his manner as inscrutable and as it should be.

Well that was fine but sitting waiting and anticipating was like being in death row. What was the verdict, which way would the pendulum swing? We got our answer and my eyes filled up. I looked at Ann and I think we could have stood up and cheered. Yes it was a highway, and the claims made by North Yorkshire County Council were proven and beyond doubt. He went on 'And now we came to the question of the verge. Is it or is it not part of that highway?'

This was the all important part of his judgment. It was crucial because if it was not, then our access was effectively a no access. It was a very stressful and nailbiting situation and my heart was pounding. This pounding has continued on and off ever since the trial. He started on his summary, we sat tense and forward on our seats. Just at that terminal point a man appeared behind the witness box and to the left of the bench. He was both apologetic and earnest and looked embarrassed. 'Did you not hear the audio alarm? Clear the court quickly there has been a bomb alert!' We didn't wait to be told twice and the next few minutes found us in the shelter of the building next door — it was a church.

Was I dreaming all this? I felt like pinching myself. My assistant had joked with me about an article we had read in the National press about a man in Germany who had taken a bomb and a gun to court. He had shot the judge and then blown the court up including himself.

I in reply had said that if I blew the court up it would be with me on the outside. She had laughed and said 'Well just don't go taking any bombs.' I just could not believe it.

We stood there in the cold, it was mid to late afternoon and only the second but what was to be, the final day. Our destiny hung in the balance. What a time to happen and what a catastrophe if we had to come again tomorrow. There would be no sleep tonight. Our legal representatives also seemed to be looking a little less confident. They thought we should win and anyway the road was proven. ... of course if the verge isn't part of it, it is going to cost you a lot of money.

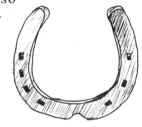

This was the worst possible few minutes of my life. The talk was 'Had the Judge gone home and if not would he carry on with his judgment at this late hour?'

Relief was at hand. An usher appeared and said we could return to the Courthouse, the area had been checked and our case was to be concluded.

We filed back into the Courtroom and took up our positions. The opposition on the left hand side and us on the right. Again the judge started to deliberate and I was shaking. This time I couldn't altogether follow the drift of his comments and I found this a bit disturbing. In front of me I had a clipboard and paper and I was doodling just to occupy my mind. A thought about luck came into my head and I was then remembering a telephone conversation only days earlier with a friend who had really experienced some rotten luck. He had been to the farm last year and asked me for a horseshoe. This recent telephone call had been to tell me how much his luck had changed since he got the horseshoe. A new job, a new baby, and good prospects. He said he now had three of them nailed to various doors.

With this in mind I started to sketch three horseshoes on the pad and elaborate them with shadings and nailholes. Just as I had finished came the verdict.

'And in conclusion and in view of the evidence put forward by both plaintiffs and other witnesses I have to find in favour of the defendants. The verge in this instance is part of the public highway.'

We were exuberant. The relief was almost too much to bear and everybody on our side was smiling. We had won!

As soon as the Judge retired it was hand shakes all round. This had not been easy for anybody and a great deal of work, thought and effort had gone into our defence.

Before the proceedings had quite ended our Counsel had responded to the Judge's verdict. He then said that the cost of this case to his clients had been considerable — well into five figures. On the other side, the cost to the plaintiff had been nil. Could he therefore ask leave of court under section 18 Legal Aid Act 1988 to seek to recover some of these costs out of the legal aid fund and directions given for further conduct of the case.

I shall not get into technical details here in case I am wrong but it seemed we may be in a position to claim help from the public purse. The Judge granted this request and then turning to the opposition he stated. 'And even had I found in favour of the plaintiffs the award for damages would have been small, no more than three hundred pounds!' If that wasn't a rebuff then I misunderstood the point he was making. A bomb scare had driven us out of court and now it seemed the opposition were being bombed out!

I must end this my third book with a comment I made some years ago when I could see a dispute developing. Take heed 'There is no such thing as victory when neighbours can no longer live in harmony!'

One previous neighbour who I have mentioned in my second book always refers to the old adage, 'Live and let live' and it is sound advice. There are some wonderful people in the world and we meet a lot of them here at the farm. Keep coming to see us and keep reading. One day I shall write about my peaceable, uneventful and tranquil life.

CHAPTER FORTY ONE
Tranquil Times

Once the trauma and sometimes despairing situation had miraculously come to an end, it was time to really move on.

An appraisal of our amenities and facilities had now to be fully carried out and this time any improvements we could provide would have a future.

Ann and I had called for a cup of tea and a snack at a recently established restaurant and cafe just outside Driffield. I found it refreshingly unusual and interesting. It was themed on a cobbled stable yard within the precincts of a rather attractive and somewhat historical farmhouse and buildings. Modern materials with olde worlde appeal had been used to good effect and blended perfectly with the existing surroundings. Pieces of yesteryear added to the illusion of the past, and the overall impression was one of restful charm. "This is just what we need" I said to Ann - and not without more than a subtle suggestion that my mind was already made up.

At that time we had a large building which was used as a general display area for our collection of carts, waggons and old farm implements. It also doubled for demonstrations on wet days and was also used as a covered picnic area. Adjoining our play area, it was both accessible and useful.

Having said all that, it had an earth floor which was uneven and presented us with other problems. The soil or earth floor was both dry and dusty, and of course on windy days our display vehicles got covered with a dirty brown film. With uncertainty about our future, it had not seemed even practical to consider some form of flooring. Now things were different - very different.

Now I could see our own covered and cobbled stable yard right here in this building - perfect - or as in the Darling Buds of May "Perfick! Well we have more than our share of May blossom here anyway, with our wild and flowering cherry trees, and that's without the vast areas of yellow flowering gorse. More than that, I wanted my new plans to be all in place before our visitors came back to enjoy the blossom. This would be a super new start, and there is more to come - read on.

Now my mind was made up, the next thing I needed was a supplier of Riven and cobbled effect pavers - Yellow pages - have you seen the TV advert? Well there it was, an actual manufacturer, and even better, he contracted to lay them. I reached for the telephone. This was not a straighforward job - but then - how many really are?

After an initial survey and costing out materials and labour, I decided to go ahead. It was a bit daunting at the time because our finances had been so badly stretched by the planning dispute - this was definitely make or break.

To begin with, we needed earth-moving equipment and a contractor to take out the top soil and level the floor. This was not an easy task working round the pole supports with a limited headroom height. However this went well, the weather was dry and very little damage was done to our nice amenity grass play area.

So far, so good. Next came a delivery of sharp sand - all 24 tons of it. Oh yes! I forgot to mention the size of this building and the fact that we needed around 1,000 large pavers. The sand was primarily to level the irregularities in the surface and then laid with cement to provide a bed to lay the pavers on.

As chief labourer, I had agreed to do all the mixing, barrowing and transportation of the pavers to the point of action - the man who was painstakingly laying them.

We had previously agreed on an attractive pattern - the black or charcoal coloured Riven pavers - (Riven is the original name given to hand hewn and dressed stone flags) - it does look very authentic. Then came the cobbled circle effect for the inner area. This provided an attractive contrast and also made far better light reflection. Altogether a very pleasing - and dare I say it - an area of restful charm.

At first the job went very smoothly, the play area was still dry so we were able to drive over it with the delivery vehicle and unload them straight into the building. The cement mixer was also sited just outside it, so all I had to barrow across from the car park was the sand - so far so good.

The sound of cement mixers is music to my ears and they have never been far from my life. Working with bricklayers and builders has always been a happy situation and I have enjoyed every minute. We used to call cement mixers 'hurdy gurdy's - (the old street organs).If DIY was the mother of invention, then I must be the father.

This project has now taken over thirty years and still continues. I have been shovelling sand and cement into a mixer for even longer, but the great thing about construction work is that it is always there to be seen and take a pride in.

Meanwhile back to the job in hand and all was going well until the rains came. In a very short time it was no longer possible to drive the pickup across the grass, so unloading of the pavers had to be done on the car park. This meant transporting by hand, in other words, in what we call our "wheelie barrow'. It is a trailer barrow, something along the lines of a single axle small car trailer - except of course pulled by hand. In this case - yours truly! No evidence of any obesity here I can tell you. It is not difficult to imagine how much effort it took to drag this thing across wet and soggy grassland. These pavers are heavy and there was still a lot of them.

However, nothing ventured, as they say and by now a wonderful transformation was taking place. This once dull and dark interior was turning into a seemingly spacious and very attractive indoor courtyard. It was enhanced by the circular patterned cobbled features which I had built into the design. This pleased me immensely and the sheer effort of carrying out this work became more of a challenge and less of a burden.

Just in case you are getting bored or even tired with all this description of what can only be described as work - let us move on.

A new member of staff had just joined the team - to phrase this event in modern day terminology. Basically I had just managed to recruit a new assistant called Claire Holliday, and I do regard these events as 'special'.

There have been very few assistants since this attraction first opened to the public in 1985. They seem to become such a part of this job in terms of input, enthusiasm and even influence that I do owe a debt of gratitude to each of them.

People or visitors as we call them, probably think these girls as having a really glamorous job working with horses and ponies and entertaining visitors. No doubt during the summer on a sunny day when we are open to the public, that would be fair comment. Behind the scenes how very different. The job is extremely demanding physically, and requires more practical skills than anybody could possibly imagine. First and foremost, a first class knowledge and ability with horses - that goes without saying. Next, practical skills - how good are you with a paintbrush and do you like decorating? Can you use a hammer and knock a nail in straight? Are you happy climbing ladders and steps? Can you stand cold weather and feeding round in a snowstorm - and not in stables - all our twenty horses and ponies live out. The list is endless, like driving a tractor, grass cutting and even road mending are all part of our regular routine. I think most young women would run a mile, but the ones I have employed didn't. They came, they stayed and they have been amazing. Where did I start - Oh yes! a new assistant, Claire and another remarkable young woman as you will hear.

She had just started, as the basic laying of these 1,000 or so pavers had been completed. "Have you ever done any pointing? Well you are just about to learn". "How" Claire grinned - "show me"!

Claire finishes off

CHAPTER FORTY TWO
Smugglers Cottage

It's amazing how projects here have sometimes been started by sheer necessity. At the start of the visitor season in the spring of 1997, I was doing the rounds for an appraisal of the jobs needing to be done. I had gone into what we then called the cottage museum.

This building contained a collection of old domestic items and artifax and was set out as a kitchen scene. It did get very dirty in there during the winter due to its old and patched up pantile roof. I looked round, and a loose pile of dust and debris caught my eye at the base of the back wall. Where did it come from? I looked upwards towards the roof - What the!!?

In a flash I took in the situation, the back wall for many years had been leaning outwards at something of a precarious angle, it appeared to have moved further. The dire consequences of that was suddenly apparent, the heavy roof principle made originally from old ship's timbers had slipped off the wall which supported it. It now hung ominously and threateningly, supported only by the purlins which were pegged into it. The whole of the roof, rafters, pantiles and all was in danger of immediate collapse. I didn't hesitate, a collapsed roof and the devastation that went with it would be a disaster for the start of the season.

A prop was needed and quickly - I ran down to what we call our re-cycled building materials department - or tractor shed and looked round desperately for something about the right length to use for a prop. The pile of fence posts offered little in this direction - too short. By now I was really getting concerned- had it all collapsed anyway? And then, there it was, a short length of scaffold pole and just about right by the look of it. Legging it back to the yard I shot into the building - relief - all still standing.

The pole was just a few inches too short but that was easily remedied by a couple of wooden blocks. I tapped the last one in, and just in time. What a miracle that I had gone in and spotted the problem.

A job here for Des of Dogs, Pans and Thruffers fame, but not this year - the show had to go on. In the meantime, Des came and looked the job over and ascertained the building was relatively safe structurely. Yes, the prop had saved the situation, and with the weight now firmly settled on it we could start and clean up the inside.

Again we must move on to another early spring, and preparation for the almost total demolition of the building. My grandsons, Simon, Oliver and Tom just happened to be looking to earn some pocket money at half term - I seized the opportunity. "How would you like to start taking the roof off, you could make a start removing the pantiles and stacking them?" The thought of climbing ladders and clinging to rafters, not to mention other precarious possibilities, brought instant approval. "Great, do we start straight away?" Well you can imagine the enthusiasm for this job, it was a sort of controlled vandalism - and they loved it.

The start of the renovation work

242

After the pantiles, the rafters, and after that the whole of the back wall had to be taken down. I didn't let them loose on that though - some of these dressed stones weighed well over 50 kilos. There was not much left standing when rebuilding finally started.1

Midway - renovation work

Des, the eternal optimist, had been on another job which had to be completed before ours could start. I really was panicking, we only had just over eight weeks to almost rebuild the whole cottage. Des was adamant - "we can do it". As usual I became the happy labourer, but of course I had my own labourer's assistant now in the shape of Claire - she was amazing.

Prior to coming to work for me, she had spent two years as a working groom at Newmarket which entailed a lot of hard riding and hard work. Her physical capacity impressed Des - especially when she sometimes collected bags of sand from the builders merchant (in an emergency). She would drive up on to the yard, flip the hatch open and in one movement lift the bag out of the boot on to the yard. Des would shout "you shouldn't be doing that!" "Too late", she would shout back.

From the start I could tell that this was going to be another happy job. We had a lot of laughs and everything progressed well. Des, who decided to retire not long after (at 75 I might add), was a very skilful and dedicated stone mason. Every stone was laid to perfection. I joked that this building had stood for 200 years. Des replied that this time it would stand 500.

When we got nearer the roof I decided to opt for some re-claimed timber for the rafters. Modern kiln dried timbers seems to have a shorter lifespan with very little of the resins left in it. Again I was lucky, and managed to get some rafters from a demolition firm not too far away. They had to be cut to size and this was a job for me and a power saw. The intoxicating smell of the pitch when I cut these angles was marvellous - a breath of pinewoods. At this point, time was at a premium and we intended painting these rafters with fence paint since they were to remain exposed on the inside.

"Do you think you could walk the plank Claire, and paint these rafters as we put them on? It will be easier that trying to do them from the inside once the roof's finished". "No problem" she said. "Just get me a brush". The end product of course was a lovely apex ceiling which adds to the historical charm and creates a nice feature.

There was still a lot to do, all the inside to plaster and a new floor to be put down. I had decided on pavers to represent authentic flags.

Inside this old building, formerly a pig sty and food store, were several built-in stone troughs and two had to be removed. In the previous chapter I have written about the laying of a new floor and creating a stable yard effect. This would be the ideal place to site these troughs and provide a nice stone surround to build them into. Des was enthusiastic. "They must stay here, it's where they belong". He was again recruited for another job, and another feature for posterity was in the pipeline.

By now the yard area was like a demolition site, broken pantiles, stone fragments and all the old rafter doors and timber - it was a formidable job. "Claire", I said "could you just get the tractor and transporter box, we need a purge on this yard". No sooner said than done. All timbers loaded and taken to the pond area for burning, all pantiles sorted and set aside for hardcore for the floor, the rest tidied up and swept up. What a transformation. Now we were making progress.

The floor went down without a hitch and Des had skilfully plastered out and scored in a stone pattern on the walls.

The next job wa s for me to re-construct the shelves in the cottage

Nearing completion of renovation

kitchen. A lot of history here because they had previously been removed from the house. They were in fact the shelves from the dairy which I have referred to in an earlier chapter, describing the layout of the house. Again another interesting feature which had to be preserved.

That done, only the decorating remained and we were just a couple of weeks from opening - we were going to make it - what a relief!

What was going to make the cottage more interesting was that it was to be themed on the Mead family and their involvement with the smugglers. More than that, the connection to the murder trial and subsequent deportation of William (Billy) Mead. Fascinating stuff, some of it already described in earlier chapters. We would call it Mead Cottage.

The reason I got so interested in Staintondale's history was that we inherited a lot of ancient documents and deeds when we bought the farm property in 1969. They gave me a real insight into the families who had lived here, right from an original indenture dated 1770. This document also referred to the manorial rights which had been passed down, would you believe, from the Twelfth century.

These manorial rights were in fact a Royalty awarded to the mediaeval order of the Knights of St. John of Jerusalem. The joint Lordship of the Manor of Stainton in Blackamoor is now passed on by documented freehold, in simple terms, with property previously owned by a freeholder.

The Mead family were recorded freeholders and we inherited the title from them. A joint Lordship of the Manor sounds very grand, but of course it is a fact. The inclosures awards of 3rd October 1829 were addressed to the Lords and Ladies of the Township or Royalty of Staintondale mmmmm .... Lord Anthony!

All the relevant documents and a facsimile of the indenture are now displayed in Mead Cottage here at Shire Horse Farm.

The completion of the renovation work on the cottage

CHAPTER FORTY THREE
Horse Murmuring

To understand something about communication between horses, we have to be able to identify what the various sounds mean to other horses. For example the whinny is a loud call and basically used for long distance communication. It appears to be used for establishing presence and possibly to establish territory. A lost foal will whinny to its mother and a mother will respond to the call - It has been observed also, that a mare can identify with its own foal from the sound of the call. There are many sounds and signals that a horseman has to recognise, particularly aggression. By nature horses are passive animals, providing their territory is respected by others. They are of course prey animals and as such basically insecure. They are constantly on the look out for predators and this is why impulsive and sudden movement by the handler can upset them.

A good example of this is when some people go to catch a horse and especially if they are in a hurry. Rushing towards a horse waving a headcollar is a positive threat, and to a horse that means a predator. You are never going to catch a horse like that.

Many, many years ago an old farm worker told me of his experiences as a lad. He had gone to work on a farm as a hired hand at only thirteen years of age. In those days they were bound by what was called a foot to seal the bargain. This was a small sum of money, a shilling or two. Hirings, as they were called took place on Martinmas Day, 23rd November. These men were paid for the whole year at the end of the period, the only recognised holiday was Christmas Day. This is a piece of history that I am priviliged to record because those days will never return. A farm lad's ambition was to become a waggoner or a ploughman, and they learned to handle and care for horses from an early age. Woe betide anybody who didn't do exactly as they were told and the welfare of horses was paramount. This was in the days before tractors took over.

Anyway, back to the story. Young Bill, as he was then, was the youngest 'lad' to start on the farm and in the pecking order, at the bottom of the ladder. He had the job of going out into the meadow at 5 am to catch the farm's five cart horses. I quote 'Gaffa said to me, don't you go rushing up towards that field waving those halters - if those horses see you coming they will be gone'.

The 'Gaffa' then went on 'Just take your time and whistle as you go - make on that you are passing by and keep those halters behind your back'.

Bill had apparently set off up the lane and he told me that he hadn't gone far when he heard a voice shouting. The 'Gaffa', intent on making his instructions stick, had shouted after him - 'and if you feel a rush coming on, sit down!' In that simple story from the early nineteenth century you have learned something about the psychology of a horse.

Today we have people who profess to be experts, but for the most part have picked up their knowledge here and there. It takes a lifetime really to understand the workings of a horse's mind - even if you ever do. Wellington, at the Battle of Waterloo, rode his horse Copenhagen for over fifteen hours on the day of the battle. When finally he slipped exhausted from the saddle, the horse rewarded him by lashing out with both feet, narrowly missing the Duke's head. His description of the horse was '... never got to the bottom of him!'

Quite the nicest compliment a horse can give is the nicker, which brings me back to the title of this chapter. It is a soft and gentle sound, low pitched and resonant. A horse nursing a foal uses this lovely vibrating sound which is probably closely related to a purr. It is a submissive sound and horses use it discriminately.

Over the years it has given me tremendous pleasure when I have had sick horses stabled. You are then custodian and keeper and above all their comfort. It is incredibly rewarding when a horse recognises your footsteps and softly nickers as you approach the stable - you are their friend. We tend to use the word or description 'Horse Whisperer' loosely as if it can apply to any situation. Basically all it means is that a horse is calmed by a soft gentle tone of voice. It is something they will respond to, simply because strong and harsh sounds present themselves as a threat. Irish lads and females seem to develop an easy relationship with horses and especially highly strung thoroughbreds - soft, assuring tones.

If you really want to relate to a horse, see yourself as the dominant factor, but respect his doubts and suspicions. Always be persistent but remain passive. Give him plenty of time to try and understand what you are asking of him and above all take everything one step at a time. You have to learn to communicate with horses, but on their terms. They are very much creatures of habit and short repetitive lessons will get good results.

Another aspect I take seriously is environment and temperament. For me these two important ingredients go hand in hand. Make a horse comfortable, give him security and friendship and see how he responds. Many people see a horse as a pleasant experience. Something to ride out on or just something to own. A horse has got to recognise you as the pleasant experience, and the provider of its well being and security.

To give you, the reader, an example of environment and temperament, I would point to two thoroughbreds that I own. The eldest is a chestnut mare called Tilly, who is 16 years old, and the younger one called Penny, (her daughter) who is 12. She is by State Diplomacy. They are both registered at Weatherbys and of extremely good blood lines. Tilly Toulousa was by an outstanding stallion, 'Roman Warrior'. He is a direct descendant of one of the three Turks - founders of the Thoroughbred.

These horses are beautiful and gentle in every way. They have both been used in the shows and demonstrations I do in my work. Surrounded by hundreds of people and children throughout the summer months, we have dressed them up in both English and Western saddlery. They have been subjected to endless photographic sessions with hordes of shoolchildren round them and never even blinked an eye. Laid back is a modern word to describe it but really it is total trust in you and what you are asking of them. Their environment is a secure one. I tell my audience 'Trust is mutual you know and it must be reciprocated'. Now then, if I were to stable these two horses at a racing yard things would be very different. By nature horses can sense urgency and expectation from their surroundings. Horses on 'their toes' as it's called, give off signals and instinct itself plays a major role. Racing is in their blood. This is why a thoroughbred is regarded generally as a highly strung animal - not so here.

You cannot treat a thoroughbred harshly either by action or voice. They soon get upset and fear shows in their eyes - this is the time for the soft tone and reassuring overtures. Ask them to put their trust in you.

Years ago a lady called Barbara Woodhouse, had a programme on television. She demonstrated how to give horses confidence and she did it very well. Looking back she was probably one of the first people to show just what so called 'Horse Whispering' is all about. Her quiet confident manner made her a leader in the horse's world and that is exactly what horses are looking for - leadership. Don't bully your horse, don't ask for submission, just ask him politely - will you?

CHAPTER FORTY FOUR
The Real Horseman

Forget about Bronco busters, Rodeo riders and even horse whisperers for a moment. Let us look at the men whose livelihoods and indeed their very existence depended on horses. It would be very remiss of me if I failed to remind readers, and pay tribute to the carters, waggoners and ploughmen who made such a tremendous contribution to our society.

Their love of horses started when they were just village lads with an ambition to work with horses. Most of them started work at thirteen and would be known in the pecking order as 'least lad'. they would soon be taught to plough and were usually given an older pair of horses that were steady workers. In fact, there was an old saying that I have heard many times about this situation 'It takes an old lad to teach a young hoss and an old hoss to teach a young lad!'

In the days before mechanisation, horses indeed reigned supreme and they were treated with respect. The farm workers regarded the horses as their own personal property and would buy horse brasses and make up decorations with their own money – from the little that they had.

A good foreman was judged by the condition of his horses and they went to great lengths to make sure they were well muscled, sleek and shining at all times. During the ploughing season and up to the end of February, a working horse would get a stone of oats each day in addition to chopped hay and straw. When work got really hard and the horses were being pushed on, this rose to a stone and a half (around ten kilos). No corn was given on Sundays. It has been my privilege to know many such people and I owe a debt of gratitude for the knowledge and wonderful stories bestowed upon me. I am sure even today, a young lad yoking two pairs of cart horses in tandem, (one pair in front of the other) and driving by sitting postillion on the near wheel horse and driving the front pair from this position, would be an impressive sight – and with the waggon loaded with three tons of corn. I have to add also that the braking system was dragging one back wheel on an iron sledge (shoe). I want to mention two people that I knew and one in particular, Fred Ulliott, whose family spanned several generations of farmers, carriers and carters. During the First World War (1914 - 1918) he left school aged 12 years and started work. His horse stories, wit and humour fascinated me. He seemed to me to be one of the most contented men I have ever met.

'When we were haytiming,' he told me, 'we used to start sometimes at 3am when the grass was heavy with dew. It was cool then you see, and the horses worked better. Charlie Beaton and me would take a few turns round the field and then swop. One of us would be sat sharpening the spare knife, while the other cut.'

The spare knife he referred to was the cutting blade of the horse drawn mowing machine. In tough grass they had to be kept as sharp as razors.

'We knocked off when the sun got up, it was hard work and the horses soon got sweated and hot. We used to go leading stone for the rest of the day and start cutting again later.'

There were no frills, embellishments or glamour to the lives of these old horsemen. Life was a drudge and little more than bed and work. Surprisingly enough, they were happy and cheerful people and always seemed to be able to laugh and joke when reminiscing about the bygone days. It has been my pleasure to have known and talked with these people. One particular quality about these old horsemen was their hands and handling of the horses they worked with. It was a necessary quality that they all recognised – a soft pair of hands. I have heard them variously described as 'hands like silk' and 'hands like velvet' when driving young horses.

One of Fred's stories I found particularly fascinating. It was to do with the 'borrowing' of a young three year old gelding. Apparently at one particular harvest time one horse in the binder went lame. The binder was a machine which cut corn and bound it up in bundles. They were noisy and unwieldy machines and hard work for horses.

Fred told me, 'when a horse went lame, you really were in trouble, we depended on them so much.' He then went on to tell me that a neighbour had a few young horses running about and from what I could gather was not always around or engaged in farming. They would 'borrow' one. Now to consider putting a young untrained horse to work, and in particular in a binder, was in itself a major decision not without risk.

'Well we put a set of blinkers on and led it out of the field – it were almost dark anyway and it didn't seem to mind. After that we geared it up and left it standing for a bit until we was ready. We put it in between two others and yoked it to binder and we were away. It jumped a bit at first but soon settled down.'

This sort of thing makes the backing of a young untrained horse more of a novelty rather than a practical reality, or should we say necessity. From the tales Fred told me and many others from his contemporaries I wrote a song – in fact it was the first song I wrote. I called it the 'Jolly Ploughman'. A title that seems to have been bestowed upon ploughmen in various forms over the centuries. What was it that made this particular job so attractive and the men so happy? I can only assume that it was being so close to nature, the smell of newly turned furrows and the sounds of nature around him. Ploughmen sang and

253

whistled as they worked and their very body rhythms would be at one with the countryside. One American country music singer who became quite famous said he learned to sing whilst working as 'plowboy'.

My song is about one such farmer who in the 1940s decided to move with the times and buy himself a tractor. He took his horses to market, hung up his collar, hames and chains and bought the tractor. Selling the horses was a sad day for him but worse was to come. He soon realized that the tractor wasn't always running as sweet as it could be, and the noise blotted out all the things he loved the most. He could no longer hear the birds singing or the Church bells, but most of all he missed the wonderful companionship of the horses. He decided to go and buy them back and restore his pride and joy. I shall let the song speak for itself.

To give some idea of the sheer size and scale of the horse ploughing operation and the workload of both men and horses, the following may be of interest.

A man's working day during the time that references in this book have been made, was eleven hours. To plough an acre with a pair of horses was regarded as a good day's work, and in the course of that day a ploughman would walk eleven miles.

At the end of his working week which again, at that time was 6 days, he would have worked 66 hours, walked 66 miles and ploughed just 6 acres of land.

To put that in perspective, in comparison with today's modern mechanical equipment, that same 6 acres could be ploughed in less than 66 minutes. It can in that time, wipe out a whole hardworking week of yesteryear.

I must finish with a lovely little story that has its roots very firmly in this byegone age. It is one that I am sure has been told over and over again.

A young lad – it could have been Fred, had arrived at his new job on the farm. After being told to go up and put his glad rag box beside his bed, (glad rag box was the name given to the box which held his precious worldly goods – his spare clean clothes). He presented himself to the foreman. 'Right lad,' he said, 'we are muck spreading this afternoon and I am going to teach you how.'

With that he led our Fred into the stable yard where old Dolly was already harnessed in a cart – a muck cart as they were called, and it already full of farmyard manure. 'Climb aboard lad and grab this fork.'

'A JOLLY PLOUGHMAN'

I am a jolly ploughman
I plough the fields all day
A hasty thought came to my head
That I should change my ways

So I parted with my horses
And laid aside my plough
And put away my hames and chains
I'll no longer need them now

It was a scene of heartbreak
At the market place that day
I said goodbye to Prince and Grace
And slowly walked away

And I bought myself a tractor
A little standard Ford
The engine sang out sweetly
At a price I could afford

But I missed the sounds of nature
And the birds no longer sang
The tractor barked and spluttered
And the church bells never rang

So I'm off to buy my horses back
To harness to the plough
I've never missed two friends so much
but I know I miss them now

The lark was me that morning
And sunshine was the day
With "C'mon old gal" and "Gee up Prince"
We were proudly on our way

So come on you jolly ploughmen
Who plod behind the plough
We'll say a prayer for yon old 'oss
And by gum, we'll say it now

With a click of the tongue the horse moved off and the foreman lifted himself up on to the shafts. Once in the field he joined Fred on the cart itself and the well seasoned horse walked slowly on. 'C'mon lad, get plenty on yaw fork and get plenty of muck on this land – taters are goin in here – hungry things is taters'. He repeated these lines throughout the afternoon and the words were ringing in Freds ears. 'C'mon get plenty on – hungry things is taters'. By teatime our Fred was reeling from the constant repetition, tired and hungry. he hoped there was more to farming than this.

The foreman's wife also fed the men and after washing himself in cold water at the pump in the yard, in to the kitchen he went. Being the least lad also meant he was the last lad – to be fed, that is. He eagerly awaited the food. It was a large pie baked in a huge dish almost the size of a baby's bath. There were ten men and three lads to share it. Somebody muttered 'Meat and Potato pie'.

At last Fred's turn came and a large portion was unceremoniously dumped on his plate. He laid into it with gusto, he was so hungry. After a few mouthfuls he became curious about the content, and with his fork he tried to lift a corner of the pastry. The foreman's wife's eyes flashed 'what's thoo looking at,' she snapped. Fred jumped back in his chair, he was so startled. 'Well Missus,' he stammered, 'foreman said taters were hungry things – I reckon they've eaten all t'meat out of this pie!'

CHAPTER FORTY FIVE
Horse Language

One of the most rewarding comments I hear from people after watching me work with the horses is 'Those horses love you.' It is a real compliment but there is nothing difficult about establishing this sort of relationship.

I explain that basically a horse's response or its temperament is relative to its environment. You, as the horse's keeper, create that environment. At this time I have bred and reared most of the 17 horses and ponies that we have. I have also had a whole lifetime's custody of several more, that have now passed on.

What a wonderful and rare privilege to have enjoyed. You give them shelter, you feed and look after them and you build a remarkable relationship. You are their leader and they depend on you – and it shows.

It does make it easy when it comes to training, because you have this complete trust – and trust is mutual. If, for example, a big Shire horse didn't want to be led by any particular person – and it has happened, it could physically just walk away. A horse has got to want to be with you to get the best results.

My favourite example of what not to do, is what I call the 'you will mentality'. It seems to be the norm around many stables and riding establishments. If people would only reverse this situation and try asking the horse 'will you?' As in any society, politeness costs nothing and persuasion is better than punishment anytime.

On no account be misled into thinking that horses are stupid. This is very often their way of demonstrating non co-operation. They are much cleverer than some people would give them credit for, and they can certainly out-think a human. Try teaching your horse to recognise you as a friend and wanting to be with you. If he's going the other way, you are not making a good job of it. We have our own special way of building up a relationship and it starts on day one, when the foal is born. At this stage it knows no fear and probably recognises you as a parent. The foal has to be handled anyway, and I usually dress its navel to reduce the risk of infection. Again, it is easy for me because I have also by now, bred the mother as well. She is quite happy for me to handle her offspring. In fact, in all probability she is telling the foal that I am a friend. One of the best even!

I go back several times during that first day and let the foal see and smell me. The foal is communicating in its own way and will not forget this encounter. After this initial introduction I 'give' the foal over to its mum. For the next few days she will become increasingly possessive and protective, and will take it away at the first sight of an intrusion. Don't rush to re-establish contact, because this situation will change.

After this period the foal, like all young beings, will start to get curious about the big world and start to approach you. I call this 'coming forward' and this is what you must cultivate. At this time the mare will be wanting to show off her baby, and when this happens, take her a bucket feed and start to hand feed the foal at the same time. The foal will only lick at first but you are sowing the first seeds of dependence on you. It won't be long before the foal is looking out for you and galloping over.

Gallop is the word and if you are not familiar with horses, you might be interested to know the following facts. A foal is usually born in seconds – and that applies equally to a big Shire. It can be on its feet within minutes and in the wild, can be galloping with the herd within hours. It would then be both suckling and grazing.

To give you a good example of an established relationship and one that I am probably most proud, I must describe the following experience.

I had taken two young fillies to be served by a stallion at Howden. It was owned by a man called Jon Martinson. They were Shire horses and I had raised them both from foals.

At feeding time and indeed at every opportunity I had whistled to call them up. I had found that on a windy day a whistle was more effective. They responded to it without fail and of course people were impressed. It is amazing what the promise of food can do! This is part of a subtle training method that I have practised over the years. The whistle was a sort of see saw sound – a high note and then a low one repeated at intervals.

I had arrived at Jon Martinson's farm with my Landrover and two-horse trailer to collect them. They had been there a month. The farm was deserted – not a soul to be seen. I discovered later that it was Howden Show Day and everybody had gone there. My first thought was to abandon the idea because even loading two young horses, without help, can sometimes be a problem.

Anyway, I decided to see if I could find my pair and then possibly just try. Oh, I found them all right – well I found horses, a field full of them. Jon Martinson kept several stallions, and there must have been fifty mares in this field and some with foals. I couldn't even see my two.

Well nothing ventured nothing lost. I started to whistle. Some of the horses looked up, I think they were used to seeing a man with a dog on hearing it. None of them moved however, but something else did – from the far side of the field, making their way slowly through the other horses, Carmen and Grace started coming towards me. I was absolutely thrilled. More than that, I took them quietly from the field and loaded them without a problem. I walked in backwards and they meekly followed me into the trailer side by side.

This was just twenty five years ago when horse whispering was unheard of and natural horsemanship was something only the Indians did. The lesson here is 'If you create a comfortable environment for your horse to live in, he associates that with you'.

I have pursued this technique through the years and it really is a very simple formula. A horse is a creature of habit. By repetition he learns quickly, and this is well illustrated by the way our foals are trained by using them in our shows at the farm.

At around three weeks we let them follow the mare on to the yard. They usually stand fairly close and can be guided just by the use of a hand. After this initial introduction to people, and also the many children around, we start to use a headcollar and lead rope. Still allowing the foal to follow the mare but with a gradual progression towards restraint.

By this time the foal is standing quietly beside Mum and we are able to touch it all over. This is very important and from its head, to all over the body, we gradually work down its legs. After that, picking up feet is a must. A foal's feet will need trimming eventually and we must prepare for it.

After weaning we start again, and by now the yearling as it is called, is a very independent being. We teach it to tie up quietly, back into a stall and be led up and down to the fields. Oh, and have a body bath and its mane and tail shampooed.

Altogether a very natural progression and at two years of age they are all backed, without fuss or formality. Depending on the type, we only lightly back them at this age but Shire horses can be harnessed to do light work. We are lucky because our horses are used to crowds, cars and many other diversions and very rarely spook at anything.

In the world of Thelwell – bomb proof!

CHAPTER FORTY SIX
Bonding

I have been very lucky because most of the horses I have owned have been home bred. It does make training and handling that much easier because horses with their excellent memory, recognise you as a family member.

Most horses have probably changed hands several times before they are a few years old and of course during this time the owners or dealers have sent out very different signals. Horses are soon confused and you cannot say to a horse 'you have had a rough time but all that has changed'. Invariably the old submission technique will have been used and the horse is by now headshy and distrusting. Can you blame them? This is when most damage is done. It is not easy to restore a horse's confidence, but with time and patience it can be done. Horses bond to each other easily and part of this relationship is down to grooming each other. You often see two horses in a field nibbling each other's lower neck - this is what is called grooming and is probably to a horse the equivalent of a cuddle. Well a symbolic gesture which says 'I want to be your friend'.

If we take a horse that is nervous and instead of tying it up tightly by a headcollar, we have a longer lead rope which will allow us to move round the horse. This way you are giving the horse some space whilst you gently work round him until you are grooming an area that makes him relax. Talking softly with rhythmic movements as you work will get results. Jabbing and thrusting with your arms and heavy handed brushing must be avoided. Don't stare him in the face and keep your shoulders and arms relaxed and lowered when possible.

This is only the start, but don't be in a hurry and keep at it until the horse sees you as a comfort zone. Don't overdo the grooming sessions - little and often is better. If your horse will eat a tasty bucket feed and stand untied, so much the better..

This book is not about re-training problem horses, but I am sure much can be learned from it. Ground work is the secret of true success and spending time with your horse - make a real friend of him and remember he wants to play sometimes. Don't see this as being unruly.

I don't think many people realize just how much influence they have on their horses, especially when the relationship is well established. I see them as my children most of the time, and talk to them on this level. This way a certain dependence develops and the horse quickly learns to recognise when he steps out of line. I wonder sometimes if facial expressions don't come into it, when your horse looks at you almost enquiringly. I do believe they can sense tension and anger and suspect body odour might be a possibility - or scent! Dependence is a real bond and as I have said in other Chapters, horses are insecure by nature, except perhaps when running with the herd. Even then the prey animal instinct is basically one of flight rather than fight. I have had many examples of dependence over the last thirty years and one in particular will always stick in my mind.

Many years ago I was at Burniston Show, a village about 6 miles away. I had taken two Shire Horses down to show in separate classes. The younger one of the two I had left in the trailer whilst I was showing the other in the first class on the schedule. The showing was quite some distance from where I had parked the trailer, but Joanna as she was called was seemingly very quiet and content left in there. Infact she was munching from a haynet. The judging had just started when a friend of mine came tearing into the ring yelling 'Tony, Tony come quick, your horse is going berserk in the trailer!' I quickly handed my entry over to him and ran like the devil. The uproar hit me before I got anywhere near the problem. A crowd had gathered and what a scene met my eyes. The trailer rocking on its springs, loud whinneying from within and worse, a forefoot sticking through a broken front window. I pushed my way through the spectators and opened the groom's door. At that moment I heard a man's voice say 'She'll be alright now, Gaffa's come'. Those words were to stick with me for the rest of my life.

The significance is clear, obviously this was a knowledgeable man from days past. A man who knew about horses. He realized the dominent influence of ownership. He was quite right. I squeezed my way inwards and upwards and surveyed the scene. Joanna was standing quietly now, sweat was running down her whole body and legs, and dripping from her underside. She was visibly shaking and shivering all at the same time.

What a mess, but my problems had only just started. She had apparently reared up and got her forelegs over the breastbar. From this position in trying to free herself she had gone up again and struck out with her off fore - it had gone through the window. I looked on with horror. Blood was running down both the inside and outside front of the box. Joanna herself was standing very quietly now and I stroked her neck and patted her. 'Hold on baby' I said 'soon have you sorted out'. It was not going to be easy. She was not standing at all really because her front legs and body were suspended on the breastbar. The first job was to get the foreleg out of the square hole that had once been a window. Fortunately that did not prove too difficult. I got a helpful friend to go round to the front of the trailer and lift the foreleg upwards. At the same time on the inside I kept quietly talking to Joanna as I threaded the leg inwards. With so much weight off the ground we managed this really well, and I was relieved to note only skin damage. Well, so far so good. I then got someone to get the Landrover tool roll out of the vehicle and see what we could use. An adjustable spanner seemed ideal. I was lucky, the nuts unscrewed easily and all I had to do was punch the bolts out. Joanna was superb, she stood quietly looking on with the big trusting eyes that those horses have. After that came the thumping and banging as I used the base of the screw jack to punch out the bolts. The horses weight was on these. As the bolts flew out, the breastbar was bent down, under Joanna's weight. Once more she had her feet on the ground. What a relief. I dropped the tailgate and led Princess, the other horse, into the trailer. A reassuring whinny all round and peace and tranquility was restored.

We headed for home with a big sigh of relief. Although I could have done without it all, experience comes in many ways. The total trust I got that day was sufficient compensation for the trauma. This story is a good example of an animal's flight behaviour pattern. Joanna had seen other horses walking past and disappearing out of sight. She had pulled back against the headcollar, panicked and – well you know the rest. I blamed myself – leaving someone to keep an eye on her would have been a good idea.

CHAPTER FORTY SEVEN
Our Mascot

One of the first lessons I learned about a horse's capacity to get himself into situations that you thought impossible, happened when Mascot was only a year old. I was teaching him to stand quietly in a stall on a fairly short tie up. He had gone through the usual stages leading up to it, and I was satisfied that he had learned his lessons well.

On the day in question I had left him for a few moments in the stall, confident that he was in a safe situation – or so I thought. No sooner had I turned my back than he decided to prove me wrong. Although I had adjusted his tie-up short, he had managed to rear up and get himself into a very serious situation.

Hearing a commotion, I rushed back into the stables and what a sight greeted me. Mascot was more or less up on his hind legs, blood was pouring from a cut in his right knee and his left foot was stuck through the bars of the corner manger. What a mess – and what a problem. A broken limb looked inevitable.

Fortunately the hay and straw barn was next door – I flew round and grabbed a bale in each hand. I then rushed back into the stall next to the one Mascot was in and piled them up against the division. Climbing on top, I found myself easily able to reach over and talk to Mascot whilst I examined the extent of the problem. 'Don't panic,' I told him, 'keep still.' Actually he couldn't do much else, although sudden panic could have been a disaster. I carried on talking to him in a soothing voice whilst I looked carefully at the bars of the manger. Would I need a hacksaw and would he stay still that long? It appeared that the width at the top of the bars was wider than that at the bottom. This was why he was trapped – his foot had slipped downwards.

'Mascot,' I told him, 'I need some cooperation here, if you could stretch your leg out a bit further and straighten your knee.' I was proceeding to manipulate his leg as I was talking. 'We might just be able to get your foot back through.' It was my lucky day once more, because a few inches higher up the bars, out it came.

What a relief as Mascot regained his normal posture. 'Bet you don't do that again,' I said. It was another instance of a horse's dependence on its keeper, and in my experience I have found that horses recognise this, once away from the herd. Well, his education continued and by the time he was 5 years old we had him well trained to most situations. At this time a young lady called Graziella Brownbridge was working for me and she was a keen horsewoman.

One day she was trying to persuade him to jump a small open ditch – he thought otherwise. 'Just tap him on his backside?' she asked, 'and see if he will go over.' I gave him a sharp smack with my hand and hey presto, over he went. Over the next few days it became his party piece, and the next thing I knew, she had him jumping small jumps. It was obvious that he thoroughly enjoyed it and needed no encouragement. The next lift was 40 gallon barrels laid on their side at first, and then stood upright. Mascot jumped them with ease. After that Graz took him to a local sand school and he took off over coloured jumps like an olympic contender.

About this time we were approached by a regional television channel – could they come and film him? Their researchers had done some fact finding and discovered that draught horses were not naturally inclined to jump. they thought viewers would enjoy seeing it. They were not to be disappointed – Mascot was a star that day as he easily cleared 4' 6". The T.V. interviewer asked her what he was like to ride and handle, compared to a normal riding horse.

'He's brilliant,' she said, 'his stable manners are superb and you can always trust him.' She went on, 'and more than that, although a big strong horse like this would normally be more difficult to turn, I only have to touch the bit and he's round. He loves jumping so much that he can't wait for another go – it's just as though he's jumping against the clock!'

At about this same time I had paid a visit to a friend, John Whitehead, now sadly and prematurely passed away. He had been training a pony to drive, and invited me to have a ride out with him. The vehicle was especially built for training young horses and the two of us chatted away as the pony trotted in front of us. I asked John if he was everworried about these ponies galloping away with him. He grinned, 'Well you would have to ask yourself what they were running away from – if its you, then change your job.' Words of wisdom indeed. It summed up my exact sentiments, a horse should be running towards you if you are a respected leader in the horses' world.

After that visit I had ideas of my own. I would build a cart very similar to John's and train the stallion, Mascot. He was a likely candidate and would be an ideal driving horse. What I needed was a substantial axle and a frame – it suddenly came to me – a touring caravan chassis. As luck would have it (again) I soon found what I was looking for and a choice of two. It seems casualties among small touring caravan owners are not unusual. Anyway I chose the best one and towed it home. It was not difficult to re-arrange the metal frame, and to lower the centre of gravity, I simply turned it upside down. A pair of shafts from an old hay rake and bingo!

Graz was an enthusiastic assistant as we started to train Mascot for his new role. We started by long reining him around a paddock, taught him to stop (whoa) and stand still. We also drove him in the long reins through gates and puddles and had him turning left, right and doing figure of eights. He was a very responsive pupil.

At last the great day arrived, we would 'put him to' as it is called. We let Mascot stand quietly with Graz holding his head and talking to him. I gently wheeled the vehicle forward on its single axle and tipped the shafts upwards. We then pushed Mascot back a couple of yards, lowered the shafts, complete with back band on to the cast saddle.

We already had Mascot fully harnessed in cart gears and so the rest was easy. We coupled the shoulder chains, then the back chains (called breeching chains) and then fitted the belly band. So far so good.

I then took the coiled reins down from the nearside harness and let them out. 'Right Graz,' I said softly, 'lead him on and I will drive from the side of the vehicle for now.' Off we went. Mascot surged forward just a little bit as he felt the collar against his shoulders, but that was all. After a few yards I was in the driving seat and after a couple of turns, Graz joined me. Mascot had proved himself once again. This was one of the most rewarding of all my experiences with horses. A real D.I.Y. job. Not only had I bred, reared and trained the horse (with help from Graz of course) but I had successfully built the vehicle, put the two together and driven it. Much more was to come. As a life and almost lifelong member of the Shire Horse Society, I had attended several annual spring shows at Peterborough showground.

A gem of an idea again entered my head. I wonder if we could manage to show our stallion in harness at this show – and at the same time show him in hand in a separate class? He did already have a premium award. Again, Graz was enthusiastic. 'He'll do it all right, let's go for it.'

The obvious choice for a vehicle was the Dales Waggon made by J. Harrison & Sons, Grosmont, North Yorkshire. It was owned originally by Mr R. M. Pearson, Egton and its size and construction faithfully recorded in a book written by Marie Hartley and Joan Ingilbey. It was first published in 1972 and is called Life in the Moorlands of North-East Yorkshire.

I acquired it in the late seventies and undertook a complete restoration. The design features are a credit to the makers and it is indeed a lasting example of village craftsmanship.

To get Mascot used to the sound of it, I towed it behind him with the Landrover, while Graz drove him forward. This is important because with blinkers on, a horse cannot see behind. The sound waggon wheels make is very special, it is called knapping. It is a sort of knocking sound and when a good, well made waggon was halted, the wheels were supposed to knap three times. A waggon in motion made a sound somewhere between a rumble and a trundle, but they ran remarkably freely on almost any surface.

The wheels themselves were all wood of course, with an iron hoop which served as a tyre. The hub or nave was made of Elm, the spokes were of straight grained Oak and the rim sections or fellos, were made of Ash.

Mascot took it in his stride and soon he was pulling it around easily. 'What we need now is crowd experience,' I told Graz. It was a joke really because crowds are hard to come by in a village with a population of only two hundred. We had an inspiration – the Boxing Day Hunt – they attract a lot of people – even a few coachloads. It was brilliant really because a Shire stallion in his striped roller and side reins, feather shampooed and coat gleaming was a wonderful sight. The spectators loved it and so did he, in fact even the sound of the hunting horn only caused him to prick his ears.

Another good example of natural horsemanship. It is all about treating a stallion as just another horse. How many of them, I wonder, could be trusted to live out all the time. Not just that, but surrounded in other fields by grazing mares?

The Amish people I know in the Holmes County, Ohio, U.S.A. treat their stallions in a similar manner and actually work them side by side with the mares

It is pretty obvious that I could write about him for a long time and still not tell his, now twenty year, life story.

He featured in a T.V. documentary when I drove him down to Robin Hoods Bay. It was a local environmental pressure group, who wanted to highlight the folly of long sewage outfalls into the North Sea.

I was the undertaker and we were to be seen picking up mock coffins from a rocky seashore only accessible at low tide. It meant driving Mascot down the slopeway where the fishing boats are launched. He wasn't too keen to go down.

After a bit of persuasion he started to edge his way down the slippery cobbles. At this point he must have felt the breeching tighten round his quarters, as the waggon pushed into him. Without warning, he just sat down. Over the years I have heard many stories about such things happening but this was my first experience – and at first hand.

I got down from the box seat and went round to his head. He seemed to be looking up at me from the top of his blinkers, it said everything. 'What on earth are we doing down here anyway – its supposed to be for launching boats isn't it?' I soon persuaded him back up and he played the part superbly. Oh yes, we got him to the Shire Horse Society Spring Show and he revelled in it, even stopping to pose each time he saw a camera.

He also did a wonderful T.V. piece with a Victorian sledge I restored – and without snow. It was really funny because the cameraman asked if he could go faster, and Mascot took off into a gallop.

It was a lovely piece and we had the sledge all decorated for Christmas. To the strains of 'God Rest Ye Merry Gentlemen' Mascot even seemed to be in time with the music.

It faded out just as Mascot had got into top gear, and Fred Ulliott, whom I have mentioned before asked me, after he had seen it on T.V., 'did that 'oss get away from you?'

I even wrote a fictitious song about Mascot called the 'Staintondale Stallion', a tribute to how clever my horses are, and what I think they may be capable of. Enjoy it.

THE STAINTONDALE STALLION

I once bred a Stallion way down in the valley
His nostrils were wide and his head he held high
His action was lively, his manner good natured
His coat shone and gleamed like the stars in the sky

This Staintondale Stallion
A horse big and bold
He warned of the fire
And saved his young foals

A Stallion endowed with instinct and senses
His wit was as keen as his eyes in the night
I broke him to saddle, to rope and jump fences
A mustang and a Cowboy and his dream of delight

Chorus
One night I awoke to the sound of his calling
A smell filled the air and I knew it was fire
I ran to the barn where the timbers were falling
A baulk jammed the door, young foals were in there

Chorus
It was then that I sensed the horse stood beside me
The Stallion had jumped the gate from his field
A rope quickly gathered was tied to the debris
And a pull from the horse soon had the foals free

Chorus (with feeling)

269

'Our Mascot'

CHAPTER FORTY EIGHT
Horse Power

Just how do we define Horse Power? if we are talking about the power of horses i.e. quite apart from their physical strength, I think my personal definition would be 'Power without aggression, presence without vanity.'

No story would be complete without a touch of sadness or even a touch of trauma. Inevitably they are both hard to come to terms with, but these experiences do tend to make us stronger and sometimes even more determined. The most traumatic period of my life was undoubtedly the threat of enforced closure by the establishment. In my case a planning authority. At the end of the day, as a small family enterprise, the only weapons you have against the almighty power of bureaucracy, are public support and the news media.

How to harness the power of the people as it were, and harness should probably be in inverted commas, is not within everybody's reach, but it was in mine.

I had two wonderful horses called Nobby and Princess and they were a very impressive and much loved pair of Shire Horses.

In 1984 they ploughed at the 31st World Ploughing contest at Horncastle in Lincolnshire. What a feast to the eye that was. Something like 32 pairs of horses strung out across what seemed like a prairie to me, heads down, shoulders deep in the collar and harness and brasses gleaming. It seemed that out of this enormous field, my pair had caught the eye of a certain photographer. He had been specially commissioned by the National Westminster Bank to take photographs of the horses ploughing.

He must have been excellent at his job and particularly unobtrusive, because I wasn't even aware of his presence.

Just before Christmas of that same year, I got a telephone call from the local branch of Nat West at Scarborough. The manager had said that he would like me to go down, and that he was going to present me with something. What could it be? Well it was unlikely that it was going to be a cheque, even though banks usually have money.

I was called into his office and given a friendly welcome. 'Mr Jenkins,' he said, 'we have had some wonderful photographs taken at the ploughing contest and it seems, two of the horses ploughing belonged to you!' I nodded, 'Yes, Princess and Nobby.' He then opened a folder on his desk and took out two splendid full plate photographs. 'It is our pleasure to present you with these, those horses looked magnificent, and they are a credit to you.' What could I say? I was completely taken aback and proud wasn't the word, I was elated. Princess, our own gentle and impeccably mannered lady and her son Nobby, who I had bred myself, had deservedly made their mark.I really was overwhelmed – but they were my proudest possession after all!

Horsepower has been demonstrated in many ways, and throughout history has become a proven fact. We have to look no further than the Battle of Hastings which took place on Saturday 14 October 1066.

A battle most of us remember from school days but really know little about the way victory came about. Both were professional feudal armies, one led by Harold, King of England, and the invaders,the Normans, were led by Duke William of Normandy. The main difference between the two armies was that the English army was comprised mainly of foot soldiers, while many of the Normans were mounted. This is clearly illustrated by the Bayeux Tapestries and also well recorded by Norman chronicles.

It was a battle hard fought over a long day, but through a clever ploy by the Normans and the sheer superiority of their cavalry and bowmen, they earned a well deserved victory. The English had no answer to the appearance of what was to become the great war horse.

It would be impossible to include all the stories relevant to horses, and especially in warfare, where they have excelled. One particular culture though, does spring to mind and I found it to be awesome – the Mongol Lordes of Genghis Khan. They struck fear, dread and wreaked terrible destruction across Asia and Eastern Europe in the early 13th Century.

Less than 100 years later, the last of these Mongol nomads under one of Genghis Khan's decendants, Tamurlane, set off to conquer the world. The death and destruction he left behind as he drove across Asia and threatened the Turkish empire, is mind boggling. At a place called Isphan in what was then Persia, Tamurlane's Tartars left behind them a pyramid of seventy thousand human skulls. Their conquests were only made possible by their brilliant and accomplished horsemanship.

Daily orders by Tamurlane, under threat of being severely beaten and put under arrest if disobeyed, included taking great care of their horses, not tying anything to the back of their saddles, and what I found particularly fascinating, was that they should ride bridleless on the march in order to rest the horses' mouths. Was this fourteenth century natural horsemanship? Failure to obey these rules by lesser mortals could result in death to the offender – they could be beheaded! The next time you are pulling on the bit and restricting a horse's natural movement –think on these things.

These impressive and awe inspiring armies could cover 80 miles in a day. Just try to imagine the largest army Genghis Khan ever put together, on the move – 230,000 mounted men.

Europe was nearly lost on account of these terrible, yet incredible people and their horses, and no other cavalry in recorded history have been so devastatingly effective.

I want to move on now to one of my favourite cultures, that of the Plains Indian.

One of the most moving books that I have ever read must be Dee Brown's 'Bury My Heart at Wounded Knee', an Indian History of the American West. I found it disturbing that greed, deceit and broken promises could practically wipe out a whole native population. The Indians were possibly the first true conservationalists, who respected the earth, the trees, the rivers and the mountains. They could not understand why the intruders seemed to want to destroy these things, and exploit natural resources. This book is about horses, and without horses the Indians would never have become the formidable fighting force that held out so long against the white man's intrusion. It seems likely that the vast herds of wild horses which spread over a region west of the Mississippi were introduced by Spanish explorers around the middle of the Sixteenth Century. They were either lost or abandoned in relatively small numbers, but in finding a natural environment that obviously suited them, they thrived and bred in considerable numbers.

To the Indian they were everything. They traded them, sold them, bought wives with them and they became a symbol of their personal wealth and status. They were recognised horse thieves as well, and in this their stealth and handling ability is well documented. By the end of the Eighteenth Century all the various tribes of the Plains Indians were mounted.

My favourite tribe must be the Comanches, who have been described as being amongst the world's most expert horsemen. It was their ability to lay their entire body alongside that of the horse, and hanging by their heel, could fire a bow and arrow under the horse's neck. They could do this with incredible accuracy and speed, and discharge arrows at such a rate as to have two arrows in the air at the same time.

The power of these small bows was equally amazing and it is said that such was the force of delivery, they could drive the shaft of the arrow right through the body of a buffalo.

From the experiences of 'moving' books I want to record a very moving experience with an account of something more relevant to this area of Yorkshire. In 1912 Sir Mark Sykes formed a horse transport unit called the 'Waggoners Reserve'. It was commandeered by the army soon after war was declared on August 4th 1914.

It was my privilege to meet one of the last surviving members of this unit who fought in the great world war. 'They were farm lads,' he told me, 'they were recruited because they were used to handling and working horses. I don't think that they had any idea of what they were letting themselves in for, it was terrible.' His voice trembled a little as he recalled the horror of war, but he went on, 'These lads saw horses blown to pieces as they drove them forward, the horse having no idea of what he was being asked to do. The lads knew though, and I have heard many of them crying themselves to sleep – it broke their hearts.'

It is a memory full of such stories that persuaded me to write my Millennium song, 'Bertie Boy.' How many war memories do we see erected in memory of fallen horses? How many miles of space would it take up. After defeating the Aztecs in Mexico in 1519 he said 'Next to God we owed the victory to the horses.' Hernan Cortes (1485-1547).

To conclude this chapter I think a story or two of sheer physical power should be recorded. One such story was possibly the largest load ever pulled by a pair of Shire horses. In Michigan U.S.A. in 1893 they pulled a load of massive Redwood tree sections weighing 125 ton. It was done on a level icy road and the horses pulled the sledge over a quarter of a mile. The massive load, the size of a house, and the two horses looking almost like a pair of ants. Throughout the Nineteenth

Century it was fairly common practice to move huge post-mill carcasses – windmills. Imagine this scene today, a gigantic task in those days with anything from 20 to 40 horses pulling a windmill along a country lane. We are not talking about a few hundred yards either, distances varied but 10 miles was not unusual.

This is horse power at its best and without horses and the overwhelming love and fascination for them, by so many people, you would not be reading this book.

'Nobby and Princess of Staintondale.'

CHAPTER FORTY NINE
Shetland Ponies

Described as the smallest and strongest equine in the world, Shetland ponies are exceptional creatures. Their hardiness and willingness to work made them indispensable in many areas of industry. In the 18th Century the coalmines of Scotland probably became the first to recognise how extraordinarily strong these ponies were for their size. After that they were used extensively all over the U.K. and out crossed with other native ponies and even horses. It really did put the Shetland on the map. They influenced the pit pony and came in all sizes and all colours. Their native natural environment had given them good strong bone and feet and their ability to do well on very poor quality feed is legendary. It is said that they actually lived on dried seaweed in the wintertime on the Shetland Isles. On lush lowland pastures they are inclined to get fat and of course the risk of Laminitis is very high. This is inflammation within the confines of a horse's hoof and is extremely painful. It can even be fatal.

One of our Veterinary surgeons remarked some time ago that the best pasture for a Shetland pony was six square feet of concrete. Having said all that, and contrary to some voices of opinion, they can be extremely well behaved and responsive. They seem to have a natural willingness to work and are very easy to train. I am of the firm opinion that their naturally affectionate nature can be spoilt at an early age, by people using unkind methods to dominate them, simply because they are small.

In fact to go even further, this is probably the root cause of so many horses behavioural problems, as so many of us are aware. A new vogue is at last sweeping the horse fraternity, it is being called new but nothing is further from the truth.

The simple fact is that there has been such a lot of ignorance involved in the understanding of horses - or the lack of it, these newly acclaimed and so called horse whisperers have managed to capitalise on something that has been around for thousands of years. A horse wants to be your friend but most of the time people send the wrong signals - try encouraging horses to come to you rather than you going to them. I will explain more about this later. At this time we have eight Shetland ponies, the oldest one is Nancy, of indeterminable age. We think she must be approaching forty. We bought her in 1985 with a black foal at foot we called Pepsi. They were an unprecedented success with visitors and more Shetlands followed.

The next to arrive were a driving pair called Bonnie and Clyde - a lovely matched pair of Chestnuts. Bonnie has a striking flaxen mane and tail and Clyde a somewhat darker colour.

Buying these two and actually trying them out before final purchase was a rewarding experience. They were at a village called Hunmanby which is several miles down the coast from where we live. The lady who owned them used them for competition work and did very well with them. I have to say that they were extremely fit and were exercised six miles each day.

She explained about the harness which was completely new to me. I was used to collars round horses'necks, but this was breast plate harness round the horse's chest. It looked a very complicated collection of straps and buckles. I need not have worried because once fitted it all became very simple.

The ponies really impressed me as she fitted the harness. They stood stock still side by side until all the harness was in place. She then crossed the traces on to their backs and I helped her draw up the four wheeled buggy until the coupling pole was lying between them. A quick connecting of the pole straps and traces and we were ready.

'Would you like to drive she asked?' Quite taken aback, I questioned her confidence in me. 'Oh you'll be all right, I am sure if you can drive a pair of Shires you will handle these O.K.'We climbed on to the box seat, it was a real experience behind two such small ponies. 'We will drive into Hunmanby and through the village, they are very good in traffic and at traffic lights'. she told me.

Off we went and at a brisk trot. The ponies fitness came across and I was amazed at the power. They hardly seemed to notice that they were pulling a vehicle and two adults. The owner was explaining, 'Oh they can easily take four adults and you should see them on cross country - these ponies can gallop through water and even swim.

Nothing stops them, they are fearless.' I was very impressed. As we came into the centre of Hunmanby we approached the traffic lights. I must admit that I was a little apprehensive but I need not have worried. The lights were at red, 'Whoa, steady', I said softly as I gently made contact with their mouths. They came to a halt. 'Stand still - good lad Clyde - good girl Bonnie.' They were wonderful. When the lights changed I asked them on and we made a neat turn to the right. There were cars, buses and people all around us but they were unperturbed. Cars gave way to us and people smiled and nodded. What a lovely sight it made and in today's world, something of a rarity.

We trotted back in splendid style, the steady clip of metal shoes ringing out and an occasional snort from one or other of two happy ponies. Needless to say I became the new proud owner of a complete Shetland pony turnout.

Now there were four ponies at the farm but as visitor numbers grew and more children fell in love with them, I decided to increase the number and perhaps buy a mare and a foal?

The opportunity came in the shape of a Falabella cross mare with a foal at foot - and in foal again to a Falabella stallion. These ponies are smaller than Shetlands and named after the family who first bred them. They originate from Argentina.

The pony we bought was called Nancy, but we changed it to Cilla because we already had a Nancy. She is lovely and became the smallest of our growing happy band. The foal she had at foot we called Candy - a lovely red and white piebald - also very pretty and affectionate.

There was more to come. The following Spring, Cilla gave birth to another foal - and it came unannounced and took us all by surprise. It had been a particularly cold day for the time of year and May is supposed to be the month of flowers. Cilla, the pony had been hugging the area around the admission kiosk all day. We knew she was due to foal eventually, but had no specific date. It was very gloomy and starting to drizzle by late afternoon, and from the farmyard I could see that Cilla was lying down - it just made me a bit curious. Was she thinking about foaling? Anyway I couldn't settle so I decided to give her a few minutes and if she hadn't got up I was going to walk down to her.

In less than that time Cilla was up and I could just make out that she was busy with something close to her head. I ran down the farm track and across the field to where she was standing. It wasn't really a surprise, but the almost desperate situation Cilla seemed to be trying to overcome, was certainly going to be a problem for her.

She had given birth to a tiny little foal which was still very wet and partially wrapped in the placenta. It was raining quite hard by this time and Cilla was fighting a losing battle trying to clean the foal up with her tongue. The foal was visibly shivering but that reaction was quite normal. Normal or not, I grabbed the foal, tucked it under my arm and took hold of Cilla by the fetlock - 'come on'I said, 'let's find you a nice warm stable and get your baby clean and dry.'

At that moment Wendy appeared - she helps Ann manage the shop and cafe.'Let me help', she said, 'it's awful for them out here,' Between us we got them into a stable and Wendy started to clean up the foal with straw. This was the birth of Pinto, who actually appeared on television as he was so tiny at birth. We hadn't even named him but the Tyne Tees television reporter had asked me what we were going to call him. Looking at his amazing markings I immediately replied Pinto - a striking example of the colour of the American Paint horse favoured by the Indians.

We now had seven ponies.

The year after that we were loaned a cheeky Shetland stallion called Rusty. He really was a super character and we had him for the whole of that summer. Our visitors loved him - well so did Cilla I think, because the following Spring she produced another beautiful filly foal. This time it was a nice sunny day with no problems - well a filly born in May - we just had to call her Milly.

So now we are eight.

Pinto is still a star, I think T.V. made him that way. With his cowboy saddle and fancy bridle with long western reins, he really does look the part.

Anybody for a photograph?

'The Author driving Bonnie and Clyde.'

280

CHAPTER FIFTY
Birthdays

You are never going to get closer to a horse than you do when you actually help to deliver it at birth. It is not surprising therefore that I often refer to my horses as being like children - and especially to me.

I have tried to be present when most of our horses and ponies have foaled. Over a period of thirty years I have forgotten just how many births I have attended.

Usually a foaling is a very smooth and uncomplicated affair and the mare can handle it. It is only when a problem occurs that help is needed - and that help is needed urgently. Once the foaling process has started it is very much an ongoing situation. Any restriction by whatever cause, can be a serious threat to the mare and equally to the foal. That is why you need to be present if at all possible. The next two accounts will illustrate exactly what I mean and why horses are so dependent on their keepers.

One of the most dramatic, occurred in the area that we now reserve for the Shetland ponies - at the top of what we now call the car park. At that time it was just a field.

Carmen was going to foal as soon as she thought practical. This was usually in the very early hours when all was quiet and still. Knowing her as I did, I didn't expect to have long to wait. At midnight she had seemed calm and comfortable - a lady in waiting. I decided to have a couple of hours in a chair and go out about 2 am.

These foals are usually born in May and the nights are usually bright and sometimes frosty. This one was no exception. A particularly bright and moonlit night greeted me as I walked out through the back door. When I got to the gate into the field I looked up towards the top where I had last seen Carmen. It is usual for mares to choose an elevated position to foal, because as prey animals, they are always on the look out for predators.

The scene that met my eyes was quite disturbing and made worse by the early hour of the morning. It did look, to say the least, a bit eerie. A long white, boney object seemed to be protruding from Carmen's rear end, and in the pale moonlight seemed to signal something ominous and serious.

I ran up the field as fast as I could and took in the scene at close quarters. It was a foal's foreleg sticking out with no sign of a head or anything else. Carmen was in excruciating pain. Sweat was running from every part of her body and literally dripping from her underside. She was walking round in a small circle, and the abundance of sweat from her body had already paddled up this circle into mud. I can't describe my reaction to all this because I was dumbstruck.

At that time our Vet lived 40 miles away and this was 2 am in the morning. I realised the timescale of getting help would be futile. Carmen on the other hand thought help was on hand. Before I had time to even think about my next move she dropped down, rolled onto her side and started to push. The pain was obvious, she was groaning and moaning with the sheer effort. I thought back to my many textbooks and the only silly comparison, seemed to be a badly presented lamb at lambing time.

Well the situation was the same - just a size difference. This was a fully fledged Shire mare weighing over a ton. No time for thought even, as I applied theory to practice. Try to push back the protruding limb to release the pressure, at the same time insert a hand and try to locate the head or the other limb.

To this day I cannot believe how lucky I was. My hand had located the forefoot and I was gently easing it into position. As soon as this foot found its opening a second foreleg started to emerge. Carmen did the rest. As she pushed, this foreleg seemed to unfold itself and at the same time, the head which was apparently tucked inside the bend in the forearm appeared. Another push and the foal was ejected in a flurry. Carmen responded with a sigh you usually associate with a deflated balloon. As I had done before, although not quite in such dramatic circumstances, I pulled the foal's head round to its mum's. Carmen was in need of a rest but she needed to see her foal. I walked back down the field. It was going to be a lovely dawn and a lovely day.

These are fairy tale endings but this one didn't even end there. Where Carmen had paddled up the ground in a very obvious circle, the grass had got severely damaged if not destroyed. At a later date a fairy ring appeared on the site of this circle. Do you believe in magic?

These are not isolated stories and it would take a much bigger book to relate them all. The next one is again about Carmen, and I think it really does illustrate the amazing power of communication that develops between a horse and its keeper.

On this occasion, Carmen's foal had not appeared to be particularly imminent, but there again nature ultimately decides that. We had at the time, a caravan in a small paddock which is now the play and picnic area We used to let it to families for a one or two week stay. Obviously we got friendly and sometimes I would walk down there in the evening for a chat. This was before we opened up the farm as a visitor attraction.

On the way past the field shelter at the edge of our car park, I heard Carmen call out to me. I must enlarge on this and tell you that it was a very foggy and frosty night. The ground was dry and as hard as bell metal.

'Strange', I thought, 'I wonder what she wants?'

Anyway I decided that if she hadn't moved when I returned, I would go and investigate. An hour or so later I went to see, and Carmen was still stood by the small gate. We always have a foaling box ready at foaling time, and I decided there was no harm in taking Carmen up and keeping her in for the night. It was very cold. I got a head collar and led her into the box. It was deep in straw and was banked round the sides. As the next few moments unfolded I was just the spectator. Carmen got straight down in the deep straw and started to roll vigorously. I just sat on the edge of the glazed water trough and watched.

She really did go at it, and my immediate concern was of her getting cast - that is with her legs up the side of the wall, so that she couldn't get up. After what seemed to be quite some time, she got up and gave herself a good shake. 'What could this mean?' It didn't take long for me to find out. After a few minutes she got down again, but this time I could see the familiar stretching of the neck. She was going to foal! I was spellbound, as I watched the whole sequence unfold. It suddenly occurred to me, what the rolling was all about. The foal seemingly had been badly presented or positioned for foaling and Carmen had to correct this. The ground in the field was hard and cold and she knew it. She had called out for help and thankfully I had been around to respond.

The only thing horses cannot do is to speak our language - but we can learn to understand theirs.

This next one is another real and true story and can be verified. Any lesson to be learned must be, that nature can never be tied down nor underestimated.

The year was 1986 and for some reason Carmen hadn't foaled that year, so 1 decided to keep an eye on developments after her first service towards the end of April. The oestrus cycle is three weeks in horses. That means they have a heat period every 21 days usually from about early May until the Autumn. At twenty one days Carmen was showing quite clearly that the service hadn't held. We served her again every other day until the heat period ended - or so we thought. A week later the oestrus indications had returned. All was not well. I decided to call in our Veterinary Surgeon. It was now almost into June.

After making an internal inspection by a method known as rectal palpation, our vet found the problem. 'Cysts,' he explained. 'There is no way she's going to hold a service until we get rid of them.'

He gave Carmen a thorough cleansing and after giving her an injection said he would return in a week or two and examine her again. In fact he made several visits but the offending problem did not show any signs of clearing up. By July, the visits and treatment were becoming expensive and the time for serving mares getting less favourable. Foals need to be born ideally in May or early June. The gestation period is 350 days.

'The best thing to do, is to forget trying to get the mare in foal this year. Let old nature take its course and let's have a look at her early next spring. They may even have cleared up!' 'I shall take a blood sample on a routine basis and have it checked. It is pretty clear it will be negative but just in case.' He left with the comment, 'I shall be in touch in a few days.'

Sure enough I got a phone call. 'Right,' he said, 'blood sample negative so here is what to do. Make a note on your calendar to contact me really early in the new year - March even. We can then make a good start by giving her a jab to induce oestrus - assuming all is well. Or we continue treatment and get the problem cleared up.'

There is another line in another song that always intrigues me.' Time goes by so slowly,' I have never found this to be the case have you? Time here flies by and it seemed to be March almost by the end of that week.

'A foal arrived in the spring'

I rang up the Surgery and within a couple of days the Vet came down. We had Carmen in the centre horse stall in the stables, warm water, bucket and towel to hand. This type of inspection had become almost routine. It is also used to determine whether or not a mare is in foal. This was not the case today and I was at the mare's head end leaning against the wall. I was talking to Carmen. stroking her head and day dreaming, all at the same time.

'You are going to be a Dad.'

His words although audible had not penetrated my thoughts. nor did I respond. He tried again, 'Did you hear what I said? You are going to be a Dad!' I heard all right, but couldn't believe my ears. 'I can't believe it, not after all that treatment and what about the blood test?' My tone was a mixture of incredulity and disbelief.

'There's going to be a lot of explaining,' I said grinning. 'For one thing I did not record the service in Mascot's service book so I shall have to contact the Shire Horse Society.' Veterinary inspections, blood samples, negative responses and now a foal!

We decided it had to be a gift horse.

The Shire Society were very good about the late notification and soon had the records put straight. Mascot, well, he had to fit into the picture somewhere, but I did toy with the idea of changing his name to 'Phantom'.

In due course Carmen produced the foal, and a lovely black filly arrived in May. This really was a bonus. We had bred fillies before from Carmen but they had all been sold. When it began to look as if she wasn't going to foal again I was seriously regretting not keeping one.

This was a real gift and a really nice well marked animal she proved to be. Since quite a few of our fillies have been born in May we have tried to give them May names. May Blossom, May Queen, etc., etc. What shall we call this one. After much thought we had it - 'May Belle', the Belle of them all. We would call her Bella for short.

Such was the wonderful temperament of this filly (she takes after her father and grandmother Princess in this respect) at only two years old and having had no attempt either to mouth her or fit a roller, one of the staff called Hilary, just quietly climbed on the wall and slid over on to her back!

It happened one afternoon when the horses were being taken back to the fields after an open day. Four girls wanting to ride and only three of the horses previously ridden. They had looked at Bella standing seventeen hands at only two years. 'Wonder what she'd be like to ride.' said one.

'Soon find out,' said Hil, 'Just push her over to that wall.'The move was made, Hilary was on her back and with the aid of the head collar and two shanks she was ridden away with the others.

Many, many times I refer to temperament and trust. Many, many times I am equally rewarded with situations like the one I have just described.

Trust is the keyword to a good relationship with horses, but it has to be mutual!

CHAPTER FIFTY ONE
Texas Adventures

'Pursuing the lives of my high riding heroes', I quote from a song that seems to sum up some of my ambitions. It never occurred to me when I was day dreaming about all these things as a young boy, that they actually would become reality. I have mentioned Roy Rogers and the comic 'Radio Fun', that I read in my childhood. Little did I realise that over 60 years later I would be standing on Hollywood Boulevard, Los Angeles, looking down on Roy Roger's footprint. Not just his footprints but his horse Trigger's hoofprints and a print of Roy Roger's Colt 45 Peacemaker, all set in concrete in 1948. We were enroute for the holiday of a lifetime and heading for San Antonio and later Bandera, Texas. The first stop was San Antonio, where I wanted to visit the Alamo museum and get a real taste of Western culture.

This in itself was an experience because San Antonio was in festival mood. It was the first fiesta of the twenty first century and what a colourful and head turning feast unfolded before us. 'They are celebrating Texas independence' the taxi driver told us ruefully 'We don't have much to celebrate though, they robbed us of our land!' He was grinning as he said it and he was very obviously a Mexican.

The Alamo itself was awesome. We explored the incredibly well restored fort and stockade, with more than a passing interest. This was for real, and the artifacts on display brought it all to life.

The Comanche and Apache Indians played their parts too, and the whole scene was of white settlers, waggon trains and Texas rangers. A schooldays dream, usually played out at the cinema, but the struggle to survive and the hardship endured along these trails was an ordeal in itself. Nothing like the glamour on the screen. They called the Colt 45 (produced in or around 1886) the 'Peacemaker'. It became a legend as fast draw cowboys became a magnet for young Cowhands to prove their prowess with a sixgun. Anyway suffice to say that Roy Rogers had one, and so did a host of other silver screen heroes, and with their white stetson hats, (the good guys always had white hats), played a very impressive role.

Next stop a Dude Ranch at Bandera - 40 miles or so out of San Antonio and located on one of the oldest waggon trails in the West. We were going to live the lives of modern day Cowboys, eat biscuits and beans and ride some of the Ranch's 60 or so horses. Oh, I almost forgot to mention the occasional Texas T. bone steak.

Ann (my wife) does not ride and although we have kept horses for well over 30 years she has only been on a horse twice in all that time. Keep this in mind, because she had said that she was determined to ride during her stay at the ranch. I had serious doubts in this direction, but as our daughters have often commented - she is quietly determined.

We arrived at the Ranch in air conditioned comfort, driven by Nancy, a daughter in law of Don and Judy Hicks, who owned the ranch. This was far removed from the trail riders who had to wear long sleeved shirts with buttoned cuffs, not to mention bandana's over their noses to keep Texas dust from body and soul. We were to experience that later.

Since this book is intended to be mainly about horses, I think we should head for the Corral and find ourselves a mount. The wrangler explains all . 'These horses are western trained and very light on the mouth. To turn, you simply lay the rein across the neck on the left to go left, and the same to the right to go right. To stop you say Whoa, and take up the rein and let go again. If you pull on the rein the horse will go backwards! Ride forward on a loose rein at all times'.

It was hot and dusty as we set off in single file of around 30 horses. Once in the trees it was shady and cool and we found ourselves tracking a river bank. It really was a dream and we chatted and laughed as we rode. We rode into the cool flowing water, it was almost up to our stirrups. It wasn't just a crossing point, we were to ride so far up the river and pick up the trail again. Most of the horses had left the water with just a few riders bringing up the rear. The wrangler was shouting to someone behind me - 'don't pull on the reins Ma'am - don't pull on the reins, just lift his head'. I turned and looked back - who should be stuck in deep water sitting on a horse quenching his thirst - you have guessed it - Ann in solitary splendour.

'But she doesn't ride' I said, 'she really has no idea what to do ....' This laid back Texan just kept talking 'lift his head, make him walk on'. At last this well schooled pony decided he had drunk enough and walked on to join us. I should mention that I was impressed - there was absolutely no panic - and that was only the horse.

It is sixteen years since I brought a secondhand cowboy saddle back from Newark, Ohio. On this trip I had taken the same saddle bag I carried it home in, back with me. I was hoping to find something really special for Burtie Boy, so I had taken it 'just in case'. I had wandered into one such saddle shop in Bandera - a town that had all the hallmarks of a dusty cow town of byegone years. I was told on good authority that they even had shoot outs up until the 1960s. The saddlers name was Lew - 'you really do want to buy a saddle?' he had enquired. 'Well I do, but I would like some advice on size and fit. They are very different from English saddles'. 'Well' he drawled, 'size is what you find comfortable and fit is for the horse. The bars of the saddle must be right for him'. He went on 'It doesn't follow that say a 16" saddle would be anymore comfortable than even a 14". It would depend on the maker'. He walked round the shop and picked up a saddle from the rack, 'Now take this old Cook saddle - it's only small but I could ride comfortably in that'. He dropped the saddle on the fitting horse 'Just sit on that'. For some of this session a local Cowboy had stood patiently waiting to have a word with Lew, I thought he must be a friend, since the saddle testing and conversation looked like going on for some time, he finally gave up waiting. He just said 'Catch you later Lew' and left.

Eventually I left the shop too, but I had arranged with Lew to call in again on the Monday, (this was Saturday) to try a saddle belonging to a friend of his that had one to sell. At around 11 am on the Monday, I am again seated on the saddle horse trying out the saddle. In walked the local Cowboy - he took one look at me, grinned and said simply, 'Aint you gone home yet?'

Now for some real luck, or are these things meant to be? On the last day of our holiday I still hadn't found a saddle that I really wanted. It had to be something really special for a really special horse.

One thing I did need to bring back was a good pair of foot nippers. I had been told I should try the Bandera Ranch store. Len and Freda our newly acquainted friends had taken us round there. As we walked in the door there it was - the saddle - I almost rubbed my eyes. It was already on a saddle horse so all I had to do was sit on it, and I lost no time in doing that. It was made to measure and I just seemed to pour into it. Comfort wasn't in it, it was pure luxury. I got off and looked it over - silver everywhere. Skirt corner plates, conchos large and small, plates on the cantle and even on the stirrups. It even had a silver topped saddle horn. Would it fit? I took it off the stand and turned it over, it looked just right. What a find - and the price was a steal. It had been used but only just, it was like new. The shop lady spoke 'That Cowboy said that saddle was just too darned pretty for roping steers'.

It was indeed a very special saddle and had obviously been presented as a star prize or trophy at a roping event in 1994. This date was mounted in gilt over the silver corner plates. The ranch store were selling it on behalf of the owner who had decided to cash it in. I joked with the store staff as I left - 'If this saddle doesn't fit my horse - then he's just going to have to slim'.

'The Saddle.'

CHAPTER FIFTY TWO
Bits and Headpieces

One of the most compelling and informative books that I have ever read is 'Horses, their role in the history of man' by Elwyn Hartley Edwards. It was based on a Channel 4 television series.

It was fascinating because of the way horses have been trained throughout history and how these methods are still practiced. A combination of brutality and kindness, which seems to recur time and time again.

It is often referred to as the carrot and stick method, but all too often the stick, together with total dominance prevails. and we read little about kindness. In later years the English were recognised as horse lovers, but in competition some of that seems to have gone out of the window. All too often we see the flailing of a stick.

It is not only the stick that can cause discomfort, and here I must consider the use of bits.

Over 2000 years ago Xenophon, a Greek general, was writing books on cavalry management and horsemanship. Even today his works and teaching are well respected. Although quiet handling and asking for cooperation from the horse was advocated, he was well aware of the horse's attitude to pain. To this end, special bits were made that could be either severe or possibly acceptable to the horse, which was 'rewarded' by the use of a mild bit once it was yielding to the hands. Xenophon was also aware of the pleasure shared by horse and rider when lightness to the hand became evident.

He was also conversant with what we now call a cavesson - a noseband made of metal, which he knew as a psalion.

It really is amazing that in over 2000 years little has changed. We still have some dreadful examples of bits and even more dreadful accounts of the way they are used. Even the noseband, which is still favoured by many as the kindest of all methods to control a horse, has been used as a weapon of torture. In some cases spikes were fitted to the inside, so that any contact with the horse's nose would be a very painful one.

An Italian nobleman by the name of Frederico Grisone was advocating in 1550 that horses should more or less be beaten into submission. He used a selection of cruel bits, some of which he designed himself. His cures for bad behaviour were anything from a footman attacking the horse from behind when it refused to go forward, to lighting a bundle of straw under its tail. He had many other 'cures', and yet insisted throughout on achieving a light responsive mouth!

Curiously enough, the straw burning technique lasted well into the twentieth century, and many waggoners have told me a tale of a horse in the shafts of a loaded cart refusing to move. Their cure - 'We used ter chuck some straw down, right behind it and light it. It soon moved.'

It is interesting to read about the development of movement, both of the horse and the rider, and what we now regard as the classical seat. Accepted by some and rejected by others.

It certainly does not make for better horsemanship, and if we look back again at the Comanche Indians, they were indeed natural horsemen and were at one with the horse.

Their reins were nothing more than a length of rope which passed over the horse's head and through its mouth. It was then wrapped round its bottom jaw and the rest of the rope formed the reins. Simple and so effective. It wasn't the equipment that made these ponies so incredibly manouvreable, it was the rider and the use of their legs. We in the western equestrian world call it natural horsemanship, and the Indians were possibly the first exponents of it.

For example, the use of a jaquima (a simple hand tied rope halter), is possibly far more effective than a bridle and bit. I have read this was really the original hackamore, but the Texas cowboys were not too hot on Spanish and couldn't pronounce 'jaquima', so they called it a 'hackamore'.

The amount and variety of bits on the market is staggering and I agree here with Pat Parelli. He says, if you keep on trying to restrain a horse by subjecting it to even more pain by the use of severe bits, you eventually have to admit defeat and sell it. There hasn't been a bit made that can control a badly disciplined horse or compensate for poor handling ability on the part of the rider.

One lovely story I can relate with all honesty. Melvyn, an American friend of mine, was watching a young ploughboy working in a field with a pair of horses. He could see from a considerable distance that the horses were straining at the bit, and that the boy was having great difficulty holding them to a steady working pace. He had walked over to take a closer look and being a horseman himself, could see that the horses already had sore mouths. To Melvyn the problem was obvious, the horses were leaning on the bits and pushing forward to try and eleviate the pain. The action Melvyn took could be a lesson to many people. He asked the boy if he could make some adjustments, and then unbuckling the reins from the bit rings, he buckled them back on the headcollars under the bridle. 'Now try that,' he said. The boy clicked the horses on, and what a difference. It suddenly became pleasure and comfort all round, with a big grin from the boy and a happy snort from the horses. Melvyn was probably the happiest of all, he had done the horses the biggest favour.

Throughout history there has been great debate about dominance, high collection and discipline. It has been variously described as an art form, showing off both your horse and yourself, and in some cases, a necessary accomplishment. My own personal view is that any attempt to make a horse perform unnatural gaits, and by whatever means, cannot be acceptable. As I have already said, it is, and has been, a controversial subject. They say that beauty is in the eye of the beholder. Well, looking at this subject through the eye of the horse, we get a different picture.

Throughout my life with horses - and humans, I have found that eyes tell the truth. If a horse, for example, shows the whites of its eyes, it is either through fear or pain. All too often I have seen horses being put strictly 'through their paces', showing the whites of their eyes. I shall let you be the judge.

Early cavalry had a reputation for wild gallops, lack of control and disaster for the horses. It was not until Cromwell entered the scene in the seventeenth century that rigid discipline and giving horses first consideration, created regiments respected and renowned throughout the world.

Later, towards the end of the nineteenth century an Italian cavalry officer, Captain Federico Caprilli, introduced a system of natural riding. He discarded the high collection and exaggerated movement of the school horse and developed natural balance. The curb bit gave way to a snaffle and he insisted the rider conform with the horse's natural movement.

His system was introduced at many other cavalry schools, and the prancing airs and graces of the French courts became less of a priority. Natural horsemanship had arrived. The bit became an extension of the voice, and not interfering with the horse's natural movement, gave it more freedom.

The end of cavalry came about in the Second World War 1939-45. One terrible example must be the destruction of the 44th Mongolian Cavalry Division near Moscow in 1941. The German army were advancing with infantry and artillery and the Russians attacked with cavalry. They charged with all the force they could muster, sabres drawn and head to head. In minutes it was all over. The startled Germans opened fire and 2000 horses and riders were lying dead or dying. It seems there was not one German casualty.

What did I say about war memorials for horses?

CHAPTER FIFTY THREE
Burtie Boy

I had reached the milestone age and was about to enter what are called the golden years. It sounds better than pensioner or O.A.P., and anyway I was definitely not ready to use a bus pass even if I had one.

Over the years I have described breeding, rearing and training an assortment of equines from Shetland Ponies to Shire horses. It has given me a lot of pleasure. At the back of my mind though, the idea of owning something really personal and special has never been too far away. Well that idea was about to become a reality.

My present to me, to mark this auspicious occasion, was to be a real flight of fancy. Do you remember my references to Roy Rogers and Trigger? Well this was my opportunity - I would look for a big, bold golden Palomino. One with a flowing blonde mane and tail, if possible!

For the next six months I scoured the columns of horse magazines and regional newspapers - nothing. Quite a few Palominos, but all far too small. It seems that big horses of this particular colour are rare. One particular Saturday night in March 1998, we were all packed to go on holiday to Tunisia the following morning. Ann, as usual had collected our newspapers from the village shop. Saturday night was equine post night, in the 'Yorkshire Post'. My weekly treat. Well it seemed a bit futile but I couldn't resist glancing down the columns. It was a repeat performance of the day we found Dusty. There it was - my dream horse.

Of all the nights, and how frustrating and annoying! Well just bad luck I suppose and nothing I could do - or was there? A germ of an idea started to develop in my mind - Claire.

Claire had only been working for me for a short time but I saw her as a very capable authority when it came to horses. More than that, I respected her opinion and would stand by her decision. If I could contact her, there was a chance .....

I rang the number and enquired about the history and breeding of the horse. The young woman who had him to sell was forthcoming and sounded honest and genuine. He was homebred, had been well handled and corn feed from birth, he was fully vaccinated and had regular foot trims. His breeding was Irish Draught crossed to an Hanoverian stallion, he would make around 17 h/h. The dam was there to be seen - perfect! Putting the phone down, only to pick it straight up again, I dialled Claire's number. Please, please let it be answered, I was almost pleading. Very often it was an answerphone, and this was Saturday night. Relief, relief - a voice, it was Claire's mum, Lizi. I quickly explained my predicament and what I had in mind - was it a possibility? Lizi's response was typical and reassuring, 'Oh I'm sure Claire will go over for you and do whatever necessary, if you leave her a note at the farm, together with the deposit you have already agreed, she will do the rest and she won't let you down'.

Well I knew I could trust her, and it was an opportunity I could not miss. But what a cliff hanger!

I suppose I could have left a contact number for Claire to let me know the outcome of our arrangement, I chose not to. It was to be left in the hands of destiny. My father always maintained that it was the anticipation of owning something rather than the ability just to acquire it, that gave you the most pleasure. With that in mind, l went away on holiday with a feeling of anticipation and guarded optimism. It was like waiting for Christmas as a child.

This was one holiday that couldn't end too soon, and since the second week had turned quite cold, we were ready for home anyway.

Claire's voice was unmistakably positive - 'yes, I've bought him for you - he's lovely. He is a bit leggy though and still looks very coltish, I hope you like him?' She went on to explain about her visit and the fact that the owner also had two Apaloosa stallions that she had fallen in love with. A very successful visit altogether.

Now, I had a horse called Burtie, he was almost two years old and a Palomino. A Palomino by the way describes the colour, it is not a breed. It would be another two weeks before I was to see him, because of the weather and arranging transport.

At last the day arrived. Claire had gone for him with her own trailer and taken her mum Lizi, with her.

Their arrival back at the farm was Claire to a tee. 'We had a job getting him in the trailer, he was bigger than I thought. I had to take out the centre partition and sort of jam him in diagonally, corner to corner. I could see just what she meant! 'Anyway he was brilliant to load so we didn't have a problem'. I laughed 'Good job too, looking in there. I'm surprised you managed to close the tail gate.'

Burtie was gently persuaded down the ramp, me at one side, Lizi at the other. He seemed to unfold himself at the same time. I looked at the trailer again and then at Burtie. It was like managing to put a quart into a pint bottle.

It was love at first sight. Burtie was not the big beautiful golden Palomino of my dreams, he was a rough looking, leggy horse with an almost white and shaggy winter coat. His head was hairy and he looked a bit nondescript. He was an ugly duckling, but I could see a thing of beauty hidden within.

It was Burtie's big brown gentle eyes that just caught my attention. This was the giveaway to his character - and what a character he has turned out to be. Full of trust and full of fun, a true friend for life.

I have read many guidelines and comments about choosing a horse, but most of them miss out on what I consider most important. First of all I would look at, and into the horse's eyes. I would then look at its feet - and then, and only then, would I start to make an assessment on its suitabilty for my purpose.

Claire you did an excellent job.

I added Boy to his name because it seemed to suit him. So he became Burtie Boy and as you will soon discover I even wrote a song about him. I spent some time getting to know Burtie Boy and for the first few weeks kept him stabled. This gave me the opportunity to handle him all over and brush out his mane and tail. I was going to train him using natural horsemanship methods, Western style. He was surprisingly nervous for quite a long time, and would almost jump out of his skin when you walked passed his box even. He showed all the characteristics of a prey animal - always aware of what his surroundings may be hiding. It was the same when he was being led sometimes, he would suddenly jump sideways. I persevered by assuming the leadership technique and calming him at every opportunity. It was obvious that he was reassured by my presence, and I enjoyed building on this relationship. When theory and practice come together it is a very rewarding experience.

'Burtie Boy - your mane is flowing.'

Within a few weeks of Summer we had Burtie working on the yard, and I started to explain about natural horsemanship training to visitors. He responded remarkably well and soon I had him saddled and bridled using a complete western rig. I got him used to a rope being swung in a loop over his head, and eventually to the rope being thrown and it actually dropping over his head. His response has been wonderful, and this does demonstrate the amount of trust that can be achieved. In addition I taught him to pick a revolver from its holster with his teeth, and disarm me technically, when my back was turned. He learns very quickly.

As I write this book we have moved into Millennium year 2000, and to mark it as a special milestone I wanted to commemorate the history of the horse. A friend, Margery Parkinson, suggested I write a song. The song is based upon the horse you are reading about, and I decided to dedicate it to the British Horse Society. It tells the story of the horses' massive contribution to mankind and the debt we owe. The whole song is printed at the end of this book.

I also want to dedicate it to the memory of four of my equine friends who have now passed on. Very few people are fortunate enough to have custody of a horse for its lifetime, but now as I move into over thirty years of keeping the horses I have bred, these partings are inevitable. They are very sad as in all family situations, and just like with children, you remember their young life in particular. So, Carmen, King, Princess and Nobby, we shall remember you, and you will always be grazing peacefully at Staintondale.

One particular happy story happened when Nobby was only one year old. He was grazing on the small grassed area at the front of our house. In the old deeds it was referred to as 'The Calf Garth' which meant a small enclosure to keep the calves in. As you will appreciate a Shire horse even at one year old can be the size of a traditional riding horse.

Quite by chance I just happened to look out of the window. I just could not believe my eyes. Not one, not two, but three small boys were sat on his back! I rushed out of the house, through the barn and round to the front. Nobby was just stood there with the three cheeky faced boys astride him. Well I could have been cross. but remembering my younger days I found it difficult. 'What do you think you are doing', I said, trying to sound angry. 'Just riding this horse mister - well he came and stood by the gate so we all climbed on.' Nobby seemed to nod in agreement. 'But he's not a horse', I started to explain - I looked at their faces, I was wasting my time!

CHAPTER FIFTY FOUR
A Golden Opportunity

"It's an ill wind" so goes the old saying "that blows nobody any good". Nobody I am sure would regard something as devastating, and in some cases, as heart-rendering as the Foot and Mouth outbreak as just "an ill wind". It caused great distress and financial hardship to many businesses far removed from farming. It was the year 2001.

This was basically a countryside disaster, and in recent years, it is these areas of the country which have proved so popular with tourists. National Parks of course were particularly badly hit and this was to affect us.

People were encouraged to avoid the countryside altogether and this resulted in hotel cancellations and abandoned holidays. Pretty chocolate box villages became ghost towns and the rural economy was in shreds. It became suddenly very apparent just how much local jobs and wealth creation depended on Tourism.

Thankfully it eventually got contained and later eliminated altogether, but the damage was done and the knock-on effect started to emerge. Recovery was being predicted as very slow and a great deal of financial hardship was becoming painfully clear. It was said that some businesses would never recover. Pressure from certain sections of the community was brought to bear and the government responded by setting up an enquiry. This was a start. Soon wheels were in motion, and what later came to be known as a rural recovery plan emerged. Any businesses who had sustained losses could apply for a grant. It was not to be a handout but a jointly funded exercise to regenerate an existing business, upgrade its status and improve its potential. It was being administered by 'Yorkshire Forward'.

The criteria was specific, prepare a detailed business plan based on developing it towards maximum efficiency, marketing, and new projects to improve and enhance potential for the area.

A tall order - but another challenge. Here was an opportunity to realise an ambition to build an all-weather show arena. Well this is England after all!

A business advisor was made available, and many long and far reaching discussions ensued. For our part it meant a substantial financial contribution towards what I considered to be a real investment in the future. It was going to be worth all the effort and as much time as we had at our disposal, not to mention learning new computer skills. I won't bore you with too much detail, suffice to say we were successful, but the timescale to fulfil the conditions seemed more like an imposition. We were made aware of the deadlines of course, and now we were going to meet them, come what may.

Planning permission (dare I say it) was needed and this meant plans being prepared and an application submitted. This time round it wasn't seen as a problem, but these things do take time and we were working to a deadline. An Architect friend of mine, Howard Acklam, took on this task. A local firm Thackray and Sons of Brawby near Malton secured the contract and the fabrication of the steel frames commenced. We jumped the gun here a bit as the planning application had not yet been approved!

What was particularly brilliant about this development was that I was able to design and tailor this building to suit our exacting requirements.

By now of course we are into 2002 and we are all very optimistic about the number of visitors returning to the countryside. We were not to be disappointed. The season progressed and planning permission granted. It had been decided to erect the new building at the end of the season in September.

It was quite funny really because I was busy outlining our plans to some visitors not long before we closed. I was explaining that building work would start as soon as we closed the following week - a voice only feet away said - "we start the week after next, standing up the frame!" It was the voice of Roger Crozier the works manager of Thackrays. He was at the farm together with his wife as visitors.

The big lift came on the arrival of the crane - what a monster. It was a real state of the art machine and I stood fascinated as the driver operator set it up. I won't go into detail but I think the picture illustrating this event says it all.

These were exciting times for me, the culmination of everything I had dreamed of. From happy childhood days in a pit village when my heroes were cowboys, to a wonderful environment where horses were supreme and I was able to live a life others could only dream of. My pleasure is in sharing this creation with others and it is never taken for granted.

The building progressed favourable, and at last after years of DIY I was able to watch something being constructed that I didn't have a hand in. Should I rub my eyes I wondered?

Moving into the summer season of 2004 and comments I thought I would never hear. It was a season of soaring high temperatures and somewhat uncomfortable situations.

The new building was our safeguard against what we call typical summer weather - wind, rain and sometimes unseasonal temperatures. This particular day it was different and Ayley, my assistant was her usual bright and chirpy self, entertaining the children. It was Shetland pony time and the kids were grooming them on the yard. It was hot - very hot and I could see the onlooking adults defending their heads and faces with anything from newspapers to handkerchiefs and scarves. They really did look uncomfortable. I walked into the middle of the yard and caught the audience's attention. "Sorry folks" I said "I'm going to move you all to the indoor facilities out of the sun". "Thank goodness for that" came the unanimous response.

As I sit writing now, we are on the threshold of yet another season and making the usual preparations. My gold at 'Rainbows End' of course up to now had been Burtie Boy - but there was more to come.

A certain Mr. R.W. Carr had been the last station master when the line closed under the Beeching plan on March 6th 1965. Only four years before we had purchased East Side Farm. Mr. Carr at that time had the Stainton Dale Station sign removed and taken it with him into retirement. For all the years we have lived here I had seen this sign stored quite close to his bungalow. It had acted as a weathershield on the roof of his shed!

Of recent years his health was suffering and he was forced to give up his home and move. The sign - what would happen to it? I, determined to myself it must stay in the village.

One of Mr. Carrs son's, Jim had an engineering workshop close to the old station. I decided to give him a ring outlining my plan to offer a safe home for the sign. I explained about the new building and my proposed site for it. It would be erected on the inside of the new arena, high up on the Yorkshire boarding facing the seating area. I went on, this way all the visitors would see it and it would be preserved and enjoyed. Jim listened carefully, when the time comes, the sign is yours.

Well the time did come and I went to collect it. "Oh! by the way" said Jim "there are some other bits and pieces you might find interesting". Well - interesting wasn't the word. For someone like me with an insatiable appetite for the preservation of history, it was pure gold. The bits and pieces now on display included some framed first (1st) class award certificates, a platelayers plan of refuge sites and other gems. The former station masters hat, possibly used for 'right Royal occasions' and suitably trimmed with gold braid was one of them.

Somebody once wrote that life was a journey, and mine is continuing. It seems very appropriate that another station has been reached - a very special one - and its called - Stainton Dale.

Left:
The start of the all weather show arena.

Below:
Tony on Burtie Boy outside the show arena

BURTIE BOY

Words and Music by Tony Jenkins

The year two thousand dawned upon us and our thanks
must go to you. You are the root of our survival
Old faithful friend we love you so.

Chorus:

Burtie Boy your mane is flowing, Burtie Boy the wind
is blowing, Burtie Boy your coat is glowing
A golden horse at Rainbow's End.

All through history you have carried us, our burdens on
your back. You have bridged our human failings
And withstood the test of time.

Chorus

For six thousand years you helped us, to survive
and conquer all. To develop our ambitions and
secure the world we know.

Chorus

On the land and in our cities, you have pulled your
weight and more. In the field of human conflict
You gave your heart as cannon roared.

Chorus

You are God's gift to all your subjects, a noble lord
above the rest. A splendid majesty and beauty
Is what you have - you are the best.

Burtie Boy your mane is flowing, Burtie Boy the
wind is blowing, Burtie Boy your coat is glowing
A golden horse at Rainbow's End.

STAINTONDALES

It's a very special place to know
where families can safely go.
It's a little off the beaten track
but that won't stop you going back
a second, or third, time to be
with equine friends, beside the sea.
Along green pathways, across the stiles,
you can walk along the cliffs for miles.
Oak and Ash saplings spread their green
near a slate grey pond in a field serene,
whilst the hiss of goose and quack of duck
compete with the trundle of farmyard truck,
filled to the brim with the happy noise
of smiling and waving girls and boys.
Tony, in stetson with toy cowboy gun,
tells a tale, cracks a joke with everyone,
whilst Penny lifts children, smiling wide
for 'photo calls', to sit astride
the back of ponies - very small -
and Burtie (who is very tall)
sneaks Tony's gun, or tosses a mat
and lowers his head for the lariat!
There's a tiny collie, black and white
so gentle (she would never bite),
and another, larger, collie - who
seeks out and takes - a treat from you.
There's a pleasant shop, selling scrumptious teas
- two tasty ploughman's lunches PLEASE!!
There are tales of smuggling and 'derring-do'
- to please the outlaw side of you!
So, if being with horses is your aim
this 'horses heaven' has a name
it's ten, too, on ponies' paradise scale
it's the Shire Horse Farm at Staintondale.

JESSICA HEAFIELD